YOUR BODY'S WISDOM

A Body-Centered Approach to Transformation

Renee Welfeld

Sourcebooks
Inc.
Naperville, IL

Published by Sourcebooks
P.O. Box 372, Naperville, Illinois   60566
(630) 961-3900
FAX: 630-961-2168

Library of Congress Cataloging-in-Publication Data

Welfeld, Renee
      Your body's wisdom: a body-centered approach to transformation/
   Renee Welfeld.
         p.   cm.
      ISBN 1-57071-147-X (pbk. : alk. paper)
      1. Change (Psychology) 2. Mind and body. 3. New Age movement.
   I. Title.
   BF637.C4W45   1997
   613—dc21   97-5371
                                                                 CIP

Printed and bound in the United States of America.
                  10 9 8 7 6 5 4 3 2 1

Dedication

To my children—Wendy, Jeremy, Jonathan, James, and Veeda. Thank you for giving me the opportunity to discover and experience the true meaning of unconditional love.

Acknowledgments

Special thanks go to my friend and editor, Jane Cromer, for her encouragement and her invaluable editorial assistance. Her insightful questions helped me clarify my theories. Her skill as a writer helped me stay focused.

A number of other people have lent their support, encouragement, and skills to this project. Thanks go to friends, family members, and writers whose feedback was very helpful: Wendy Farley, Barbara Gibson, Susan Kulp, Kathleen McCue-Swift, and Helen Belitzky.

I thank Fred Madeo, my seventh grade teacher, who told me that I wasn't stupid and taught me the meaning of empathy; Dr. Steve Stein, my first therapist and the model for the aspects of Self, known as the Nurturing Parents; Franklyn Smith, my beloved friend and teacher, who taught me about impeccability and what it means to walk one's talk; the revered Bhagwan Shree Rajneesh for opening my eyes; and all of my clients, who constantly inspire, instruct, and give me the opportunity to speak the words I need to hear.

I also acknowledge Irving Welfeld, my former husband. Without his financial support, I would not have been able to take the time I needed to complete this book.

My deep appreciation goes to the staff at Sourcebooks, and especially to my editor, Todd Stocke, director of marketing, Karen Bouris, and publisher, Dominique Raccah, for the care and attention they gave to birthing this book.

Author's Note

The use of either 'he' or 'she' throughout the book seemed inappropriate, so I have used 'she' in the odd-numbered chapters and 'he' in the even-numbered chapters. I hope that this will make readers of both sexes feel welcome.

CONTENTS

Conscious Breathing As a Tool for Relaxation
—*Exploring the Breath*
—*Expanding the Breath*

Recognizing and Releasing Chronic Tension
—*Tension Inventory Exercise*

Meditation As a Tool for Relaxation
—*Meditation for the Busy Executive*
—*Are You Looking at the Mirror or Is the Mirror Looking at You?*
—*I Am the Center of My Universe*

Experiencing the Interval
—*The Stillness at the Center of All Movement*
—*The Silence That Surrounds All Sound*
—*The Emptiness That Envelops All Form*

We are a biological life process that thinks, feels, has needs, is able to have highly specialized responses, able to dream and to act. We are a chain of events, an entire ecological system with many life environments, from tidal pools and ancient biochemical seas to highly complex, brain-organ action systems. We are continually on the move, continually forming, reorganizing ourselves and our surroundings. By living from our process, we can commit ourselves to the evolution of the living, the forming of the self, the culture, the planet.

—Stanley Keleman
Somatic Reality

PREFACE

wanted to produce this book in order to share some of the theories and tools that have helped the people with whom I have worked. All of these men and women wanted to mature, to grow up and out of habitual ways of perceiving and behaving that no longer served them. They wanted to create a new home for themselves, to explore and improve the quality of their lives.

I see myself as a guide for people on a journey of meeting themselves and embracing their uniqueness. To facilitate that journey I combine body work, meditation, ritual, prayer, and various counseling techniques. These tools create an atmosphere in which insight occurs. These insights can shed light on unresolved traumatic events from the past and help a person to release emotions related to those experiences or to more current events. Insight allows us to revise distorted beliefs that were established by emotional traumas. Insight also moves us toward the realization of personal and professional goals that have been thwarted due to unexplored feelings, emotions, and beliefs. And insight opens us to our connection with God/All That Is.

The material in this book is the result of years of study, practice, and personal discovery. I include relaxation techniques; introduce the concept of the Interval; offer an expanded way of looking at our feelings and emotions; posit theory concerning the six aspects of Self; explore life issues; teach the technique of Silent Listening/Intuitive Response; and, finally, present reflections on what I believe to be our evolutionary imperative—to discover who we are and to contribute to the Universe that which is uniquely ours to give.

In the course of using the theory and the exercises to explore your emotions, you may come in touch with hidden memories from your past. As children, some of us needed to bury recollections of traumatic experiences. We employed such psychological mechanisms as denial or suppression to forestall dealing with those experiences, seeking to protect ourselves from emotional pain that was unbearable to us then.

These rekindled memories and the feelings and sensations associated with them, while painful, contain the precious gifts of insight and self-discovery; they are well worth your time and careful attention. As adults, we are fortunate in that we can create caring and supportive environments from which to confront the past and heal our old wounds. We can reach out to friends, people who have had experiences similar to ours, trained professionals, and/or spiritual advisors for support. That support may come in the form of discussion and feedback, a physical presence, psychological counseling, or spiritual guidance.

I encourage you during the course of your reading to be open to the assistance and loving attention that others can provide. Inviting and accepting their help is a way to be good to yourself, and it will soften and hasten the learning process that you have embarked on. The information and techniques outlined in this book will, I hope, provide you with the tools to welcome these memories, feelings, and sensations so that the gifts contained within them can manifest for you.

As you become familiar with the archetypal figures known as the Nurturing Parents, you will have constant access to a powerful internal support system. These two beings help you focus on those things that affirm your sense of worth and lovability, your wholeness, your irreplaceable contribution to the unfolding of the Universe. By making their qualities and habits your own, you will move into your most integrated and commanding self. You will become a conscious co-creator of the Universe.

In *The Reluctant Messiah*, Richard Bach says that we teach best what we most need to learn. I agree. Clearly this project was not only a way for me to make a contribution to my readers, but also an invitation from God/All That Is to become a student once again, to explore, learn about, and unify within myself the elements of body, mind, emotion, and Spirit about which I was attempting to write. I feel very grateful for all that I have learned in the course of writing this book.

Organizing the material and writing it down has helped me to consolidate and integrate at even more subtle levels all I have learned during twenty-five years of studying, practicing, and teaching meditation, body/mind therapies, ritual, and religious philosophy. Writing this book has made me a more effective teacher and a more enthusiastic pupil. Through it, I have developed new skills and perspectives about living with illness (I have had Crohn's disease since childhood). Writing about tools for coming in touch with feelings has naturally helped me to explore my own more deeply. With those tools, I have been able to resolve and release feelings of fear, grief, and anger related to my own childhood. In doing that, I also have been able to experience greater compassion for myself and my parents.

In the realm of Spirit, working on this book has profoundly strengthened my sense of being connected to and nourished by the Source. When I sit in front of my computer in preparation for writing, I quiet myself and begin to move between prayer and meditation. This movement is the path of exchange between me and the Source, God/All That Is. When I pray, I give thanks for the many gifts that the writing has brought me. I try to convey my needs and desires to the Source and ask for assistance to continue and complete the project. When I meditate, I silence myself and listen quietly into the Universe. In my silence, the Source communicates with me through my Intuitive Self. Soon the writing begins, and I become deeply aware of the intelligence, love, abundance, and support that flows from God/All That Is into me.

I have felt encouraged and guided at every point along the way, and my sense of the abiding presence that revealed itself to me as I worked continues to deepen with each passing day. I wrote this book to help you strengthen your own sense of unity with God/All That Is. By embracing this unity, you will come to know your body, your thoughts, your emotions, your desires, and your spiritual sense of self in the most nourishing and empowering ways.

I assure you that in the process of reading this book, integrating the theory, and practicing the exercises, you will become more generous and less critical of yourself. You will find it easier to interact openly with others. You will become aware of the areas in your life where you make choices, and you will perceive many more options from which to choose. You will find yourself making decisions with more confidence and clarity because you will sense your interconnectedness with God/All That Is.

Welcome to what I know will be a rich learning experience. The information and techniques you find here will help you transform your life and the world around you.

INTRODUCTION

ince the beginning of time, men and women have been delving into the nature of their own existence. During the second half of this century, this exploration into the self took on new proportions. In 1956 in *The Art of Loving*, Eric Fromm wrote, "Modern man has transformed himself into a commodity; he experiences his life energy as an investment with which he should make the highest profit.... He is alienated from himself, from his fellow men, and from nature."[1]

In the 1960s, many of us came to realize the truth of Fromm's statement. Suddenly life seemed hollow and devoid of meaning. Consumerism and recreation had replaced activities that nourish the soul. We came in touch with feelings of emptiness, tinged with fear and confusion. We were no longer in charge of our own lives. A deep need and desire to take our lives back rose into our consciousness, and we began to ask the big questions, "Who am I?" and "What, if any, is my role in the cosmos?" Our feelings of alienation, and isolation prompted an unprecedented, universal search for meaning.

Those who were drawn to find answers to the question, "What is my role in the cosmos?" became deeply involved in issues of global concern. They began to examine their relationship to their brothers and sisters on the planet, as well as to the life of the planet itself. The peace movement, the peace corp, Greenpeace, the Green Party, consumer rights, and the movements to end racial and gender discrimination, fired the minds and hearts of people all over the world, moving us closer to a planetary consciousness.

Those who awoke to the question, "Who am I," moved in the opposite direction. Seeking answers and solutions on a more personal level, they turned inward and began exploring the workings of the mind, the soul, and the body, and their relationship to God/All That Is.

The ancient saying, "When the student awakens, the teacher appears," proved itself to be true. Suddenly the concepts of Freud, Jung, Adler, Rogers, and many other students of the mind, became a subject of study even for the uninitiated. These teachings, once the domain of an elite few, were now available to the average person. Psychiatric principles were being applied not only in the care of the mentally disturbed, but in the lives of the general population as well.

Psychiatry, analysis, and numerous forms of psychotherapy helped bring us in touch with the unconscious mind. We learned that much of what we feel and believe about ourselves and about life lies hidden deep within the unconscious mind, influencing our behavior and creating the emotional atmosphere that surrounds us. "Yes," we said, "this is the answer." "We are the product of our unconscious mind, and knowing what we feel and believe will empower us and help us create meaningful lives."

To our chagrin, many of us discovered that knowing *what* we feel and believe—and *why*—had little effect on changing our feelings and beliefs. Nor did it influence the choices we made, or change the way we behaved. We still felt isolated and fragmented; for the most part, were unable to take charge of our emotional lives.

This revelation led us to explore the workings of the body, the keeper and transmitter of our feelings and emotions, and we discovered that the body has an unconscious mind of its own. Once again, many teachers appeared to enlighten us on the subject of the body and its mind. Stanley Keleman, Eugene Gendlin, Moshe Feldenkrais, Ida Rolf, and others offered us a myriad of ways to understand the unconscious body/mind connection, and to experience its relationship to our feelings, beliefs, and behavior.

We learned that worry, fear, shame, and confusion express themselves as tension in our muscles, joints, and organs. We learned that our feelings and emotions are experienced as a movement of energy within the body, as various sensations rising and passing. We learned that thoughts, feelings, and sensations rise simultaneously, clarify one another, and affect the way we move in the world, physically and emotionally. We thought, "Yes, now we have the answer to our question, 'Who am I?' We are both the mind and the body, and understanding how the mind and the body interact, and the affect this union has on our feelings and behavior, will empower us and help us create meaningful lives."

But a piece of the puzzle was still missing. Knowing about our feelings and having a meaningful encounter with them are two very different things. Most of us were unable to maintain significant contact with the actual physical experience generated by our feelings to learn from them or change them. The rawness of our feelings brought us in touch with our vulnerability and mortality, and we recoiled in fear. Our fear kept us one step removed from intimate contact with ourselves, and our deepest wisdom remained inaccessible. If we were to become fully integrated beings, available to ourselves, we needed a new way of being with ourselves and our feelings.

In response to this need, we began to investigate the Source within, and God/All That Is. Before we could withstand the fear and discomfort our feelings and emotions generated in us, we needed direct experiences of love, compassion, and non-judgment. We needed to discover something larger than ourselves—God/All That Is. World religions, responding to our need, rose to the challenge; and new religions appeared for those of us who were unaffiliated.

AA, an outgrowth of Christianity, triggered a plethora of Twelve-step programs. Twelve-step programs appeared all over the country, helping people recover from every manner of addiction and abuse. Christian writers such as Henri Nouwen, Thomas Merton, and Hugh and Gayle Prather encouraged us to open our hearts, and experience life through the eyes of love.

Eastern religions such as Buddhism, Taoism, and Sufism found their way to the West. Teachers like Thich Nhat Hanh, Joseph Goldstein, and Bhagwan Shree Rajneesh introduced meditation to thousands of people. Yoga and meditation, once considered exotic practices, became accessible and acceptable. We were taught how to relax the body and silence the mind. Hundreds of different forms emerged, appealing to every kind of mind. Today, some form of yoga or meditation is being taught in almost every city in the world.

Judaism produced many new teachers. Rabbi Zalman Schachter launched "The Jewish Renewal Movement," introducing modern Jews to a form of personal spirituality previously unknown to them. A modern Chasidic troubadour, Rabbi Shlomo Carlebach, quickened the hearts of Jews all over the world by transforming spoken prayer into songs of celebration. Rabbi Aryeh Kaplan began teaching the Kabbalah in English, introducing many Jews to Jewish mysticism.

Channeled works, like those of Jane Roberts and Ruth Montgomery, expanded our understanding of the metaphysical universe. New Age teachers such as Jean Houston, Fritjof Capra, and Deepak Chopra made the body/mind/spirit/Universe connection in ways we could all understand and use.

Our journey has been an evolutionary one. As evolving beings, in a constant process of growth and change, we have begun to realize that we are in a profound and mystical partnership with our evolving Universe. Each teacher moved us closer to this realization. Each teaching prepared us to experience ourselves as fully integrated mental/physical/spiritual beings—part of one another and the Universe.

We have been shown the way. Yet many of us still struggle with feelings of isolation and fragmentation, and are unable to answer to the question, "Who am I?" Many of us are still one step away from accessing the guidance that lies within us and within the Universe, the guidance that will help us create the lives we envision for ourselves.

What must we do to integrate everything we have learned so far and discover who we are? The question, "Who am I?" can only be answered when we understand that who we are changes from moment to moment. As we move into the twenty-first century, we are being guided to step into the body and perceive it in a new and more profound way. Our next evolutionary turn is moving us toward experiencing the body on an inner, visceral level by maintaining significant contact with everything that rises in us. As we do, we experience the internal shifts that inform us of who we are at that very moment. By remaining exquisitely present to everything that is occurring within us from moment to moment, we experience our holism, and become on with our bodymindspirit nature.

Your Body's Wisdom will teach you to come in touch with yourself as an energetic organism. It's exercises are designed to help you refine your senses, and its theory expands your consciousness to include the energy that moves through your cellular being. The cells of your body are a conduit for the electrical impulses that are your thoughts, memories, feelings, sensations, and emotions. Within your energetic, cellular structure also floats the voice of your Intuitive Self. Your intuitive voice speaks not in words but in a holistic way. It rises from within you, revealing a deeper form of knowing—much deeper than words can convey.

By learning to relax the body and still the mind, you will deeply touch this movement of energy and tap into your body's wisdom. Your experience will be direct and immediate. Engaging all your senses, you will be able to communicate with the unconscious mind and with your Intuitive Self. Turning inward with interest, tenderness, and compassion, you experience all your thoughts, feelings, and sensations without discrimination. You have the opportunity to reintegrate those aspects of self that have been denied, and transform your feelings of fragmentation and isolation. You discover what you want, and what is in the way of achieving it. Fully awake to everything that is happening within you and around you, the interconnectedness between your inner and outer selves reveals itself.

With practice you come to feel exquisitely at home in your body, and in the Universe. You discover the love that is the foundation of your being, and the foundation of the Universe. In touch with your own wisdom, you recognize those aspects of your self that are in need of transformation and require your devoted attention, those aspects that need to be healed or matured within the privacy of your own heart. You learn to distinguish between those aspects of your self that serve to create the life you desire and those that do not. The fear and confusion that once prevented you from using your free will in a creative way begins to dissipate. Taking charge of what you project and reflect into the Universe, you are able to take charge of the life you create. A feeling of trust in yourself and in the Universe begins to emerge. You are able to embrace your own vulnerability and mortality, and to engage life with enthusiasm.

By practicing the exercises and assimilating the theory, you become *real* and alive to yourself. Your awareness becomes centered in your body, and you feel the space that you occupy. Your senses become more refined and you notice many different sensations, subtle movements of energy within you—tingling, pulsing, churning, heat. All of your experiences become sharper, clearer, more deeply felt. The sun on your face, a cool breeze, water to soothe a parched throat, the taste and smell of your favorite food, the tender touch of a child's hand in yours, your lover's kiss. Each of these moments becomes a moment of fascination, a cause for celebration.

As you refine your senses you experience the breadth of joy, excitement, delight, passion, warmth, tenderness, and ecstasy. You also experience the touch of grief, rage, anguish, terror, greed, guilt, shame, and despair. You feel the full range of human emotions. To do this takes courage and compassion. As you awaken to your body's wisdom, both of these qualities become available to you, and you have a sense of belonging and a reverence for everything that is of the body.

You feel a tremendous tenderness toward your body and a deep compassion for yourself.

Centered within your body, you hear your intuitive voice, advising you, helping you to make wise decisions, and to take very good care of yourself. You think with greater clarity, creativity, and confidence, and you learn to express your feelings in positive ways. You become available to the wisdom of the Universe, and experience revelation—the "Aha!"—that propels you along your evolutionary path. A deep sense of harmony and balance rises as you know yourself to be—body, mind, and soul—at one with the Universe.

What causes some of us to disconnect from our bodies and lose access to the wisdom contained there? For many of us it is a question of time. We are so busy that we simply do not take time out to notice our bodies. And if your body is a healthy one, if it takes you where you want to go and performs the tasks you ask of it, it is rather easy to ignore it.

Another explanation for not feeling connected to our bodies has to do with our focus on intellect and our belief that *mind* is superior to *body*. Of course it is obvious that we could not have a *life of the mind* without the body. But many of us still see and treat our bodies as an aside; the body is something to be tolerated while we go on with the more interesting and compelling life of the mind.

Some of us disconnect from the body because of our religious training. Perhaps you were taught that the body is a burden you must bear until you die and are delivered to a place where you can let go of the demands and limitations of the physical body. Perhaps you were taught that the body is "bad," the source of original sin, or the source of sexual feelings and the desire to express them. Even if you do not hold to such beliefs, you may be influenced by them in subtle ways and disconnect from your body on some level in response to these teachings.

Not liking your body is yet another reason for disconnecting from it. You may not like your body because it is a source of discomfort due to illness. Or you may not like the way your body looks. Cultural notions of beauty can affect your ability to feel good about your body. If your body does not fit the ideals that are put forth by magazines, film, and advertising, then you may find it difficult to like your body. When you compare yourself to those ideals, you may see yourself as too thin, too fat, or the wrong height. Maybe you do not like your nose, your hips, your belly, your hair (or the fact that you are losing it). If you are not as beautiful, as strong, as graceful, or as young as you would like to be, then you may find it hard to feel at home in your body.

Denying our feelings is one of the most common reasons for disconnecting from our bodies. As children, many of us were told that certain feelings were bad, and that we were bad if we felt them. Even as adults, each time we feel sad, angry, frightened, or ashamed, our body produces sensations to let us know that this feeling experience is taking place and if we perceive that experience as something undesirable, we resent the messenger—our body. Our response will be to pull away from both the messenger and the message—the sensations and thoughts that we are having in that sad, angry, frightened, or shameful moment. When we pull away from the messenger and the message, we are no longer centered in our body: in a sense we have run away from home.

Finally, many of us have chosen, consciously or unconsciously, to disconnect from our bodies as a way of avoiding the pain that accompanies certain feelings. This pain may be emotional, mental, or physical. Some of us make such a decision when we are very young. If we are exposed to abuse or neglect, disconnecting from our body can help us to survive the pain we are experiencing. Unfortunately, this childhood coping mechanism of dissociating from the body becomes a habit for many survivors of abuse. As adults these abuse survivors continue to disconnect from their feelings and from other aspects of being centered in the body. But the childhood memories, feelings, and sensations that these grown-ups are trying to distance themselves from remain buried just below the surface of their conscious minds, waiting for release and usually creating many problems in their lives.

For those of us who want to come home to our bodies, what does that process look like? What do we discover along the way? The process of awakening to your body is one that you engage in from moment to moment throughout your life. It is an ongoing journey that begins with becoming a student of yourself, a student in love with your subject. You can begin this exploration by asking yourself a few questions about what you believe and how you feel about your body.

When you stand in front of a mirror, are you generally pleased with what you see? Or do you have feelings of dissatisfaction, dislike, or even shame? If you had the money, would you consider plastic surgery to change some feature of your body? When you walk down the street, do you make eye contact with people you pass or do you pray that no one will notice you because you do not feel good about your body? Do you think of the sexual feelings that stir you as a gift or a curse? Do you experience your body as a vehicle for self-knowledge or as a source of uncomfortable feelings? Do you feel vulnerable when you experience the sensations that move through your body, or do you revel in the vitality inherent in those sensations? Knowing what you think and feel about your body is the first step to accessing its wisdom.

The next step is to become aware of your body. You accomplish this by stopping all self-talk and bringing your full attention to the physical experience of the moment. Within that moment, notice how your feet feel as they touch the ground. When you move, feel the sensations on your skin as your clothes slide over your body. Experience the coolness in your nostrils as air rushes in and the warmth there as it leaves. Feel your belly and chest expand and contract as air moves in and out of your lungs.

Accessing your body's wisdom means inviting the awareness of tension or relaxation in your muscles. It means becoming aware of your posture, the tone of your voice, the expression on your face. It means inviting an awareness of all the sensations in your body, wherever you notice them—in your throat, chest, belly, head, limbs, back. It means embracing all your thoughts, feelings, beliefs, motives, and intentions, those you would like to identify with, as well as those you would prefer to deny. It means noticing the relationships that exist among these phenomena.

When you access your body's wisdom, and begin to explore all your feelings, you experience the depth of human suffering, your suffering. This new understanding and acceptance of your own suffering brings you to a place of the most tender compassion for yourself and for all humanity. This compassion then surrounds you in each moment, supporting your efforts to remain aware of your own suffering and the suffering of others.

Knowledge of your own suffering becomes a treasure when you no longer react to life through that suffering, but respond through the compassion that rises in its place. Moving from suffering to compassion, you step into your adulthood. As you release your suffering and reclaim the energy that this storage required, you are then free to focus your energy into creative action.

From that profoundly, persistently compassionate place—your body, the home of your deepest wisdom—you are able to take responsibility for everything you feel, think, and do. You notice and own what you are feeling and thinking. You notice how you are inclined to act. You explore the choices before you, examine your motives and intentions with respect to each of those choices, and then you act. One of the greatest treasures of being an adult is the freedom to choose and to express yourself through the choices you make. When you are at home in your body, you consciously participate in the world around you and shape that world. You step into your role as a conscious co-creator of the Universe.

I believe that we cannot be truly "response-able"—able to respond—in any of these areas if we are not centered in our bodies, at one with ourselves and the Universe. I am convinced by my work as a body/mind practitioner and by my personal journey of discovery that coming into our bodies and directly experiencing our thoughts, feelings, and sensations enables us to act with clarity, compassion, authenticity, courage, and creativity. By coming home to our bodies

10

we experience the integration of our feelings, our thoughts, and our actions. By coming home to our bodies we strengthen the cooperation that is meant to occur among these realms of our experience, but may be thwarted by unresolved feelings related to past hurts.

I also believe that we cannot become conscious co-creators if we do not explore those hurts and the events that established them. If we do not examine our self-defeating beliefs and the behaviors that limit our vitality, creativity, and sense of worth and possibility, we cannot live a full life. We cannot claim the gifts of consciousness—compassion for ourselves and others, the freedom to act, and the opportunity to find out who we really are and to contribute to the world that which is uniquely ours to give.

Begin this journey toward achieving unity within yourself and within the Universe: take a deep gentle breath, let your body soften, see and feel yourself within the space that surrounds you. In other words, come home to your body and unearth its wisdom.

RELAXATION
IS A KEY

elaxation is a key to accessing your body's wisdom. When you are relaxed, you become aware that your body, mind, and soul are fully integrated, and that they are constantly engaging in a dynamic, creative exchange. When you relax, the body softens, breath deepens, feelings, sensations, and emotions calm, the mind quiets, and the soul is at peace. From this peaceful place, you feel less vulnerable, more expansive. You feel at home within yourself and within the Universe.

At home in your body, you become aware of so many things— thoughts, ideas, plans, opinions, feeling states, memories, body sensations, impulses to act, and your Intuitive Self. You experience all of these phenomena because you live in a body that is designed to experience them in all their complexity within each moment. This is one of the miraculous features of your existence.

Each thought, feeling, and sensation you experience is your body's way of keeping you informed of your mental, physical, and emotional state. The subtle voice of your Intuitive Self speaks to you through these experiences. These body/mind phenomena—your thoughts, feelings, and sensations—rise simultaneously in response to every occurrence. They are your advisors reporting on the condition of your realm. Your realm consists of everything that is happening inside you and all around you.

The voice of your Intuitive Self is extremely subtle. To hear it requires that you stop, feel, sense, and listen—in other words, you must give it your fullest attention. It also requires that you turn down the volume of your other internal voices, the voices of your Nurturing Parents and Maturing Aspects. The voices of your Maturing Aspects are usually accompanied by intense feelings and emotions, which easily drown out the voice of your Intuitive Self. If you are not very familiar with the body/mind phenomena your intuitive voice generates, it is possible to confuse it with the voices of your Nurturing Parents. Distinguishing the differences between these other voices and the voice of your Intuitive Self is a challenge. You meet this challenge by learning to recognize the different body/mind phenomena they each generate. Each one creates a unique body/mind experience. In Chapters Four and Five you will become familiar with these other voices and learn to recognize the effect they have on you.

The challenge of adulthood is to remain present to these body/mind phenomena, your surroundings, and your intuitive voice. When you remain present to yourself, you notice your thoughts, feelings, and sensations. You are able to decipher their meanings, and to integrate the information you receive into your knowledge of yourself. Remaining present to your surroundings allows you to understand the relationship between what you bring to a particular moment, how your actions affect the situation, and how the situation affects your actions. Listening to the voice of your Intuitive Self enables you to use your deepest wisdom to guide your actions.

The process of remaining present to your body/mind phenomena, your surroundings, and your Intuitive Self faces two challenges: the fast pace of your life, and your penchant for getting lost in your own self-talk to the exclusion of living each moment.

The first challenge is made difficult by the complexity of your life: there are always various and simultaneous situations calling for your attention. Trying to keep up with all that is expected of you, you are continually rushing through one event to get to another, through one moment to get to the next. When you are moving at breakneck speed, it is extremely difficult to notice what you are thinking, feeling, or sensing. Without time to savor the moment, it is hard to extract the wisdom inherent in it.

Each situation you encounter also creates its own confusion of body/mind phenomena. When you are rushing through one situation to another, you cannot distinguish one set of phenomena from the next. After a while all the various thoughts, feelings, and sensations get mixed up with one another. Is it any wonder that most of us have difficulty sorting out how we feel, what we think, what we want, or how we want to respond to any particular situation?

The second challenge is, I believe, even more difficult: to control your self-talk and to keep from getting lost in it. The very nature of the mind is to engage you in a constant stream of self-talk. You talk to yourself about everything you notice, incessantly comparing and judging. You talk to yourself about what you've done, what you're doing, and what you're going to do. You have inner conversations with a multitude of people, some replays of past conversations, and some "scripts" of what you think someone might have said under certain circumstances. You have conversations with your inner aspects: your Nurturing Parents—the Parent Who Listens and the Parent Who Leads (discussed in Chapter 4), and with your Maturing Aspects—the Emerald Child, the Suffering Child, and the Critical Detractor Child (discussed in Chapter 5). You review old conversations, revisiting triumphs or defeats. Or, you review old conversations to change them in ways that better integrate with your self-image.

When your self-talk becomes more imaginative, you tend to lose yourself in the world of the scenario. Similar to a daydream, a scenario is a story you construct that is either related to some past event that is incomplete, or has not been fully integrated. Or, it is a drama related to some future event you wish or do not wish to happen. These scenarios are accompanied by feelings and sensations, creating a very compelling experience that distracts you from everything that is happening at that moment.

Many of us move through our entire life lost in self-talk. What happens when you become lost in self-talk? When you are lost, your vision narrows. Your entire awareness is focused on the internal conversations. You do not experience your internal or external environment. It is as though you have lost your senses. You stop hearing the birds singing, the rain falling, and the wind blowing. Your sight turns inward, upward, or to the side, and you become unaware of your surroundings. You lose sight of time. You, the observer, are no longer present.

How do we function when we are lost in self-talk and not fully present to our immediate experience? When you are lost, you shift into automatic pilot. And because you are such a sophisticated being, you are able to accomplish some very complex tasks while operating in this mode. Let us take driving for example. You have all had the experience of driving to a familiar location, and upon arrival, marveling that you reached your destination safely. You have little or no recollection of the journey. Most likely, you were lost in self-talk. Your safe arrival can be attributed to your having been successfully operating on automatic driving pilot.

There is a very harmless and enlightening experiment you can do to experience what happens when you are lost in self-talk while operating on automatic pilot. Choose something you really like to eat, something that takes at least five minutes to consume. Notice what happens after the first few bites. Are you still aware of the flavor and texture of the food, or have you become lost in self-talk? Has your automatic eating pilot taken over while you talk to yourself about what happened at work today or while you make plans for the evening?

Getting lost in self-talk, realizing that you are lost, and coming back home to your body is a continuing cycle. Becoming aware of this cycle allows you to take charge of it. The sooner you realize you are lost, the sooner you can return home. The longer you stay home, the more you are able to tap into your body's wisdom.

Let us return to the experiment of your favorite food and use it to practice getting lost in self-talk, realizing you are lost, returning home, and remaining home. Ask yourself, "What do I need to do to savor the flavor and texture of each bite of food?" Each time you place food on your spoon or fork, look at it. Watch yourself as you bring the food to your mouth. As you close your lips around the food, close your eyes and take a deep breath. Feel the food in your mouth. Chew the food slowly, roll it around in your mouth, press your tongue into it, and experience its texture. Now inhale through your mouth and notice how the flavor becomes stronger. Remind yourself to remain aware of the food until you swallow it and for as long as it takes the flavor to fade. Imagine that each bite of food is the last food you will ever taste. Savor the entire experience.

Each time you realize you have chewed and swallowed without experiencing the flavor or the texture of the food, begin again. Notice how many consecutive mouthfuls you can feel and taste completely. Remind yourself to remain present to the chewing, the smelling, the tasting, the swallowing, and the savoring. Give yourself a goal. Promise to remain aware of one mouthful, then two, then three, and so on. This is an excellent tool for practicing what it feels like to get lost, to realize you have gotten lost, to return home, and to remain home as long as you can. Remaining aware of all of the eating processes throughout an entire meal can be a transformative experience.

When you are able to notice the rising and passing of body/mind phenomena, remain aware of your surroundings, and recognize the voice of your Intuitive Self, you discover the treasures of adulthood. You use the information you receive to make wise decisions. You more easily respond with loving kindness to situations that present themselves. In a crisis situation, you find it easier to rise to the occasion. You also actively influence the atmosphere in which you live. You can best meet these challenges and reap these rewards when you are relaxed. In fact, relaxation is the key to meeting these challenges.

We have all had opportunities to experience the benefits of remaining relaxed while in the midst of a stressful situation. Parents can readily bring to mind many occasions where remaining relaxed was a necessary ingredient to successfully dealing with a crisis. Supervisors and managers who frequently deal with crisis situations know that remaining relaxed is the only way they can effectively meet the demands being made on them. Meeting deadlines is a very common occasion where remaining relaxed is a necessary component for completing the task on time. Doctors and nurses who work in emergency rooms are constantly faced with the need to remain relaxed while dealing with life and death situations. Regardless of the nature of the crisis we find ourselves in, the words, "stay calm, be cool, don't lose it," immediately come to mind. We instinctively know that remaining relaxed increases our chances of successfully meeting the challenge.

The benefits of remaining relaxed in a crisis situation are many. When you are relaxed, it is easier to remain calm in the midst of the frantic pace created by the situation. Your body remains flexible and you are able to act more quickly. Your mind is also more flexible and you see more options. The turmoil that may be going on inside you can be contained, and has less chance of spilling over into the situation The gentle voice of your Intuitive Self is distinguishable from the voices of your other aspects. You are able to use its guidance to make the decisions that are being called for. And you feel confident in the rightness of those decisions. Relaxed, you are able to observe, listen, and act with greater clarity.

When you are not in a crisis situation, and are relaxed, your ability to notice more detail about the circumstances that surround you enables you to perceive patterns and themes in your life much more easily. You notice the subtle connections between a situation, your thoughts, your emotional experience, your response, and what unfolds as a result of your response to the situation. When you are relaxed, the information gleaned from this constant flow of experience is easily integrated and used in making future decisions. It refines your "emerging self"—the person you are becoming as a result of integrating new information. When you are not in a crisis, being relaxed makes it easier for you to revel in the rich experience of being alive. Quite simply, you experience your life more completely, and you are able to respond in more positive ways, positively affecting the situations in which you find yourself.

When you are tense, everything feels like a crisis situation. It is easy to get lost in the thoughts, feelings, and sensations that rise in response to a particular moment. Job interviews, first dates, or having the boss to dinner can cause you to become lost in thoughts, such as, "They won't like me. I'm not smart enough for this job." Or, "I'm not attractive, my last date was a total disaster." Or, "The house isn't nice enough, and there won't be enough food." You become fixated on the thoughts, feelings, and sensations that are presenting themselves, and lose your perspective. When your body and mind become tense, you may stumble over your words, or the furniture. Some of you may even have become so tense in a moment of crisis that you felt frozen to the spot. Unable to move both physically and mentally, you could not meet the challenge with which you were faced. During moments of tension, you are unable to identify with your Intuitive Self, and your actions reflect the predominating body/mind phenomena you are lost in.

When you are tense, you lose sight of yourself and your relationship to the moment. You lose sight of the thoughts and feelings that are motivating your actions. You lose sight of your intentions, and are unaware that your actions are the result of unconscious fear or anger. You forget what you hoped to accomplish. You cannot hear the voice of your Intuitive Self, and the guidance you need to proceed is unavailable to you. Your actions, and their results, reflect your diminished presence. You are, in fact, not acting but reacting. Frequently, after moments such as these, I hear myself saying, "I wish I hadn't done that. Why didn't I do this instead? It would have been so much better." Or, "I wish I hadn't said that. What could I possibly have been thinking? Where was I coming from?"

Being told to relax is always extremely good advice. It is the simplest and most direct action you can take to be in a state of mind to solve a problem, deal with a difficult situation, or enjoy the life you're living. But I'm sure you all have discovered that "simple" is not synonymous with "easy," especially in a moment of crisis. We all live very complex, busy lives. We are expected to play many roles. Unless you live on a mountain top, removed from all the cares and responsibilities of life, relaxing and remaining relaxed is a difficult challenge.

I was thirty years old before I became aware of the constant tension I carried throughout my body and mind. When someone said to me, "Renee, relax." My response was to snap, "I am relaxed." I could never understand why they would shake their head and walk away. My body/mind tension was so chronic, that state felt perfectly natural to me. Most of us are unaware that we are living in a chronic state of body/mind tension. If we are to approach life with a relaxed body and mind—if we are to remain home and discover our body's wisdom—it is important that we create tools to help us recognize our tension and release it.

Releasing tension in the body has a reciprocal effect on the mind. The body and the mind move together. When you relax the body, the mind relaxes. When you relax the mind, the body relaxes. Some of you may find it easier to relax the body first; others, the mind. Below I offer you a variety of techniques to relax both body and mind. Choose the ones that are easiest for you and practice those. If you have certain relaxation techniques that already work for you, use them also. Once you experience the gifts of a relaxed body/mind, you will want to incorporate these practices into your daily life. Those moments of relaxation will become as precious to you as air, food, water, and love.

CONSCIOUS BREATHING AS A TOOL FOR RELAXATION

Each of us has constant access to a simple yet powerful tool for relaxing—breathing. Breathing is always with us, occurring continually throughout each day. We cannot leave it at home in a drawer or pocket. Since breathing is your constant companion, you do not have to remove yourself from everyday activities to become aware of it. All you have to do is slow yourself down, bring your eyes forward, and pay attention to the components of breathing.

As you read the exercise below, notice how alert you become. Notice how your body begins to relax. Imagine the benefits you will feel when you actually practice the exercise and give it your full attention.

◇ ◇ ◇

Exploring the Breath

In preparation for this exercise settle into a comfortable chair. Let yourself sink into the chair. Allow yourself to be completely supported by it. If you notice tension in any part of your body, send your breath into that area. Imagine that your breath is loosening any tension there and moving it out through the pores of your skin. Continue to breathe in this way until your entire body feels completely relaxed. Feel your body sink into the chair even more. Give yourself to the chair as though you were lying in the lap of someone you trust completely.

Now bring your attention to the breath itself. Notice the coolness in your nostrils as you inhale. Then notice the quiet, motionless space at the end of the inhalation. As you breathe out, notice the feeling of warmth in your nostrils. Then notice the quiet, empty space at the end of your exhalation.

Continue to breathe normally. As you do, notice any tension in your chest, your belly, or your diaphragm. Muscular tension in any of these areas will prevent you from taking in a full breath. With each breath, soften your belly and let it gently rise and expand. Release the tension in your chest and let your rib cage expand upward, outward, and to the sides. This will allow you to take in an even larger amount of air. Next, as you exhale, pause for a moment when you reach the space at the end of the breath and notice what you are feeling in other parts of your body. Take a deep breath and send it into those parts so

21

◇ ◇ ◇

exploring the breath (cont)

that they can expand and soften. Repeat this process of breathing into areas of your body that seem tight until each one you have identified becomes softer, lighter, warmer, more relaxed.

Bring your attention back to the rhythm of your breathing. When you come to the end of the exhalation, surrender yourself to that moment. Rest there, with a relaxed attentiveness, until your lungs spontaneously begin to take in air. Do not hold your breath. Simply let go and rest at the end of the exhalation. Repeat this process several times, each time resting at the end of exhalation until the body chooses to breathe in once again.

After a few cycles, you will notice that with each subsequent inhalation the space between the breaths has expanded. At this point let your awareness drift into your eyes and your ears. Do not strain in order to do this. Simply let your awareness move into those two areas. Listen to any thoughts and watch any sensations that are moving through you. Notice any impulses to act. Notice what happens to your breath, and to your body as these different thoughts and sensations rise and pass. If your body tenses or your breath becomes shallow, take a deep, cleansing breath and invite your body to relax once again. Continue to softly watch, listen, and feel. Trust that you will remember anything of importance that you are noticing now, and tell yourself that you will address it later on. Right now you are simply learning about the connection between relaxation, the breath, the body, and the mind. When you are ready to end this exercise, take one more deep, cleansing breath. Hold it for a moment, then exhale completely. While still relaxed, explore how you feel different from when you began this exercise.

◇ ◇ ◇

There is a very useful reciprocal relationship between the breath and relaxation: in order to breathe deeply you must be relaxed, and in order to relax you must breathe deeply. Without even realizing it, most of us do not inhale as deeply or exhale as fully as we might. The next simple exercise can reveal the subtle ways in which you prevent yourself from taking in a complete breath.

◇ ◇ ◇

Expanding the Breath

First, revisit the previous exercise. Sitting in a chair, take a slow, deep breath. Notice the cool feeling in your nostrils. Hold the breath for a moment and then exhale. Inhale again, allowing your belly and then your chest to expand. As you exhale, notice the sensation of warmth in your nostrils as air passes through your nose. Notice how the muscles of your abdomen and chest contract to push the air out completely.

Breathe in again and notice if this time you can take in more air than before. Hold the breath for a moment, then release it slowly. Repeat this sequence of inhaling, holding, and exhaling three more times. Each time you do, try to notice how deep and smooth your inhalation is. Also notice if the space between breathing in and breathing out is a restful one for you. Pay attention to how completely your lungs empty when you exhale.

Now you will learn to expand the breath. Inhale again and this time notice if there is a moment during the inhalation when the breath seems to 'catch' somewhere. You will experience this 'catching' as a slight hesitation or block in the flow of the inhalation. It will feel as though the breath wants to go deeper but for some reason cannot. Your attention will be drawn to the precise place where the inhalation catches. At that place you will notice sensations such as tightness, thickness, or heaviness in the muscles of your throat, chest, or back.

◇ ◇ ◇

expanding the breath (cont)

As soon as you have identified the place where the inhalation catches, exhale slowly and fully. Pause for a moment, and then inhale once more. When you reach the point where your breath caught before, hold your breath right there for a brief moment. Focus your attention on the 'catching place' and then exhale with an open mouth and a deep sigh. As you exhale, visualize the tension in the 'catching place' being dispersed. You will probably have the urge to yawn. Do so. With the next breath you take in after yawning, you will notice that you are able to take in a much larger breath than you could before. You will also notice that your exhalation is longer and smoother, more complete. This means that the 'catching place' is already starting to loosen up.

Inhale once more. Observe the point where your breath seems to be blocked. Inhale ten short, soft, pumping breaths directly into that point. At the end of these pumping breaths exhale as deeply as you can. When you take your next breath, you will notice that you can take in an even deeper breath than before. Hold the breath for a moment at the end of the inhalation, then exhale completely. You can repeat this process of INHALING/FINDING THE 'CATCHING PLACE'/SENDING SHORT, PUMPING BREATHS INTO THE 'CATCHING PLACE'/EXHALING as often as you need to in order to inhale fully, smoothly, and completely.

By exploring and expanding the breath through exercises such as these, you learn how to use the breath to relax your body. You develop a detailed understanding of the breath and its relationship to your body's ease or disease. You develop a detailed understanding of the components of the breath—inhalation, the space that follows, exhalation, the space that follows—along with their relationships to, and reliance upon, each other.

Within the process of breathing, each component has a symbolic meaning. When you expand your awareness of your breath, your understanding of the symbolic nature of breath also expands. Each time you inhale, you reestablish the cycle that initiated life for you outside of the womb. In a very real sense, you begin life anew each time you breathe in. Within the space that follows inhalation, the promise that marks the beginning of life can be deeply felt.

Exhalation, on the other hand, represents the emptying out that must precede becoming full again. It is a moment in which you surrender, trusting that the next breath, and much more, will be made available to you. Each time you exhale, you surrender the gift of life back to God/All That Is and rehearse the final release of the life force that takes place at the moment of your death.

The space at the end of exhalation is given to you as a moment in which to pause, reflect, and gratefully acknowledge your relationship with God/All That Is. The mind becomes quiet, you establish a connection with the source of all creation, and you hear the gentle voice of your Intuitive Self. You experience a profound sense of well-being. Feeling protected and watched over, you feel confident that the circumstances of your life are intended for your benefit. In this space you invite not only the next breath but all of life to begin anew. You reaffirm your desire to be alive.

When you bring your attention to the breath, you experience a deep connection with the creative force. You come in touch with the ultimate source of the breath, God/All That Is, and its life-giving intentions toward you. In a sense you remember that the vital force within the breath, or "chi" as Eastern philosophies refer to it, is an offering to you from God/All That Is and an affirmation of your partnership with God.

The Bible recounts, "Then the lord God formed the man of dust of the ground, and breathed into his nostrils the breath of life; and the man became a living Soul."[2] This passage tells how God's breath initiated life for Adam and for all humankind. The teachings of Judaism hold that God is continually renewing our covenant with the creative force by blowing His/Her breath into wo/man. I believe that we play a very active role in renewing that covenant, that wo/man and God are constantly entering into an ongoing mutual agreement. Under its terms God/All That Is promises to share His/Her vital force with us, and we in turn promise to use it well, in ways that honor our partnership with Him/Her.

When I become aware of my own breath, I also reflect on the breath of God. I am reminded of the constant collaboration that goes on between us. I see each moment of my life as an opportunity to make a contribution to the Universe unfolding. The details within each of those moments become precious to me. I become more present to those details and to myself. I experience my body and my surroundings in a very profound way. Immediately I am at the center of my personal universe, at the center of all that exists inside me and around me. Resting in the stillness, the silence, and the emptiness that the breath affords me, I realize that relaxation is much more profound than letting go of physical tension. Relaxation is feeling free to let go completely, in every sense of the word and in every direction, because we know that we are constantly being nurtured and supported.

RECOGNIZING AND RELEASING CHRONIC TENSION

Most of us lead very busy lives in which stress is the norm. Perhaps you are already a good manager of stress. You take time out for rest and relaxation, eat well, exercise with some regularity, nourish your support networks, pace yourself, and are creative about juggling the different roles you play. But even if you consider yourself to be a skillful stress manager, you probably have areas of chronic tension in your body. This is the tension that we carry around with us even when we think we are relaxed. In a sense this form of tension exists underneath the tension which we can rather easily identify when we stop and listen to our bodies for a moment.

You may be surprised to discover where this tenacious, long-term form of tension has taken up residence. Many of us walk around with our jaws clenched or our shoulders hunched up and do not even notice these habitual reactions to stress. This is what makes chronic tension so insidious: it becomes the norm for us. We do not notice it, so there is no cue for us to investigate or try to release it. In a general sense, we may notice at the end of the day that we feel "stressed out" or "wound up," but we seldom take the time to thoroughly investigate the details within such an assessment.

The following exercise is designed to help you locate areas of chronic tension and begin to release it. Eliminating chronic tension will not happen overnight, of course, but you will be amazed at how different you feel after practicing this exercise just once. If you repeat it regularly, you will be able to map out areas where tension tends to collect for you. With that information you can observe your posture, your movements, and areas of physical discomfort, with an eye toward recognizing and releasing all manifestations of chronic tension.

◇ ◇ ◇

Tension Inventory and Release

The more you practice relaxation techniques such as this one, the more you will understand the precise ways in which you experience and store tension. Shallow breathing, awkward movements, stiffness in muscles and joints, eyes straining outward in what I call 'the figuring out look'—all of these signs of underlying tension will become more obvious to you. You will be able to let go of these manifestations of tension and the defensive postures they produce. You will become less guarded physically and more open in every way to each moment. Coming home to your body at different times throughout the day, you will be able to take a quick tension inventory, release whatever tension you discover, and relax.

◇ ◇ ◇

Tension Inventory Exercise

Start this exercise by looking at yourself in a mirror. Study your face. Is your brow furrowed? Are your eyes and mouth pinched with tension? Do you have any tics or muscle spasms? Now, find a quiet, comfortable place where you can lie down undisturbed. Whatever you lie on should be firm enough so that you can feel your muscles and skeleton as they rest against the surface.

Rest your hands gently on your belly. Take ten slow, deep breaths, encouraging your belly and chest to expand. Notice the rhythm of your breath as it comes and goes.

Notice the position of your body. Where does your head touch whatever you are lying upon? Is your head turned slightly to the left or right? Is your chin pointing toward the ceiling or your chest? Are both of your shoulders touching the surface? What parts of your back touch the surface and which do not? Are your buttocks tense or relaxed? Are your feet turned in or out?

As you observe these things, let your inventory be free of any judgmental dialogue such as "Why can't I just relax?" or "Why am I so uptight?" Such self-talk will simply add to the existing tension and make it harder for you to stay open to what you are observing. When thoughts that are not specifically related to this exercise rise, let them drift out of your mind just as leaves floating down a river pass out of your sphere of vision. Let go of these thoughts and return to your awareness of the body.

While taking a deep breath, tighten all of the muscles in your body. Try to contract every muscle, from the top of your head to the

◇ ◇ ◇

tension inventory exercise (cont)

ends of your toes and fingers. Hold this posture for three seconds, then slowly and deliberately release your breath and muscles. Take a deep breath and release it. Repeat the process.

What areas of tension do you notice immediately? Bring your full attention to one of these areas and examine it fully. Breathe deeply, as if you were actually breathing into that part of your body. Feel this area expand each time you inhale. Continue to breathe into that area until you feel the energy moving and the tension releasing. Remember, areas of chronic tension will need your repeated attention and permission to soften before they can return to and maintain their natural state of fluidity.

After you have dealt with the most conspicuous area of physical tension, begin a general review of your entire body. As you do this, remain conscious of your breath coming and going. Start at your head and move down toward your feet in a more thorough search for remaining areas of tension. Be sure to sweep your entire body, very slowly, reviewing each part of it.

Notice if there are any parts of your body where your awareness does not want to go. Make a mental note of them. These may be places in your body that are holding repressed memories. It will be useful to come back to these areas for deeper investigation at a later time.

Give yourself permission to soften and release any constriction or rigidity that you find in your muscles, joints, and organs. Continue paying attention to your breath and notice how its rhythm changes when you become aware of an area that is tense. If your breathing becomes shallower when you come to an area of tension, let your chest and belly expand so that you can take a deeper breath. If your breathing becomes more rapid when you come to an area of tension,

◇ ◇ ◇

tension inventory exercise (cont)

slow it down by allowing the space at the end of the exhalation to last a little longer before you inhale once again.

Pay special attention to your face. What sensations do you notice in your mouth and jaw? Are your teeth clenched? If so, release your jaw so that your upper and lower teeth are not touching. Let the tip of your tongue rest gently against the back of your teeth. Are your lips parted or pulled together? Let them part and feel your jaw drop. Can you feel a facial expression underneath your skin? Let the muscles that are maintaining that expression relax, become longer. Let them stop working.

Bring your attention to your forehead and brow. Let the muscles beneath the skin of your forehead elongate. Let the muscles that surround your eyeballs loosen so that the eyes have more space in which to rest. Notice if your eyelids are tightly closed or softly relaxed. Let the small muscles within your eyelids become longer, more relaxed.

Continue to move your awareness into different areas of your body. As you become more and more relaxed, try to visualize your bones and the muscles that surround them. Can you see where your bones and muscles come in contact with each other? Try to feel that place of contact. Imagine the fluids within you that bathe these bones and muscles, that make the places where they meet soft and slippery.

Place your hand on any part of your torso and feel the rhythm of your breath as it moves in and out. You will notice the rise and fall of your chest and belly as air moves in, rests for a moment, and moves out again. This flow of air is the "wind" that moves within us. It cleanses the blood and other fluids that constitute our "waters," the internal ocean that is the setting for the chemical reactions which

◇ ◇ ◇

tension inventory exercise (cont)

spark and maintain our life processes. Take a moment to sense the wind and waters that move within you. Notice images or sounds that come to mind as you do so.

Now bring your attention to your breathing and send each breath throughout your entire body. Let this breath sweep over you from head to toe, like a wave sweeping over the sand as it comes onto the shore. As you imagine this wave coming onto the shore, try to visualize the waters that move within you—blood, lymphatic fluids, hormones, and other fluids that bathe your cells. Imagine them flowing slowly and evenly, into and out of every part of you, nourishing the many processes that sustain your life force. Each time you breathe in and send the breath throughout your body, you are also sending the nourishing waters within you into the cells of your muscles, bones, and organs. Imagine that with each breath you are sending life into every part of your body.

Now close your eyes and imagine yourself getting up and slowly moving across the room. Notice how gracefully you place one foot in front of the other, how easy it is to move through space. Your body feels so much lighter and freer. All of its parts are cooperating, working in unison. Take a slow, deep breath. Let your belly and your chest rise as you breathe in. Experience the wonder and awe of this amazing creation—your physical self.

Slowly, open your eyes and look around. Then begin to stand up. Notice how the body needs to organize itself. What muscles start to constrict and what parts need to shift in order for you to stand? As you begin to move, recall how your body moved in your imagination. Notice if you are bringing more effort and expending more energy than is actually required. Try to keep your movements simple and stay as relaxed as you can.

◇ ◇ ◇

tension inventory exercise (cont)

Walk over to a mirror and look at your face. What do you see? Does this face seem quieter, calmer, fuller than before you started this exercise? Speak to yourself out loud, telling yourself that you will be able to maintain this state of relaxation throughout the day and return to it at any time by recalling the details of how you feel at this very moment.

◇ ◇ ◇

Using the Tension Inventory Exercise, I have learned how to locate my own areas of chronic tension and recognize the first moments when those areas begin to contract. When I notice tension in my neck, back, and shoulders, I breathe deeply into those areas, encouraging my shoulders to drop and my head and neck to move more freely. This exercise has had other positive effects for me. My gait is less burdened and more fluid. Instead of struggling to meet the moments of my life, I can soften my eyes, expand my awareness, and gently invite my surroundings to enter my sphere of vision. I function with fewer defenses and am no longer troubled by images of myself as an old woman, head bent toward the ground, taking small, stiff steps forward. Instead I see myself upright, lithe, with arms outstretched, dancing and smiling.

Fortunately there are many forms of "body work" and "movement release" that can supplement your efforts to release tension. Body work consists of techniques in which another person manipulates your limbs and tissues. Cranio-sacral therapy, deep tissue massage, Rolfing, Trager, Functional Integration, and other forms of manipulation belong in this category. Movement release, on the other hand, refers to techniques in which you move in new ways without the intervention or assistance of another person. Yoga, Feldenkrais' Awareness Through Movement, the Alexander Method, Continuum, and Authentic Movement are all examples of these techniques.

By helping you to release physical tension, these forms have positive effects in other areas, too. When you are physically relaxed, you think more clearly. You find it easier to notice your feelings and express them. You feel more connected to the presence of Spirit in your life, however that reveals itself to you. In general, when you are relaxed you find yourself living more fully, with more spontaneity and creativity.

MEDITATION AS A TOOL FOR RELAXATION

Meditation is a means of remaining present to the moment-to-moment experiences of your life. Its practice can include any activity that allows you to concentrate and reflect on the present, and which soothes the body and quiets the mind.

Meditation is an ancient practice and a central aspect of many Eastern religious systems. In the western world many people have added meditation to their own spiritual practice or have been introduced to it through classes in relaxation, stress management, wellness, and cardiac care. In his book *Freedom from the Known*, J. Krishnamurti points out that meditation is simply a matter of paying attention. This means that turning your attention to any activity can become a form of meditation.

Observing the sensations that move within you, concentrating on an aspect of your physiology such as the breath or the heartbeat—or using techniques such as visualization, massage, and movement release—could each be considered forms of meditation. Likewise cutting vegetables, weeding a garden, singing, walking in the woods, or being present to the experience of physical pain could be considered meditation, too. Whatever the activity, it is your effort to be consciously aware of what is taking place that transforms that activity into meditation.

There are many formal ways to practice meditation, including zazen or Buddhist sitting meditation, Sufi dancing, Transcendental Meditation (TM), Vipassanna, and contemplative prayer. Some of these utilize the silent repetition of a word or phrase while others involve chanting aloud. While meditating, a person might sit very still or might move about—or even dance and shout as in Rajneesh's "Dynamic Meditation." One form may be practiced with eyes closed while another involves gazing at a flower or some other object.

The goals of meditation vary. One may emphasize devotion and use the practice to communicate with God and experience His/Her love. Other forms may direct the practitioner toward experiencing the unity of all being, discovering one's true self, or learning to experience the moment. Some types of meditation seek to still the mind or call it back from its wanderings in the general stream of consciousness, while others encourage us to let the mind wander as we observe.

Each technique that we can name is slightly different, yet all forms of meditation share similar ends and all can help you to relax. By providing a way to "turn down" the rational, problem-solving functions of the brain, meditation opens a channel to your creative and Intuitive Self. When you are in touch with your Intuitive Self, you experience a deep sense of inner peace. Meditating teaches you that you do not have to avoid or put aside what you notice. There is no reason to move away from any thought, any feeling, any physical sensation that comes into your awareness, even when you consider it unpleasant or uncomfortable. Through the practice of meditation you can use the details of any experience to become centered, aware, and relaxed.

Because uncomfortable feelings, sensations, or thoughts are so compelling, they can rather easily provide the focus which is at the heart of many forms of meditation. You do not have to "send these phenomena to their rooms" in order to meditate; they become your meditation. The details within them become what you notice, and that noticing is meditation. When you experience these uncomfortable thoughts, feelings, and sensations in the context of meditating, you can sit with them a little longer and learn from them. By focusing and learning, you can act—not react. Being in control and making decisions—rather than being buffeted by outside stimuli—takes the sting out of the discomfort.

The spaciousness that exists within the meditative space surrounds each thought, feeling, sensation, and impulse to act. This allows you to "step back" a bit and examine each of these body/mind phenomena more carefully. At such times you recognize in a very profound way that you are not your thoughts, feelings, sensations, and impulses. They exist and can be very powerful indeed. But they are only a part of who you are. They do not define you, rather you can choose how to be in relationship to them.

Through the practice of meditation you become very aware of your participation in the realms of body, mind, emotion, and Spirit. Meditating enables you to notice and describe more fully your experiences of sight, sound, speech, movement, thought, feelings, sensation, and memory. You can use meditation to come in touch with everyday aspects of self and with your most profound attribute—God within you. Meditation also can assist you in looking within yourself for information and insights that can release you from unresolved pieces of your past. Through meditating you can come in touch with memories, images, thoughts, feelings, and sensations and examine them more carefully in order to resolve psychological issues associated with them.

The benefits of meditation can be applied to many areas of your life. You can use it to create a quiet inner space from which to gently observe yourself and the world around you. By meditating you can become aware of tension and agitation and learn how to release both. You can become more skillful at relaxing and staying relaxed for longer periods of time, even when the circumstances surrounding you are chaotic. Meditating also facilitates your contact with God/All That Is, thereby making you available to inspiration and revelation. In the peaceful moments that meditation affords, you experience the total support which The Source extends toward you. You sense that The

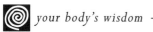

Source is constantly encouraging you to move in directions that will be in your best interest.

◇ ◇ ◇

THREE NEW MEDITATIONS

As we said earlier, simply paying attention can transform any activity, or any moment for that matter, into an experience of meditation. In the meditations below you will be asked to pay attention to the changing numbers on a digital clock, your reflection in a mirror, and the space around your body. You can practice these three meditations at any time.

◇ ◇ ◇

Meditation for the Busy Executive

This meditation will increase your ability to focus and expand your awareness of the relativity of time. Sit facing a digital clock. Take several long, slow, deep breaths to relax you and focus your attention on your body. Now stare at the numbers displayed on the clock, trying to take in all of them at once (instead of seeing one-four-five, see 1:45). Keep your eyes focused on the numbers while you allow any distractions such as thoughts, sensations, or sounds to fade away. If you allow your attention to follow a random thought, you will lose sight of the numbers and miss the changing of one minute to the next. When your thoughts wander off, simply bring your attention back to the numbers on the clock.

Start practicing this meditation by committing to one minute, then two, then three, and so on. At first one minute will seem like a very long time, but as you become more practiced the time will pass more quickly. Once you are able to stay present to the changing of

◇ ◇ ◇

meditation for the busy executive (cont)

the numbers for ten to twenty minutes, you will begin to notice that
your mind is much more focused. You will be more insightful and
experience clarity amidst complex interactions. Over time you will
notice that you feel more sure of yourself. You will experience less
pressure in situations where decisions must be made, and have more
confidence in those decisions.

◇ ◇ ◇

Are You Looking at the Mirror, Or Is the Mirror Looking at You?

By practicing this exercise you will learn to look out at the world
through your eyes. You will become centered deep within yourself.
You will know yourself as you are, not just as you are reflected back
to yourself through the eyes of others. This meditation is designed
to help you see in a new way.

Seat yourself in front of a full-length mirror. Look into the mirror and notice what you see. Notice the quality of the eyes in the mirror image. What do you see? Is there vitality or life in them? Ask
yourself the question, "Am I looking at the image in the mirror, or is
the mirror image looking out at me?"

Now close your eyes for a moment. Take several long, slow,
deep breaths. Open your eyes and look down at your body resting in
the chair. Feel the pressure against your muscles where your body
and the chair meet. Now, while you continue to feel your body in the
chair, look up into the mirror once again. What do you see? Once

◇ ◇ ◇

are you looking at the mirror?... (cont)

again ask yourself the question, "Am I looking at the image in the mirror, or is the mirror image looking out at me?"

Continue to stare into the eyes that you see in the mirror as you silently ask yourself this question. At first you may not be able to tell if you are looking into the mirror or if the image in the mirror is looking out at you. If you persist, however, you will eventually understand the question. You will experience a very rapid shift in focus. First it will feel as if you are looking out from the mirror into the room at the person sitting in the chair. If you continue to concentrate on the image in the mirror, there will come an instant when you suddenly realize that the direction has changed. You notice that you are now looking through your eyes and seeing the image in the mirror as though you were looking at a stranger. The light that you noticed in the eyes when they were looking out at you is now gone.

As you become adept at looking out through your eyes into the space around you, you will learn how to bring your full focus to each moment. You will achieve a new breadth and depth of vision that will enable you to make decisions based on the most complete information.

◇ ◇ ◇

I Am the Center of My Universe

This meditation teaches you to concentrate on the space around objects rather than on the objects themselves. It is designed to help you experience your place in the Universe. Begin by taking several long, slow, deep breaths. Next, relax the muscles around your mouth, nose, eyes, and forehead.

◇ ◇ ◇

i am the center of my universe... (cont)

Now, become aware of the boundaries of your entire body: from the tip of your head to the bottoms of your feet; from the front of your body to the back; from the right side to the left side. Feel yourself encircled by the space around you.

Now, hold your pointer finger in front of your eyes. Hold it about ten inches away from your face. Look at your finger for at least sixty seconds. Slowly remove your finger from your field of vision, off to the side or down onto your lap. As you do, continue concentrating on the space your finger occupied. Notice your sense of your body in space. Slowly bring your finger back to its original position, then bring it several inches closer to your face. Focus on your finger's new position in space, again slowly remove it, and continue to concentrate on the now vacant space. Repeat these steps until your finger is almost touching your nose. Do you notice any changes in your sense of your body in space?

Practice doing this exercise several times until you feel that you can stay focused on space and not have your eyes automatically move to settle on an object.

Now close your eyes for a few moments. Imagine your eyeballs softening and expanding to take over your entire forehead. Imagine that your entire forehead is now one huge eye and you are looking out through it. Open your eyes slowly and look out at the world through your entire forehead. Keep your eyes soft and relaxed as you focus them on the space immediately around your forehead. You may need to bring your finger up in front of your face and remove it in order to remind your eyes where to look. Notice what happens to your sense of your body in space. Has anything changed?

◇ ◇ ◇

i am the center of my universe… (cont)

By practicing this exercise you will become conscious of your body in space. You will remain present to yourself in a powerful way. You will become the "Center of Your Universe."

◇ ◇ ◇

All of the techniques outlined in this chapter will help you to relax and tap into "your body's wisdom." You will become very present to yourself and your surroundings. You will participate in every activity and every exchange with more awareness. You will think more clearly, experience your feelings more vividly, and notice the sensations in your body more readily. In a state of relaxation, you will be able to perceive and participate in all of these body/mind phenomena with exquisite patience and clarity. In short, you will discover the treasures of adulthood.

In Chapter Two, **Entering the Interval,** we will explore the Interval phenomenon. The Interval teaches us about the stillness at the center of all movement, the silence that surrounds all sound, and the emptiness that envelops all form. Within the Interval you notice and experience every detail that comes into your field of awareness—thoughts, feelings, sounds, sensations, patterns of energy, other people—while you remain centered, balanced, and expansive. Resting in the Interval also prepares you to mobilize your energy, examine your intentions, and then act wisely.

CHAPTER TWO

ENTERING
THE INTERVAL

Breathe deeply and gently.
Let your body soften.
See yourself within the space that surrounds you.
Feel yourself within the space that surrounds you.
Who is doing the seeing? Who is doing the feeling?

Hen you are truly relaxed, you enter into a space which I call the Interval. The Interval is a space of exquisite peacefulness and complete being-ness. Within it you have nowhere to go, nothing to do, no problems to solve, no one else to be. You simply exist, and everything occurring inside of you and around you simply exists too. The Interval is the domain of your Intuitive Self.

Within the Interval you experience the stillness at the center of all movement, the silence that surrounds all sound, and the emptiness that envelops all form. You become one with the stillness, the silence, and the emptiness that are at the center of you and at the center of the universe. You become one with everything that exists in creation.

Within the Interval you experience an interesting paradox. On the one hand, you become very conscious of the boundaries of your body. You sense clearly where your body stops and the rest of the world begins, and you feel yourself to be separate and distinct from the rest of the world. At the same time, however, you sense your boundaries dissolving. You no longer feel separate from the world around you. Instead you experience yourself as an intrinsic part of the world; the two become one.

Each of you has had many spontaneous Interval experiences even though you did not label them as such. An Interval experience can occur after a long period of trying to sort out a complex situation that is surrounded by intense feelings. When you stop and sit quietly after a period of trying on different scenarios that have brought no resolution, then you are experiencing the Interval. When you stop trying to figure it all out and let go of thinking (often out of sheer exhaustion), you experience the Interval. You might recall that at that very moment of surrender, the situation clarified itself and an acceptable solution rose into your mind. This is the result of giving yourself over to the Interval.

Many of us experience the Interval when we are immersed in the silence and majesty of nature, while hiking, camping, or sitting by the ocean. We also experience the Interval during passionate lovemaking. When two people are utterly present to themselves, to each other, and to the exchange between them, they are within the Interval. The love experience that all of us long for happens when neither partner is defending against *nor* pulling away from the other. Neither one is rushing through the experience in hot pursuit of orgasm or some other aspect of the experience. During this deep surrendering, our boundaries dissolve. We can no longer differentiate our body from that of our lover's, our touch from theirs. It is no longer clear who is initiating and who is responding. When we allow ourselves to be utterly present to our body and its sensations, without any judgments or agendas interfering, we experience the Interval. Each partner feels a part of something infinitely larger than the space defined by his or her physical body. We become one with God/All That Is. We are living within the Interval.

I first became acquainted with the Interval some years ago when I worked as a conservator of art objects for the Museum of African Art in Washington, D.C. I was thirty-three years old, and the youngest of my five children had just entered school. Excited about the prospect of going back to work, I started out by volunteering with the Museum. I soon discovered that my supervisor, the museum's curator, was not thrilled to be taking on a new volunteer. Clearly she expected me to be a burden rather than a help and she made no effort to hide from me her low expectations and her lack of enthusiasm. She immediately tried to make it easy for me to back out of the position by assigning me a very difficult project. But I was so eager to be part of the outside world again that I rather easily put aside her less-than-welcoming ways and quickly became immersed in my new role.

My responsibilities were to help care for the collection, including the repair of damaged objects. My first project, which would last for two months, was to restore a clay pipe that had shattered during the installation of a recent exhibit. Most African clay objects are not fired, so they are very susceptible to crumbling when broken. When this one was dropped, three of the five faces that had been embossed on its surface were destroyed, and what was left of the pipe had broken into six separate fragments. Restoring this badly damaged piece was a formidable challenge for a volunteer. I would have to recreate the missing faces and integrate them into the fragments that remained. Instead of feeling discouraged, though, I became even more attracted to my new job. I was ready for this challenge and for the chance to once again use skills that I had put aside for many years.

On my first day I was shown to my work space, a small, well-lit room with only a desk and a chair, and given some tools, the fragments of the pipe, and a book that illustrated what the pipe might have looked like when it was intact. Completely alone for the first time in twelve years, I was in heaven. No one had any expectations of me. Without my intervention, the pipe would end up in the trash. Therefore I had nothing to lose by trying to restore it. There was no pressure. I had all the time I needed to complete my assignment, so I felt totally relaxed.

The first few weeks were devoted to treating the surfaces of the six fragments to prevent further deterioration and studying the contour of each fragment, the clay itself, and the photograph of the similar intact pipe. I came to know that pipe as intimately as I knew the faces of my own children. Soon I began to make a plan about how to restore the piece. There was no phone in my office to disturb me while I was working. Hidden away, I had few opportunities to interact with other members of the staff, and they made no effort to get to know me, probably because they felt that this new recruit would not last very long.

As the days went by, I noticed that while I was working on the pipe I was empty of any thoughts. I felt at peace, enveloped by a deep sense of calm. My boundaries disappeared and I became one with the pipe. I understood its nature and its needs completely. The level of attention I brought to the work created a feeling akin to love for this inanimate object. Although I did not know it at the time, I was having a profound Interval experience. Each time I worked on the pipe I became aware of the changes that would take place within me. My thoughts stopped, my breathing became slower and deeper, my entire body became very relaxed. I especially noticed my eyes; they were softly focused on the object of my attention, as I engaged in an intimate and very compelling interaction with the pipe. While I was working, it was as though time had disappeared. Often, when I looked up from my work, I was shocked to discover that two or three hours had passed.

As I became familiar with these Interval phenomena, I began to realize that I could induce this way of being. I did not have to wait for it to come to me; I could invite it. By focusing my attention, relaxing my body, and emptying my mind of thoughts, I could experience the sense of being perfectly calm and present whenever I wanted to, not just at work. Hoping that I could achieve the peacefulness and equipoise that I had known while working on the pipe, I began to invite the Interval experience into the rest of my life.

I quickly discovered that it was much easier to experience the Interval when I was alone in my office at the museum than when I was immersed in the demands of being a wife and mother. But I continued to try to create Interval experiences when I was away from my office sanctuary, while interacting with members of my family or with other people. At work or in other settings, I noticed that all of my experiences in the Interval had certain features in common. Resting within the Interval, I felt calm, focused, and unusually perceptive. I was very aware of my thoughts, feelings, sensations, and inclinations to act or react, but I never got lost in any one of those phenomena. The actions I took after I had been resting in the Interval were always more creative and successful than those I would take without having visited that place of stillness, silence, and emptiness.

Within the Interval you become the quiet observer. You notice areas of stillness in the midst of movement and activity. You notice the many moments of silence in the midst of sound. You notice your thoughts, feelings, and sensations with great clarity, but you also notice the space that exists between each of these body/mind phenomena. You quietly observe the stillness, the silence, and the emptiness within yourself and all around you.

Just as the space between the notes of a musical composition gives form to the piece, the Interval gives form to your life. The level of awareness you achieve when you are in the Interval transforms your life from a collection of discordant fragments into a harmonious whole. Through your experience of the Interval, you surrender to the stillness, the silence, and the emptiness at the core of your being. In surrendering, you become centered.

Within the Interval you feel very oriented. You are totally present to your body. You are conscious of your position in space. You are aware of your feet touching the ground, your breath coming and going, the sensation of clothing resting on your skin. You feel at home in your body and you experience a sense of belonging there, even when you are in physical or emotional pain.

Viewing your life from the perspective of the Interval expands your field of vision. You have a larger space in which to sort out the many thoughts, memories, feelings, sensations, and impulses to act that arise within the space of a single moment. When you look at these internal phenomena from the perspective of the Interval, you experience clarity rather than confusion. You are less likely to become lost in a particular phenomenon of your inner life, less likely to be carried away with a particular feeling, sensation, or thought. You see and feel everything around you and each detail within that totality, yet you do not feel overwhelmed by all you experience.

Resting within the Interval is the best vantage point from which to observe the circumstances that surround you and the body/mind phenomena that rise within you. In addition, it is in the Interval that solutions to a conflict or dilemma reveal themselves most readily. When you enter into the Interval, you see clearly because you can recognize and release extraneous issues and incorporate important ones. You discover solutions to problems more easily, as though the Interval has delivered them up to you. You also find it easier to recognize the deeper meaning, along with opportunities for growth that exist within a conflict.

The following exercise is designed to help you experience the Interval. It is separated into three sections. The first will help you to discover the stillness that is at the center of your being where you become the quiet observer. The second section will teach you how to listen in to the silence that surrounds all sound. The third section will help you to experience the emptiness that envelops all form.

EXPERIENCING THE INTERVAL

Fully experiencing the Interval is one of the most powerful, peaceful activities you can undertake. It not only offers the opportunity to relax and focus, it is a tool for taking control of your life. It teaches you to remain centered while in the midst of the turmoil created by the continuous bombardment of sights, sounds, events, and stimuli that abound in every moment of life. Like any worthwhile tool, it takes time to master. When you were a child, it took many lessons to learn to read, but that effort has paid off many times over. The ability to read allows you to glean wisdom from many sources. Likewise, spending time now to master the following three-step exercise will pay off in your ability to go to the Interval immediately any time you wish. It will help you shorten, and eventually eliminate, the time you lose being buffeted about by outside forces or random internal feelings and sensations.

First, read each section of the exercise. Next, choose the section that appeals to you the most, or feels the easiest to do, and practice that one for at least twenty minutes. When you have the available time, move · on to the other two in whatever order you like. When you do, try to practice each one for at least twenty minutes. Go back to your favorite one as often as you can and practice it while you remain aware of the other two. Eventually, the stillness, silence, and emptiness will occur simultaneously each time you return to any one of the sections.

◇ ◇ ◇

Step 1–The Stillness at the Center of All Movement
(20 minutes)

In this first part of the exercise you discover the stillness at the center of all movement. To be more precise, you discover the stillness within you while you are observing the movement of your body sensations, your thoughts, and your feelings.

Begin by finding a quiet place where you will not be disturbed. Sit quietly for a few moments. Feel the boundaries of your body from the tip of your head to the bottoms of your feet, from the front of your body to the back, from the right side to the left side. Take several long, slow, deep breaths. With each breath let your body soften and relax.

Next, bring your awareness to what your eyes are seeing. If your eyes are closed, become aware of the darkness behind your eyelids. If they are open, choose an object in the room on which to focus your attention. Be aware of the sounds around you.

While remaining aware of your entire body and of what you are seeing and hearing, feel the coolness in your nostrils as the air comes in. Feel the way your belly and chest expand as you inhale. Pause and notice the moment of stillness that comes after you breathe in. Now as you exhale notice the warm feeling in your nostrils as the air leaves.

◇ ◇ ◇

step 1—the stillness at the center of all movement (cont)

Feel how your chest and belly contract as you exhale. Pause and notice the moment of stillness that comes after you breathe out.

Breathe in once more and this time when you exhale, notice the space of stillness at the end of the exhalation. Let this space last as long as it wants to. Rest quietly within it. Feel the absolute stillness within this moment of pausing between breaths. Listen in to it. Do not rush to take in the next breath. Instead wait patiently for your breath to come in of its own accord. Settle into this space of stillness at the end of the exhalation and invite it to expand. Now, call your name silently to yourself, as if you were inviting yourself to become more present to the experience you are about to create.

Continue to breathe in and out slowly, deeply, and gently. As you are breathing in and out, notice all of your body sensations, thoughts, and feelings as they arise. Let them pass without engaging any one of them. Now you are being the quiet observer, the essence of stillness, the eye of the storm.

Next, imagine that you are the sovereign of your own kingdom. Your realm consists of everything in your awareness, all of the circumstances that surround you and all of your thoughts, feelings, and sensations. Each thought, feeling, and sensation is a message concerning the state of your realm and its needs. Your responsibility as the sovereign is to govern the realm. The safety and well-being of the realm depend on your ability to be receptive to all of the messages that come before you.

Now, bring your attention back to your breath and the space between the breaths. When you exhale, rest quietly for a moment in the space of stillness at the end of exhalation. Allow this space to expand. From within this space of stillness imagine yourself seated on your throne.

◇ ◇ ◇

step 1–the stillness at the center of all movement (cont)

Now invite the messengers who come in the form of your thoughts, feelings, and sensations to come before you. Remain present to each one. Experience each one fully and then let it pass so that you are ready for the next one as it arises.

Continue watching and listening to everything that enters your awareness until you are ready to end this exercise. Remind yourself that whatever you notice is of use to you. Assure yourself that you have taken note of each message and that you will give it the attention it requires at the appropriate time.

When you are able to notice every detail that comes into your field of awareness thoughts, feelings, sounds, sensations, patterns of energy, other people, objects without becoming lost in any one, you are being the sovereign of your realm. You have become the stillness at the center of all movement.

◇ ◇ ◇

Step 2 - The Silence That Surrounds All Sound
(20 minutes)

In this next stage of the exercise you will focus on hearing. Set aside at least twenty minutes for this exercise. Begin by finding a comfortable place to sit. Take several long, slow, deep breaths. Rest quietly in the space at the end of each breath. Rest there until your lungs spontaneously begin to take in air. With each breath, let your body soften and relax.

Now, become aware of the boundaries of your entire body from the tip of your head to the bottoms of your feet from the front of your

◇ ◇ ◇

step 2–the silence that surrounds all sound (cont)

body to the back from the right side to the left side. Notice all the sensations that move through your body. Throughout this section, try to stay aware of your entire body and all of its subtle sensations. Remain conscious of your breath coming and going.

Now, call your name silently to yourself, as if you are inviting yourself to become more present to the experience you are about to create. Next, relax the muscles around your mouth and nose. Then pay attention to your ears, your jaw, and your neck. Do you feel any sensations moving within these parts of your body? You may experience subtle vibrations, pulsing, or tingling. Breathe into the sensations you are noticing. Each time you exhale, send your breath into these sensations to quiet them. Do this several times.

Begin to notice the sound that is all around you. Let it wash over you. Feel yourself at the center of all of that sound. Pay attention to the specific sounds that make up this wash of sound. Take as much time as you need to do this. You may notice a humming refrigerator, the footsteps of someone on the floor above you, the sound of a clock ticking. As your listening deepens, you will be able to pick up sounds in the background that you were not aware of just a moment before. These sounds could be traffic noise, a bird song, a child's laughter, a barking dog, or music coming from the open window of a passing car. By sitting quietly and listening, you become aware of the many details of sound that surround you.

As you become aware of specific sounds within all of the sound that surrounds you, you will begin to notice the silence that surrounds each sound. Some of these moments of silence are very short. Others are longer. These moments of silence help to define each sound that you are noticing. They help to define the mixture of

◇ ◇ ◇

step 2–the silence that surrounds all sound (cont)

sounds that is surrounding you. At this moment you are hearing without straining to listen. You are at the center of all of the sound that surrounds you, peacefully noticing each sound and the silence surrounding each sound.

Right now you are doing several things at the same time. I want you to notice what they are. First, you are noticing your body as a whole, with all of its attending sensations. Second, you are aware of your breath, especially the space at the end of exhalation. Third, you are aware of the specific sounds that surround you and the silence between each of those sounds. As you move into the next stage of the exercise, you will add to these three things the awareness of seeing; you will see in a very particular way.

◇ ◇ ◇

Step 3 - The Emptiness That Envelops All Form
(20 minutes)

In this last part of the exercise you will learn how to stay aware of your body in space no matter where your eyes move and no matter what they are taking in. Set aside at least twenty minutes for this exercise. Once again breathe rhythmically and call your name silently to yourself, as if you are inviting yourself to become more present to the experience you are about to create.

Now, slowly bring your attention to your eyes. Notice the sensations in and around your eyes. Notice your temples and your forehead. If you feel any tightness or pressure in your eyeballs, temples, or forehead, release it. Imagine that your eyeballs are becoming softer,

◇ ◇ ◇

step 3 - the emptiness that envelops all form (cont)

that they are resting lightly in their sockets. Imagine that the muscles in your temples and forehead are relaxing, letting go.

Your eyes are completely relaxed now. Feel yourself at the center of the experience of being completely relaxed. Next, imagine that you are surrounded on all sides by a bubble that extends about one foot around every part of you. This bubble keeps your field of vision concentrated on the space that is immediately around you. Take a moment to become familiar with this space. While you are doing this, breathe in and out, slowly, evenly, and deeply.

Now that you are very familiar with the space within this bubble, notice your body within that space. See yourself at the center of the bubble. Notice what it feels like to know that you are at the center of the bubble. Now, in your mind's eye, make the bubble slightly larger, large enough so that it can include an object that is at least two feet away from you. As the bubble surrounding you becomes larger, let your vision become larger, too. Let your vision broaden.

Looking out from your place at the center of the bubble, be aware of your body. Be aware of the space between you and the object. Be aware of the object you are looking at.

Now, looking out from your place at the center of the bubble, see if you can do all three of these things at the same time: notice your body, the space between you and the object, and the object itself.

Now expand the bubble to include the whole room. Allow your eyes to come to rest on an object at the far end of the room. Continue to remain aware of your body, the space between you and the objects closest to you, and the space between them and this distant object.

When you are simultaneously seeing yourself, the space around you, and the objects within that space, you are seeing without straining *step 3 - the emptiness that envelops all form* (cont)

to look. When you are aware of your breathing, your hearing, your seeing, and your body as a whole, you are deeply centered in the Interval.

⟡ ⟡ ⟡

The more you practice all three sections of this exercise, the easier it will be to enter the Interval and remain there for longer periods of time. As you practice, you will begin to experience your body in a profound way. It will come alive for you, revealing all of its wisdom. You will become the center of your universe, not in a selfish, narcissistic way, but in a totally integrated way. You will become one with everything in you and around you because nothing will be excluded. You will know the stillness at the center of all movement. You will hear the silence that surrounds all sound. You will see the emptiness that envelops all form.

You will internalize the Interval experience. Resting in the Interval is a profoundly tranquil experience. At the same time, though, it energizes you and helps you to mobilize your forces when you need to take some action. Because the Interval is such an inclusive, inviting space, it is also an excellent learning environment. When you are in the Interval and take in information as you are resting there, the process of learning becomes effortless and fluid. You find that you can take in much more information. You can also integrate the new with the old much more easily and quickly. There is a lightness, an ease, a gracefulness to the process of acquiring and arranging new bits of information.

In Chapter Three, **Listening to Your Feelings,** we will take a closer look at the emotional realm of your experience. Just what are feelings and how can they become tools for accessing your body's wisdom? To answer these questions we will create a dictionary of terms related to the complex phenomenon of emotion and explore some examples of people using their feelings to investigate conflict, make decisions, know themselves better, and improve their relationships with others.

LISTENING TO
YOUR FEELINGS

Breathe deeply and gently.
Let your body soften.
See yourself within the space that surrounds you.
Feel yourself within the space that surrounds you.
Who is doing the seeing? Who is doing the feeling?

hen someone asks you how you are feeling, you usually reply with a quick, "Very well, and you?" or "I wish it were Friday!" If you are asked a more pointed question about what you are feeling, you will probably respond with a general "feeling word" such as angry, happy, sad, or scared. But angry can refer to a wide variety of feelings ranging from slight irritation to rage. One person who reports that she is happy could be feeling mildly pleased while another using the same word might be wildly ecstatic. Sad could mean anything from blue to despairing, and scared can refer to a hint of nervousness or abject terror. The constant about feeling is that it is a state of awareness characterized by certain inclinations and desires, *and is always accompanied by the experience of sensations in the body.*

Feelings are very subjective and unique for each person—circumstances that evoke them, the strength with which they are felt, and the way each person describes and expresses them. No moral judgment is attached to our feelings; they are neither right nor wrong—they simply exist. However, we are accountable for the way in which we display them.

While standards of acceptable emotional expression vary from one family system, community, and culture to another, there is usually some consensus within each of these contexts as to how we are permitted to express our feelings. Yelling at someone who has made you angry, for example, may be considered justifiable, while knocking them unconscious would not be tolerated. Sharing your most intimate feelings over lunch with a close friend seems quite fitting, but it might be considered inappropriate for you to do this at the office with a co-worker.

DEFINING FEELINGS

Assigning a "feeling word" such as glad or sad to what you are experiencing is a good beginning. Your description becomes more useful, though, if you go one step further and specify the depth and strength of your feelings. To say that you are "annoyed," for example, is very different from being "outraged." The distinction between the two can give you some important clues about what provoked your feelings and what action you can take to resolve them.

Sometimes difficult to label, feelings are not always easy to define either. For our purposes, though, we will define a feeling as a state of awareness that is characterized by certain inclinations and desires, and is always accompanied by the experience of sensations in the body.

Most of us are not in the habit of including our physical sensations in a description of our emotional state. "I'm mad!" seldom gets expanded into "I'm mad and my heart is pounding and my face feels hot and I can feel a hard knot of muscle at the base of my skull." But sensations do accompany every feeling state, and your willingness to notice them makes your experience of emotion richer, more authentic. When you allow the physical sensations within your feelings to be fully present, you create the opportunity to have an integrated body/mind experience. You encourage the sensations within your feelings to reveal the wisdom they contain.

The variety of sensations that you can experience as a component of feeling is limitless. Any physical sensation that you can imagine could be an accompaniment to any feeling state that you can imagine. On the skin these sensations could include temperature changes, the impression of being touched, or the sense of something resting on a part of your body. If a person is feeling anxious, for example, she may describe the sensation of a heavy weight resting on her chest.

A person also may experience temperature changes inside of the body as large or small areas of heat or cold that remain in one area or move around. Other internal sensations include churning, pulsing, fluttering, gripping, or pressure. Trembling, shaking, shivering, and spasms create sensations within the muscles. In addition, many people I have worked with describe the sensation of an object or a shape "materializing" within their body.

Each time I listen to someone speak of such an experience I am fascinated and struck by the richness of detail in their descriptions. They may tell of a metal plate blocking the lumen of their throat, a trap door appearing in their chest, or a tunnel connecting one part of their body to another. We explore details like these in order to find the "feeling word" (glad / mad / scared / sad) that describes those sensations. These details of sensation help to paint a picture or tell a story about what has provoked a person's feelings and how those feelings may be connected to a significant event from their past. In a way these sensations become story-telling tools.

Clearly the sensations within your feelings are very useful tools. You can use your awareness of them to create a state of mindfulness and enter into the Interval. Dr. John Kabat-Zinn, in his book entitled _Full Catastrophe Living: Using the Wisdom of Your Body and Mind to Face Stress, Pain, and Illness,_ defines mindfulness in this way:

> Simply put, mindfulness is moment-to-moment awareness. It is cultivated by purposefully paying attention to things we ordinarily never give a moment's thought to. It is a systematic approach to developing

new kinds of control and wisdom in our lives, based on our inner capacities for relaxation, paying attention, awareness and insight.[3]

In a state of mindfulness you can relax and let the energy within your feelings move at its own pace, disentangle itself, and dissipate. Then you are in a better position to calmly review the situation that provoked your feelings. You are less likely to act out your feelings in automatic—and often inappropriate—ways. Instead you can take the time to consider a variety of emotional responses to your situation and choose the one that will be most beneficial for you and for anyone else who is present.

Noticing the details of your sensations can help you to stay grounded in your body while you examine your feelings. When you are having intense feelings, there is a tendency to "go up into your head" and talk about or around your feelings instead of experiencing them. But if you focus your attention on your sensations when you are having intense feelings, the whole experience of 'feeling' remains *centered in your body*. This "in-the-body experience" enables you to hear your body speaking. The information that rises into your conscious mind from your sensations contains a deeper knowing than the mind's evaluation of your feelings.

Your sensations function as clues in the therapeutic puzzle of identifying significant events from your past. Such events can continue to influence your feelings, your self-concept, and your behavior long after they occur. If you can name these experiences and resolve the feelings associated with them, then they have less power to insinuate themselves into the present and distort your perception of a current event. You find it easier to stay oriented to the present and respond with clarity and flexibility, even when your feelings are running high. You can resist the pull to respond as though you were once again in the past. Instead you can take your time and consider a variety of responses to your situation.

Sometimes your efforts to recall such an experience by drawing on memories alone will be unsuccessful or sketchy, whereas letting go of your thoughts and listening instead to your sensations may allow a clear memory to rise. Many of my clients experience this phenomenon. Let me share one of their stories with you.

For several months before we started working together, Janet had begun to feel increasingly anxious, despite the fact that she was in the midst of many positive changes in her life. She had recently become engaged to a man with whom she was deeply in love and she had just been actively recruited for a job that was perfect in terms of her interests and professional goals. But instead of feeling excited about these events, Janet was feeling anxious. She was having trouble sleeping because of disturbing dreams. At work she was finding it hard to focus, and away from work she noticed that she had begun to pull away from her fiancé and friends. Given the choice between socializing or staying at home alone, she felt more inclined to stay in by herself. She also complained that her neck and shoulders were constantly tense, even though she practiced yoga every day.

In her dreams, Janet repeatedly saw herself as a child of four or five, running on the beach at night beneath a full moon. In these dreams she felt ecstatically happy and free. She could recall and describe in great detail the sense of being completely in her body—muscular, powerful, and strong. She was intensely aware of the smells of the ocean and the way in which the full moon lit her path as she ran along the water's edge. She felt invincible, completely in touch with the vast, profound energies of nature and with her sense of unlimited personal power.

At first Janet was not sure if the details of this dream were part of an actual event in her past. But she became more and more convinced that at some point she had really been on that beach, running at full speed, delighting in her little girl strength and the experience of communing with nature. She felt frustrated, though, because she could never get past a certain point in her recollections. If she reached for the rest of the experience with her mind, the images would immediately stop. But if she stayed with the internal sensations that rose as she recalled whatever she could, the story would unfold a little more each time.

Eventually Janet was able to recover this memory completely. When she shared it with me, it was obvious why she had suppressed the rest of the details of that night. It also became clear why in recent weeks her anxiety, physical tension, and tendency to isolate herself had increased as events in her life consistently took a more positive turn.

Janet remembered that she had not been alone on the beach that night. Both of her parents were there when she had started to run down the beach, and neither seemed to mind that she had gone on ahead of them. They could see her under the light of the full moon so there was no possibility of her getting lost. She remembered hearing them call out to her at one point, but she had not wanted to stop and interrupt the sense of physical strength and independence that she was experiencing.

Suddenly her father caught up with her. She barely had time to notice that he was walking beside her when he yanked her up off of the sand by the arm so forcefully that she screamed out in pain. He began to yell at her, and as he did she could smell alcohol on his breath. She was crying and repeating over and over that she was sorry, but her father continued to yell and become even more angry. By this time her mother had also caught up with them. She did nothing, however, to try to stop Janet's father from removing his belt and beating the backs of their daughter's tiny legs so badly that she had to be carried back to their cottage afterwards.

In recalling the details of that night, Janet had a powerful insight into why she would become terrified when things were going very well for her: one of the most vivid, pleasurable, and validating experiences in her life had quickly been followed by one of the most abusive and traumatic. Remembering this event rekindled similar events in her childhood. The little girl in Janet's past who had seemingly been punished for simply enjoying herself continued to expect the worst whenever she was feeling especially happy or confident. This painful expectation and the anxiety it created changed once she recalled these traumatic events from her past and was allowed to let go of the grief and rage associated with them.

Paying attention to the sensations that accompany your feelings can also help you to identify and work through psychological issues that you have not even named yet. By focusing on body sensations, you can discover the roots of persistent feelings, such as guilt or shame, and release the tension and emotions that have been stored in your body as a result of unresolved aspects of your history.

One of my clients, a man whom we will call Joel, discovered this when we worked together several years ago. A pianist, Joel began to experience debilitating lower back pain just two months before he was to set off on his first concert tour. Joel had gone through the standard battery of orthopedic evaluations and no structural problems were found. He was treated by a chiropractor, an acupuncturist, and a physical therapist—still with no relief. By the time we met, his pain level had increased so much that he had to drastically cut down on his practice time. Afraid that he might have to cancel the tour, he was also feeling depressed at the prospect that his condition might never improve and that he might even have to give up his musical career.

Combining bodywork and other techniques, Joel and I worked at relaxing the muscles in his back. We began by having him experience his body as he lay on my work table. I instructed him to bring his attention to his breath and to the points of pain he noticed. While he described the sensations he was experiencing, I moved my hands from place to place, gently cradling the areas that were painful. This helped him to focus more intently on those areas while also releasing some of the tension there. I asked Joel to describe in as much detail as possible what images, thoughts, or feelings were accompanying his physical sensations. I suggested that he speak to the sensations themselves, welcoming them and asking them to give him as much information as they could.

Most people feel rather self-conscious when they first practice this technique. "You want me to talk to what I am feeling in my body? How do I do that?" they say. But they tend to pick up the technique rather quickly, despite their initial discomfort. In my experience, people who work in fields that call more upon the right brain—painters, musicians, sculptors, and dancers—are especially quick studies when it comes to learning this technique: Joel was no exception.

He began by describing a burning sensation in the skin over his coccyx (tailbone) and a deep ache like a toothache in the center of each buttock that continued down into the backs of his thighs. This was accompanied by a pulling sensation under his shoulder blades and a vibrating pain in his arms.

I reflected back to him what he had described: "There is burning at the base of your spine, an ache in your buttocks and the backs of your thighs, a sensation of pulling under your shoulder blades, and a vibrating pain in your arms. As you notice these sensations, are there any images or sounds that come into your mind?"

"Yes," he said immediately. "I see myself standing by a large table. I am wearing a tallit (a Jewish prayer shawl) and reciting the shacharit (the morning prayer)."

He paused.

"And then?" I prompted.

"Hmmm…" he said, surprised. "My Uncle Joel—both of us were named after my great-grandfather—just walked into the room and sat down at one end of the table." He paused for a moment.

"Now the table is turning into a beautiful grand piano, and he is playing a favorite piece of mine by Grieg. This is so strange."

"Strange in what way?" I asked.

"Strange because Uncle Joel had one of his arms amputated when he was younger, but now I see him as a much older man with both arms. And he played the violin, not the piano—before he lost his arm, that is."

Joel let out a deep sigh. His upper body was trembling, and his legs and arms became very stiff.

"What are you feeling now?" I asked.

"I feel angry," he answered through clenched teeth.

"And what do you feel in your body?"

"I want to make a fist and pound on the piano, but if I do, then Uncle Joel will stop playing. I don't want him to stop. The music is so beautiful."

For the next hour Joel continued to describe his feelings and the sensations that accompanied them. I encouraged him to release some of his anger by pounding on the massage table, making sounds, and letting the words behind his feelings come out. Raising his clenched fist toward the ceiling, Joel opened his eyes and then his mouth. A hissing sound emerged, then transformed into a growling that grew in volume and suddenly stopped.

In a rumbling, deliberate voice that seemed to come from deep within his chest Joel demanded, "Where were you? How could you allow such a thing?"

"Who are you speaking to?" I asked him.

"To God," he replied.

We continued in this way for another hour, Joel reporting what he was feeling in his body and seeing in his mind's eye, while I placed my hands on different areas of his body, depending on where he was experiencing sensations. At no time did I offer any interpretation of the feelings, sensations, and thoughts that he was recounting. Instead I simply encouraged him to notice what he was experiencing, describe it, and freely express his feelings through crying, shouting, and physical movement.

The session lasted for almost two hours. When it was over, I left the room and Joel stayed behind, quietly integrating the experience. Soon he joined me in the outer office, where we sat silently together for a few minutes. He was much more relaxed now and laughed when he looked at his watch and realized how long we had been engaged in our process. It seemed to him that no more than ten minutes had passed since the session had begun.

Sitting back and settling into the sofa, Joel began to tell me more about his uncle. Joel's uncle and his parents were survivors of a concentration camp in Poland during World War II. Before he was imprisoned, Uncle Joel had been a devoted student of the violin. After years of hard work, he had been accepted to study with a renowned teacher in Vienna, Austria. All of those plans had come to a rapid halt, however, when Uncle Joel and other members of his family were gathered up and sent to live in the ghetto. Several months later they were shipped to a camp.

Uncle Joel had managed to take his violin with him and for a while was able to win small favors for himself and his family by entertaining the guards at the camp with his musical talents. Unlike some other members of his family, Joel survived his time at the camp and was eventually released. But soon after his release he was wounded, developed a serious infection, and lost his right arm. With the amputation, Uncle Joel's dream of returning to his studies and becoming a concert violinist—the dream that had sustained him throughout his imprisonment—became impossible.

As a child, Joel had noticed that whenever a conversation began to move in the direction of World War II, all of the adults present would steer it in a different direction. References to family members who had died in the camps were quickly put aside to discourage the children from asking questions about what had happened to their missing relatives. Looking back on this time, Joel remarked that he was certain the adults in his family had agreed never to speak of the Holocaust in front of the children. "Perhaps they were trying to protect us," he said, "or they may have been trying to protect themselves from memories that were just too painful to relive."

For some reason, Joel's uncle later decided to break this family rule. When Joel became a Bar Mitzvah at the age of thirteen, his uncle invited him to his home, where they sat together in the garden. There Uncle Joel spoke about his experiences during the war and in the camp. For the first time, the younger Joel appreciated the horror associated with the tattoos he had seen on the arms of some of his family members. He had known for some time, of course, what the tattoos meant. But now the experiences surrounding those marks became real for him.

As he sat and talked with me, Joel recalled the profound feelings of terror, grief, rage, admiration, and tenderness that had washed over him that day in the garden with his uncle. He also remembered his uncle's excitement about Joel's music studies. "You will be able to see it through," his uncle had said. "You will be able to finish what I could not." From that moment on, Joel felt even more inspired to pursue his studies. The long hours of practicing and each recital became an offering to his uncle, a way for Joel to show him that he would not waste the opportunity given to him.

Less than a year later, Joel's uncle passed away, but their conversation in the garden remained vivid in his memory. Looking back on this period, Joel realized that even before his uncle's death, the excitement which the older man had aroused in him that day had already begun to transform itself into a form of survivor guilt. His uncle had survived the war, but his life as a musician had not. Joel had all of that possibility before him. Of course it could be cut off by some unexpected tragedy, just as his uncle's had been. But Joel was not being forced to live through war or genocide as his uncle had.

As an adolescent, Joel could not explore his feelings of guilt and unworthiness with his parents because they refused to talk about the war or the Holocaust. These guilt feelings had quietly continued to grow over the years. Now, when he was close to succeeding in the arena that his uncle had been forced to abandon under such tragic circumstances, Joel wondered if perhaps he was relieved at the prospect of having to let go of his musical career. If he had to give it up because of back problems, then he would no longer feel guilty about succeeding in the area his uncle had been forced to relinquish.

"Why should I have the chance to realize my dream when he did not?" he asked me. "And even if I perform this concert for him, in memory of him, and do that exceedingly well, it cannot change what he lost."

Joel wept openly for the missed opportunities of this man and for all of the unspoken suffering of his parents and other relatives and of course for himself. Then he spoke through his tears in a quiet voice.

"My uncle and I share a name. I have his gifts. But no matter how good I am or how hard I work, I will never be able to make up for what they suffered."

Joel concluded that these unresolved feelings affected other areas of his life as well and needed to be explored further before they could be fully released. We decided that when the tour was over we would work together to look at these and other feelings related to his beliefs, motives, and behavior. Within a week his back pain receded significantly. He was able to go back to his long practice schedule and proceed with the tour as planned.

The pain that Joel felt in his back was his body's way of containing and expressing the pain he felt in his heart for his uncle, his parents, and himself. Touching the pain with his awareness caused it to open and release its secret grief and guilt. When his feelings became conscious and he expressed them through crying and yelling, the tension that was needed to contain his feelings was free to dissipate.

Of course listening to your feelings and sensations also can assist you in coping with situations that are very much rooted in the present. In a workshop that I led last year entitled "Your Body as Guide," one of the participants shared a powerful experience in which her awareness of feelings and physical sensations may have saved her life.

Barbara lived in a large East Coast city where she worked as a nurse with a hospice home care agency. She frequently made visits at night to the homes of her patients and their families and had always felt very comfortable in doing that. Not overly paranoid about the potential dangers of being out after dark, still she chose to take some precautions whenever she was on-call at night. She was careful to park in well-lit areas, would call her husband to let him know when she was leaving a patient's home and when she expected to arrive home, and she would always ask a family member of the patient to escort her to her car.

One night she was called to the home of a favorite patient whom we will call Mrs. Bee. After months of struggling with ovarian cancer and then the effects of chemotherapy, Mrs. Bee was very close to dying. She lived in an affluent neighborhood where Barbara had always felt safe. Although Mrs. Bee's house was usually filled with friends and family whenever Barbara visited, on this particular night only Mrs. Bee's husband was there.

For some weeks Barbara had been working closely with this family to let them know what the last days and hours of Mrs. Bee's life would look like so they would be comfortable with letting her die at home as she wanted to do. That night a number of things seemed to indicate that Mrs. Bee would die within the next few hours, so Mr. Bee was especially attentive toward her. He lay next to her on the bed, holding her sweetly, gently stroking her head and face, and quietly reminding her that he was there and would stay with her all through the night. As she watched them together, Barbara was suddenly overcome with grief. She knew she felt sad about this lovely woman's suffering, but she also felt relieved that it would soon come to an end. So why was she feeling so grief stricken?

Mr. Bee's voice brought her back into the room. Knowing that Mrs. Bee might die before the morning came, he asked Barbara to call other family members who he felt sure would want to come over. Putting her feelings aside, Barbara made the calls.

Preparing to leave, Barbara also called her husband to let him know that she was on her way home. She then stuck her head into the bedroom one more time to say goodbye and remind Mr. Bee that he could call her at any time during the night if he had questions or needed her to return. Not wishing to pull him away from his wife, Barbara did not ask Mr. Bee to escort her to her car.

It was after midnight when Barbara left the house. Since everyone's attention had been focused on what appeared to be the last hours of this much loved woman's life, no one had remembered to turn on the lights that usually illuminated the large and thickly-planted front lawn. As she made her way down the path toward the driveway and her car, the grief she had felt earlier moved through her once again. Preoccupied with her thoughts and feelings, she did not notice that the yard was shrouded in darkness.

Suddenly she became aware of a tingling sensation in her back, a sort of buzzing in her ears, and a sensation that she described in the workshop as "a large bubble filled with heat hovering next to my left side." She felt that she was in danger and experienced a powerful surge of adrenaline. Instinctively she reached into the pocket of her jacket and grabbed the police whistle that she carried there. She blew into it as hard as she could, at the same time pulling her medicine bag across the front of her body toward the "bubble filled with heat" that she had sensed at her left. For a brief instant she thought to herself, "If there is no one there, I am about to make a real fool of myself."

Indeed there was someone there. When Mr. Bee ran outside in response to Barbara's ear-piercing whistle, the man who was about to attack her was lying on the grass. He had lost his balance and fallen to the ground when Barbara swung her bag in his direction. At the sight of Mr. Bee running toward them, Barbara's would-be attacker jumped up and fled. Two hours later the police found the man and identified him as the one whom they had been seeking in connection with a rape in the neighborhood two weeks before.

In the discussion that followed Barbara's account of her experience, the men and women at the workshop described the feelings that listening to her story had evoked in them. Admiration, tenderness, gratitude, grief, apprehension, panic, and relief were some of the feelings they cited. I encouraged each of them to also describe, in as much detail as they could, the physical sensations that accompanied their feelings. For example, what did they feel in their bodies when they experienced panic? What sensations were they having as they noticed relief? Members of the group formed pairs and each person had an opportunity to discuss for a few minutes with an attentive partner the feelings and sensations she had noticed in herself as Barbara's account of this powerful experience unfolded.

In telling her story, Barbara once again came deeply in touch with many of the feelings and sensations she had felt on the night of the attack. Within the safety and familiarity of the group (many of the people there also had attended other workshops I had led), she was able to release the emotions associated with her feelings through crying, shaking, and role playing in which she verbally and physically confronted her attacker.

As soon as her body was free of the feelings and emotions related to the attack, she became aware of the grief she had felt the night Mrs. Bee died. While sitting quietly with the sensations related to her feelings of grief, Barbara saw the face of her sister, Kathy. Four years earlier, while traveling in Central America, Kathy had become ill and died in a small rural hospital with none of her relatives present. Seeing Mr. Bee's tender ministrations for his wife triggered Barbara's feelings of anguish about her beloved sister dying alone, surrounded by strangers.

DEFINING EMOTIONS

Although we often use the word emotion as a synonym for feeling, it would be more accurate to distinguish the two terms. *Emotion is the manner in which we outwardly express or release our feelings.*

Joel's feeling of grief in relation to his family became emotion when he wept. His anger about the suffering that his parents and his uncle had endured was released when he pounded the massage table on which he was lying, roared, and demanded of God, "How could you permit this?"

Barbara's feelings of fear and anger became emotions while acting out a fantasy before the group at the workshop. She cried, yelled at her attacker, threw him to the ground, handcuffed and arrested him, and locked him in a jail cell. Her feeling of grief about not being with her sister when she died was translated into emotion when she wept while acting out a final meeting with her. With the help of another woman in the workshop (who bore a striking resemblance to Kathy), Barbara created a scenario in which she held and spoke to her sister in the same way that Mr. Bee had held and spoken to his wife. At that meeting, Barbara told Kathy how much she cherished her and how much she would miss her. Her experience with Mr. and Mrs. Bee had awakened her feelings about her sister's death and the workshop provided an opportunity for her to bring some emotional closure to that experience.

As children many of us were told that demonstrating our feelings of anger, fear, or sadness was unattractive and unacceptable. Some of us were discouraged from expressing even the more positive emotions like exuberance and excitement. If you yourself were raised with these sorts of admonitions, then you may recognize phrases like these from your past:

"You're acting silly."

"Big boys/girls don't cry."

"Why are you being such a sour puss?"

"Stop crying, I'll give you something to cry about!"

"You're such a scaredy-cat!"

"Don't you dare yell at me young lady!"

The list is infinite. After years of reproaches like these, we become experts at ignoring our feelings and suppressing our emotions in order to please those around us. There is, however, a price to be paid for this suppression. When you are not free to express your emotions, you become detached from your feelings, from the sensations that accompany them, and from the vitality within them. Your body becomes stiff and rigid from your efforts to contain the feelings and emotions that you have been told are wrong or inappropriate. A lifetime of physically holding yourself back affects your thinking as well. If you have stored up physical tension in response to strong feelings, it becomes harder for you to "flex your mind" and find new ways to resolve emotionally-charged situations when they arise.

The fact that you can control or shut off your expression of emotion by contracting parts of your body is proof of the deep connection between the realms of body and emotion. You can arrest the energy flux within your feelings and control your expression of emotion if you suck in your breath, hold it there, and stiffen your body. I had an opportunity to witness this phenomenon in action earlier this year.

While driving to meet a friend for an early morning walk in the park, I happened upon a two-car collision. Standing beside one of the cars at the side of the road was a young woman holding a child in her arms. He looked to be about three years old. As I pulled over, I leaned out of my window and asked if she was all right and if I could be of assistance. She said "no" and offered that someone had already called the police and that help was on the way.

As she spoke, I began to notice her son, who was watching me very closely. Looking directly at me, he started to speak in his baby voice and words. I could see his fear rising as he told his version of the accident. When he began to sob, his mother's facial muscles tightened, her eyes widened, and her breath became shallower. It seemed as though her fear about the accident had been activated by his tears. She gripped her child more tightly and began hushing him by gently shaking him up and down. He gulped air, sucked in his breath, stiffened his little body, and suddenly stopped speaking and crying.

This sequence of events demonstrates how we can begin at an early age to accumulate unresolved feelings and unexpressed emotions. Surely this mother had good intentions when she held her child closely and tried to make him quiet down, but she also made it impossible for him to release his terror and have a healing catharsis. His need to talk and cry in response to the accident was quite natural. In discouraging him from doing so, she short-circuited his emotional expression and deprived him of the opportunity to fully integrate the experience.

While describing my meeting with the mother and child to my friend just a few minutes later, I suddenly burst into tears. It seemed odd in a way that I should be crying, but I wondered if perhaps my tears were an expression of the fear and tension that were briefly displayed and then held back by the woman and her son. Perhaps I was having a "surrogate reaction," emoting for the two of them because they had suppressed their own emotional response to the accident.

Oddly enough, in the months to come, I would cry each time I spoke of this encounter in the park. I wondered why the experience continued to affect me and finally concluded that it must be linked to events in my own past. Somehow, recalling the details of my exchange with the mother and child unlocked a reservoir of suppressed feelings. I became very curious about what those feelings might be attached to and decided to use meditation to explore them further.

Each time I found myself recalling this experience, I would become very still and focus on my breathing. I would ask God/All That Is to surround me with protection so that I would feel safe to come in touch with memories related to my encounter with the mother and child. By paying close attention to the physical sensations that would arise each time I meditated in this way, I was eventually able to recover a memory from my childhood that explained why the incident in the park continued to be so evocative for me.

Many years before, when I was eight years old, I too had been in an accident. It had taken place one July morning while riding with my father in his truck. During the summer months my parents operated a bakery in an upstate New York resort. They worked long and hard at this job and managed to bring in more than half of our annual income through it.

Often my father would begin his baking in the early evening and work all through the night. At seven in the morning, he would load up the delivery truck and begin his rounds to the nearby stores and hotels that were his customers. This hectic schedule took its toll on him and the rest of us, too. All of us came under the influence of his fatigue, his irritability, and his increased outbursts of rage and criticism.

My job was to sit next to my father in the cab of the truck while he made his deliveries and make sure that he did not fall asleep at the wheel. If I saw him nodding off, I was supposed to call out his name and hit him on the arm to bring him around. This was a big responsibility for such a young girl.

One morning while en route to a nearby town, my exhausted father dozed off for a moment. But before I had time to wake him up, he had already started to veer into the oncoming traffic. The lurch of the truck startled him back into consciousness; he quickly spun the steering wheel in order to avoid the car that was heading straight toward us. Thanks to his quick reflexes, we missed the car but went off the road into a ditch. As we did, the trays in the back of the truck fell onto the floor, and most of the pastries he had made the night before were ruined.

Immediately I began to cry and shake. My father was so distraught that he started yelling, "Stop that right now! This is all your fault for letting me fall asleep!" His frustration was so intense that he yelled and cursed for several minutes. At first his curses were directed at me, then at fate, and finally at himself. Watching him carefully, trying to gauge whether or not I should run, I gulped down my tears and tried to become invisible. When he calmed down, we got back on the road and returned home.

Back at the house he told the story of what had happened, omitting his loss of control and his raging at me. For him the whole incident had become an exciting adventure. Everyone who listened was so thrilled that we were both alive that no one thought to question me about my experience. I was never invited to share the terror I had felt at the prospect of being killed by an oncoming car or at being the target of my father's rage. I was left feeling guilty that I had somehow caused the whole incident, that I was responsible for the extra energy and money that it would cost to replace the damaged pastries. Those feelings remained locked inside of me.

Years later when I recalled this incident in all of its detail, I came in touch with my terror over the accident and my rage over the fact that no one in my family had declared that I was not at fault nor noticed my need to ventilate my feelings. In a very real sense, I was coming in touch with those feelings for the first time, because only now was it safe for me to revisit the experience and my feelings about it. This time I did not want to be alone with my feelings and the sensations within them. I called a dear friend who came over and held me in her arms while I cried and shook in an effort to release the emotions I had been carrying for all these years in relation to this "forgotten" event.

When you are discouraged from expressing your emotions, as the child in the park was by his mother, and as I was by my father, you are drawn to certain conclusions:

- that paying attention to your feelings (and their related sensations) may be harmful to you;
- that feelings should be avoided, as an actual experience or as a topic of discussion;
- that by pushing your feelings aside you may be able to protect yourself from an uncomfortable and potentially dangerous experience; and
- that you may be able to protect others from experiencing their feelings if you shut off your own.

If you are exposed to these notions repeatedly while you are grow-ing up, there is a good chance that you will come into your adult years carrying the burden of many unresolved events from your past—events whose emotional content was never fully explored and whose emotional charge was never sufficiently released. Just below the sur-face of your awareness, though, the memories and emotional content associated with these events are stored in your mind and your body and can reemerge many years after the event itself. They may surface spontaneously, or you can actively pursue their retrieval through psy-chotherapy, hypnosis, Authentic Movement, or bodywork techniques such as somato-emotional release or deep tissue massage.

ENCOURAGING YOUR FEELINGS TO REVEAL THEMSELVES

Your feelings are a natural and desirable part of life; they are never "bad," even when the sensations that accompany them do not feel good to you. However, if you grew up surrounded by messages that contradicted these natural expressions, it may still be difficult for you to tolerate certain feelings and express your emotions openly.

If coming in touch with your feelings is a relatively new experience for you, there are several helpful things that you can keep in mind. Remember that there are no wrong answers to the question "What am I feeling?" If you greet each feeling as a cherished friend and guest, with curiosity and gratitude for the gifts it brings, your feelings will reveal themselves to you. Be patient with yourself and with your feelings. Take as much time as you need to come in touch with your feelings and name them. And assure the feelings themselves that you will receive everything they bring to you in a totally nonjudgmental way.

Many of us come to the process of exploring our feelings after hav-ing spent a lifetime avoiding them and we unconsciously resist chang-ing that pattern. This resistance is natural and is often an attempt to move away from the sensations within our feelings. Acknowledging that resistance can help you to transcend it. It also may be useful to remind yourself that there is no need to hurry. Your feelings will reveal themselves to you in their own good time, as they feel safe to do so and as you acquire more skills with which to receive, utilize, and release them.

As you become more familiar with the many different sensations that can occur along with your feelings, you will naturally become more open to experiencing all of them. You will be less and less inclined to label these sensations as "bad" or "good." They will simply become more information and thus another instrument in your emotional tool kit.

In Chapter Four, **Meeting Your Nurturing Parents,** you will discover the Nurturing Parents who exist within you: The Parent Who Listens and The Parent Who Leads. Together, these two aspects of Self teach you how to wisely and lovingly parent yourself. They help you integrate the wisdom of your past experiences, and they help you emerge into your adult Self.

MEETING YOUR
NURTURING PARENTS

Breathe deeply and gently.
Let your body soften.
See yourself within the space that surrounds you.
Feel yourself within the space that surrounds you.
Who is doing the seeing? Who is doing the feeling?

hat does it mean to parent? To parent is to protect and guide a child as he or she grows into adulthood. To parent is to nurture that child's body, mind, heart, and soul. To parent is to help a child realize his or her possibility and potential. In the highest sense of the word, to parent is to love and educate a child in preparation for greatness, to treat that child in such a way that he or she is encouraged to reach his or her fullest potential. Parenting yourself means giving yourself the same love, support, acceptance, and guidance you would offer your child.

In the mystical tradition of Judaism, it is believed that the Messiah is born into every generation. Imagine what our and our children's lives would be like if we parented every child as though he or she had the potential to be that Messiah. How would those of us doing the parenting feel about our role as parents? Would we see that role differently? Would it not become a more sacred challenge? And how would the children who were parented in this way be different? Would they not see themselves in a different way, too?

When describing how she wanted to be parented, one young woman I worked with said, "I want my parents to know me, to listen to me, and to understand me. I want them to accept me for who I am and to love me even when I make mistakes or do something wrong. I want them to help me protect myself from physical and emotional harm. I want them to help me learn how to live successfully in the world and make choices that support my growth and creativity. I want them to cherish me. I want them to teach me how to cherish myself. I want them to teach me how to wisely and lovingly parent myself."

In this chapter you will acquire the tools you need to wisely and lovingly parent yourself. I will introduce you to the Nurturing Parents, and describe in detail the Listening and Leading energies that the Nurturing Parents express. We also will explore the process by which you integrate these parental figures into your sense of Self, your way of perceiving situations, and your style of problem-solving and decision-making. You will discover how assimilating the attributes and goals of the Nurturing Parents enables you to love yourself as you have never done before, and prepares you to make the choices that support your growth and creativity.

MEETING AND INTEGRATING THE NURTURING PARENTS

The process of integrating your Nurturing Parents into your sense of Self is a gradual one and a very interesting one. It unfolds in a slightly different way for each person who engages in it but, in a general sense, there seem to be four stages in the process. The first is getting to know the Parent Who Listens and the Parent Who Leads in a theoretical way. To do so, we must answer some questions. In the purest sense, as absolute models, what do these Nurturing Parents stand for? What qualities do they embody? If they were actual people rather than archetypes, how would they behave? What goals would motivate their behavior toward you as an emerging being?

The second stage in the process of integrating your Nurturing Parents is a visual one. Through a guided meditation, you will create pictures in your mind's eye of your Parent Who Listens and your Parent Who Leads. You will make these two figures visible and real for you. Then, in the third stage, you will endow them with the qualities that the theory assigns to each one. In the fourth stage, you will invite the Nurturing Parents to participate in a situation and see how their influence changes your experience of it.

As you move through these stages you will begin to acquire a "felt sense" of your Nurturing Parents. You will feel the energy that they bring to a situation, separately and together. You will sense how your physical experience of a situation changes when you are consciously aware of them. You will notice changes in your body sensations when you imagine them being nearby. You will notice how your thoughts and feelings change when you see them in your mind's eye. They will begin to come to life for you.

As this "felt sense" grows, you will notice that these Nurturing Parents no longer feel like archetypal figures who exist outside of you—theoretical parents only. They are becoming part of you. You have been quietly taking them into yourself. You begin to see situations as they would, through their eyes, but all along you know that you are looking through your own.

In quiet times and in crises, the Nurturing Parents are constantly present, inviting you to exhibit a deep tenderness and appreciation for yourself. They encourage you to come in touch with what a creative and powerful being you truly are. They prepare you to take the next step and invite the circumstances that will move you closer to becoming your most compassionate, organized, and commanding Self. Guiding you toward the fulfillment of your evolutionary imperative, they encourage you to discover who you are, and to contribute to the Universe that which is uniquely yours to give.

I have intentionally made each of the Nurturing Parents genderless so that each one can come to life for you as a composite of all the caring adults you have known, male or female. To acknowledge their

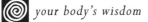

androgynous quality here, I will use the pronoun 's/he' when I refer to these two figures.

Neither sex has exclusive domain over the inclination or the ability to listen, just as neither has exclusive domain over the inclination or the ability to lead. Hopefully you have been lovingly listened to by adults of both sexes and lovingly led by both, too. As you read about the Parent Who Listens, try to recall the men and women who behave toward you as this Nurturing Parent would. As you read about the Parent Who Leads, try to recall the men and women who behaved toward you as that Nurturing Parent would. In this way, you will come to know both the listener and the leader energies within yourself, and both of those energies will become stronger.

BECOMING THE NURTURING PARENTS

As children we rely on the parent figures in our life to care for us, to be responsive to our needs, to make decisions on our behalf, and in general to steer us in the right directions. These parent figures may consist of one, two, or more parents or stepparents, depending on whether we grow up in a single-parent household, a two-parent household, or become part of a "blended family" when a parent remarries. Other adults who "parent" us include grandparents, aunts, uncles, older siblings, foster parents, teachers, coaches, counselors, and community leaders.

As we grow older, we become less dependent on all of these parenting figures. Through the process of growth and development, we acquire the knowledge and life skills that allow us to take over more and more features of the roles these adults have played for us. In this way, we let go of our dependency on them and essentially become our own parents. In this way, we also acquire the aspects of Self known as the Nurturing Parents.

In the process of growing up, we internalize the attitudes, inclinations to behave, and actual behaviors that significant adults in our life have demonstrated toward us. If these adults were caring and skillful in parenting us, then later on we will find it quite natural to parent ourselves in those ways, too. On the other hand, if significant adults in our life had gaps in their parenting and other life skills, then we will probably have gaps in the same areas, at least until we can recognize them and fill them in. The process of identifying these gaps and actively pursuing the means to acquire missing skills is one of the ways in which we continue to grow up even after we have chronologically become an adult.

Regardless of the parenting we received, however, we all have an internal sense about the qualities that loving parents demonstrate. I believe we are each born into this world with knowledge of love. We instinctively feel when we are in the presence of loving beings. We see it in their eyes, hear it in their voice, and feel it in their touch. In the presence of a loving being we feel calm inside, expansive, and free to be our playful, child selves. We know our spirit is safe. In the company of someone who is callous, we feel anxious, contracted, and afraid to show ourselves. We know our spirit is in danger, and we instinctively withdraw into our Self.

As adults we frequently lose our ability to discern a person's intentions toward us. Years of denying the truth of our actual experiences, years of suppressing our feelings and emotions, has dulled our senses. We have difficulty feeling when we are not being treated lovingly, and we have difficulty feeling when we are being unloving toward ourselves. How do we regain our ability to recognize a loving intention? And how do we learn to respond to ourselves in loving ways?

If, as a child, you were surrounded by adults who behaved in loving ways, then you already have some sense of who the archetypal Nurturing Parents are. In a way, you have met them. Each time an adult listened to you without criticizing what you were saying, or trying to impose his or her agenda onto yours, you met the archetypal Nurturing Parents. Each time you felt validated for just being who you are, or felt supported during the process of making a decision, or encouraged to follow through on a project that was important to you, you met the archetypal Nurturing Parent. Each encounter helped you internalize some of the Nurturing Parent qualities discussed earlier. Remembering moments such as these is helpful in strengthening the presence of your own Nurturing Parents.

Do not be concerned, however, if you did not have good role models for the Nurturing Parents. It is never too late to create them. As you read the following description of what nurturing parents are, invite yourself to internalize these qualities. Pause at the end of each sentence, and let its meaning sink in. Take a long, slow, deep breath, and imagine a situation in which you are being treated in this way. Give yourself a moment to see how that might feel.

The Nurturing Parents we all need are attentive, affectionate, and available. They value your thoughts and opinions. They encourage you to articulate your feelings and express your emotions. They behave as your advocates when you need support. These loving parents patiently help you to set goals that will create learning opportunities for you. They cheer you on as you take the steps that move you toward accomplishing those goals. They express confidence in your ability to succeed at whatever you attempt. They applaud your successes and urge you to be gentle with yourself in the face of your failures.

You may want to reread the previous paragraph several times. Stop each time you notice thoughts, feelings, and sensations rising. Hold onto the description of the Nurturing Parents while you examine these body/mind phenomena. Give yourself the opportunity to experience the presence of the Nurturing Parents while you are experiencing your thoughts, feelings, and sensations. If you can imagine parents such as these, if you can feel how their presence might affect the way you feel toward yourself and affect the way you respond to the world, you are on your way to internalizing the Parent Who Listens and the Parent Who Leads.

TWO HALVES OF THE SAME WHOLE

Like the principles of yin and yang in Chinese philosophy, each of the Nurturing Parents represents one half of a unified whole—the listener and the leader. The following passage from a text on Chinese medicine describes the relationship between the concepts of yin and yang. It is also a metaphor for the collaborative working relationship between the Parent Who Listens and the Parent Who Leads.

> "In reality these two are one, but one may be more or less apparent at a certain time. For instance, when night is upon us we do not at that moment experience the day, and yet the day emerges from the night. This we call the dawn; a moment when the yin/yang is in nearly perfect balance. When the night emerges from the day, we call this time the dusk, another moment of near perfect balance. We could not know day if not for night, and night if not for day."[4]

In every situation, your Nurturing Parents work together as a team, each one waiting for a signal from the other to step in and escort you through the next phase. They perform this pas de deux in a graceful way and repeat it as often as you need them to in order for you to come to a place of resolution. The Parent Who Listens is on the front line, attending to the emotional tone and content of a situation. The Parent Who Leads encourages you to ask two questions, "What needs to happen next?" and "What have I learned from this experience?" to act on the insights which the listening parent's intervention has made possible.

To help you choose the right path, the Parent Who Leads encourages you to notice and thoroughly process all of your thoughts, feelings, sensations, and impulses to act. When you are stuck and have difficulty making a decision and acting, s/he steps back, and the listening parent steps in. The listening parent then guides you through the process of exploring all the body/mind phenomena that might be in the way of acting wisely, creatively, and decisively. When that is accomplished, s/he steps back and the Parent Who Leads comes forward again.

As energetic forces living within you, the Nurturing Parents influence you to be completely present to a situation, while helping you to remain balanced and relaxed. You do not have to deny or suppress your feelings and stay exclusively in the realm of thoughts and logic, nor do you have to run off with your feelings and cut yourself off from the benefits of analyzing your situation from a cognitive perspective.

When you are in touch with these two aspects of Self, you can easily move among your thoughts, feelings, sensations, and impulses to act, without succumbing to the turmoil they may be generating. You can take all the time you need to process these internal phenomena and then act decisively and wisely. You become like a master of the martial arts, graceful at combining qualities that seem to be in opposition but which actually complement each other.

THE PARENT WHO LISTENS

The Parent Who Listens is closely aligned with your inner life. This Nurturing Parent is focused on helping you become aware, and remain aware, of all your thoughts, feelings, sensations, and impulses to act. S/he focuses on helping you develop an attitude of compassion for yourself, regardless of what is occurring. S/he knows that you cannot possibly remain open to all your thoughts, feelings, sensations, and impulses to act if you are not totally accepting and forgiving of everything you discover. As you learn to treat yourself nonjudgmentally, you are then in a position to use these body/mind phenomena to understand and explore the emotional content and symbolism within a situation. The Listening Parent validates your experience of these phenomena and helps you to elevate them to the place of importance they deserve.

As this quality of compassion becomes stronger within you, you feel more at ease. Relaxed, you find it easier to notice the details of your thoughts, feelings, sensations, and impulses to act. You also find it easier to perceive the many shifts in sensation that occur throughout your day. As you will see in Chapter Nine, "Silent Listening/Intuitive Response," these shifts are important markers within the experience of insight. They signal the rearrangement of thoughts and feelings that occurs when you have an insight. They are there to guide you in making decisions.

THE PARENT WHO LEADS

The Parent Who Leads helps you to become aware of the decision-making moments in your life, to notice the many different choices that lie before you, and to recognize the voice of your intuitive self. S/he stirs your impulse to act and encourages you to follow through on a chosen course of action.

The leading parent shows you how to be completely focused in the moment, yet also aware of the bigger picture, with respect to what is happening and what you would like to have happen. S/he helps you to perceive the small details and the larger patterns that make up your life. S/he encourages you to maintain your curiosity about the significance of such patterns and to be open to the spiritual lessons contained within them. S/he illuminates the major life choices that come before you as well as the many smaller decisions to be made each day, and s/he helps you to see the connections between these two realms of decision-making. This sense of the gestalt and your place within it permits you to maintain balance in the face of tense situations or important decisions.

With practice, you learn how to deal with every situation just as the Nurturing Parents would—patiently, purposefully, extending the utmost compassion to yourself at every step along the way. You become more and more confident about your ability to deal with demanding situations and difficult people. You no longer feel so intimidated by either. You may even find yourself looking forward to such challenges so that you can observe your adult Self exercising your new skills.

Knowing who your Nurturing Parents are is an important first step in becoming an adult. Knowing their qualities, and the role they are meant to play in your life, takes you one step further. Each time you invite them to participate in an activity, you strengthen their presence. Experiencing how their presence affects your life encourages you to call on them more often. When you internalize their qualities, and express those qualities in your life, you have succeeded in learning to wisely and lovingly parent yourself.

The following exercise, *"Bringing Your Nurturing Parents to Life,"* is designed to help you create a detailed image of your Nurturing Parents. Before you begin, however, let me share some insights based on my experience with people who have practiced this meditation. When people use this meditation to "create" their Nurturing Parents, they almost always think about their birth parents. If your parents demonstrated the tender, loving qualities that we ascribe to the Nurturing Parents, then the archetypes you create through this exercise may look and behave very much as your own parents did. Most of the people I work with in my practice, however, have been abused and mistreated by their parents. For them the very juxtaposition of the words "nurturing" and "parent" is confusing. They have never known a nurturing parent, or their experiences of being nurtured by their own parents were infrequent and unpredictable.

In order for people with negative parenting experiences to begin to paint a picture of their archetypal parents, they must first send away their birth parents. They may send them to an island in the Caribbean, to another planet, or to an eternity of torture in hell. If you think that you need to send your actual parents away in order to make a space for your Nurturing Parents, stop now and take a moment to do that. Imagine your birth parents standing in front of you. Tell them what you are about to do. Notice any feelings that rise as you do this. Be firm. Imagine the place to which you would like to send them, and picture them there. Instruct them not to intrude on your thoughts during this exercise.

Perhaps you would locate yourself somewhere in between having had nurturing parents, and having parents who were not always loving or available. In that case, you can endow your Nurturing Parents with the positive qualities that your actual parents had, add missing qualities, and send away those qualities that you found negative. The important point to keep in mind is that this exercise is designed to give you complete freedom in creating your archetypal Nurturing Parents. Whatever you choose to do in terms of including your actual parents or not is absolutely correct.

People who examine their childhoods and explore their feelings toward their parents often find that if they let themselves grieve over what was missing, then they come in touch with positive memories that had been overshadowed by their sense of loss. On the other side of their grieving process, they recall some specific positive qualities that their parents demonstrated toward them. These positive memories also may begin to emerge when they start to behave in loving ways toward themselves. In giving to ourselves what our parents withheld from us, we may remember ways in which our parents really loved us the way we wanted them to.

On the other hand, there are those who have had the sad misfortune of being born to extremely disturbed and abusive parents. As a result, they have no positive memories to unearth, and feel the need to sever all connections with their birth parents before they can create the loving parents they have always deserved. By completely freeing themselves from their birth parents, they honor the courageous child who persistently survived that abuse and is now compelling them to investigate and heal those childhood experiences.

Then there are those people who feel that they are betraying their real parents by creating imaginary ones. They experience feelings of guilt and shame, as though the exercise represents a disavowal of their actual parents. I suggest that you use the exercise to come in touch with whatever feelings are evoked—gratitude for the way in which your own parents took care of you; sadness and anger for the times you were not lovingly parented; rage at having been abused; guilt, shame, or fear for creating your own internal parents. As your Nurturing Parents become more firmly established within you, they can help you to explore all of these feelings, and much more.

◇ ◇ ◇

BRINGING YOUR NURTURING PARENTS TO LIFE

The following meditation is designed to help you create a detailed image of your Nurturing Parents. As part of the meditation, you will endow them with certain qualities.

◇ ◇ ◇

Creating a Visual Image of Your Nurturing Parents
(30 minutes)

Begin by finding a quiet place where you will not be disturbed. This should be a place where you feel safe and at peace. I suggest that you sit in a comfortable chair instead of lying down.

Close and relax your eyes. Sit quietly for a few moments. Take several long, slow, deep breaths. As you begin to breathe naturally, notice the breath coming and going. As you breathe in and out, notice how your body feels. Feel the gentle pressure on your muscles where your body meets the chair. Feel your clothing as it rests on your skin. Notice the air that is touching your face and your hands.

Make yourself as comfortable as you can. Invite your body to soften and relax. Notice your breath. Breathe in and out slowly and deeply. As you inhale, let your belly and your chest expand gently. As you exhale, let your belly soften and your chest expand. Now focus your attention on the cool feeling around your nostrils as you inhale. Again exhaling, follow the breath as it leaves your chest and your nose, and notice the warmth in your nose.

Notice the space at the end of each exhalation. Let this space last as long as it wants to. Rest quietly within it. Do not rush to take in the next breath, instead rest and wait patiently for it to come in of its own accord. Note any thoughts, feelings, and sensations that arise as you

◇ ◇ ◇

creating a visual image of your nurturing parents (cont)

are breathing in and out, then let them pass. If you become lost in self-talk, reconcentrate on your breath.

Each time you breathe in and wait for air to leave your lungs, you are resting in the Interval. Notice how it feels to rest in that space. Each time you breathe out and wait for air to enter your lungs once again, you are resting in the Interval. Notice how it feels to rest in that space.

Now, from this space of relaxed awareness, imagine that you are about to enter a room where you will meet your Nurturing Parents. As you reach for the door knob, turn it, and step into the room, notice how you feel. Once you have entered the room, look around slowly. The walls are painted in your favorite color, and there are a number of objects in the room from your childhood. What a cozy, welcoming space this is, and it is yours.

Each of the objects in the room is something that once gave you pleasure and comfort. There might be an old rocking chair, a favorite toy, or some book you especially enjoyed as a child. Perhaps there is an old stuffed animal or a comfort blanket that you had when you were small. There might be pictures of people who are very dear to you, people you love very much, people who have shown you that they care for you deeply. Go ahead and pick up some of these objects. Take as much time as you need to explore whatever you find in this room. As you move around the room and examine the objects within it, notice how you are feeling. What do you feel in your throat, in your chest, in your belly? How does your face feel? Take a few moments to be present with the rising feelings and sensations. Notice them and let them pass. When you have explored the room, experienced the feelings and sensations, and are back in the Interval, move on to the next part of the exercise.

◇ ◇ ◇

creating a visual image of your nurturing parents (cont)

As you come to the end of your explorations, you realize that sitting on one of the sofas at the far end of the room are two beings. When you look in their direction, they give you a warm, welcoming smile. You realize that they have been there all along, watching you as you looked at each treasure. You now feel as drawn to them as you were to the room itself. You have an intense desire to know them and have them know you.

Take a seat facing them. Make yourself comfortable in the chair and take a long, deep breath. Begin to study their faces. They might resemble your birth parents or remind you of other people you know. They might resemble a slightly different version of yourself, or they could be total strangers. They could be half human and half animal. They may even appear to be from another planet. Each of us has a unique image of our Nurturing Parents. Whatever these two beings look like is just fine.

As you read the next part of this exercise, begin to imagine what your Nurturing Parents look like. Take a moment to study the Parent Who Listens. Is s/he tall, short, thin, or round? What sort of clothing is s/he wearing? Does s/he have long or short hair? Is it curly or strait? What color is it? Is s/he broad shouldered and powerful looking or is s/he delicate and graceful? Now ask the same questions about the Parent Who Leads. Take as much time as you need to find the words that describe how your Nurturing Parents look. As they become clearer in your mind, let their images sink in. For some of you, the images you get may come quickly and be very clear. For others, they might be fuzzy and take a long time to come through. You may not get a visual picture of them at all, and that is perfectly all right. An image may come through at another time, or you may simply get a feeling of their presence.

◇ ◇ ◇

Endowing the Qualities of Your Nurturing Parents

In the second part of this exercise you will decide what qualities you would like your Nurturing Parents to have. Ask yourself what qualities are most important to you? Are there certain qualities that you want to make sure they do not have? Take all the time you need to find the words that will describe who your Nurturing Parents are. This is your chance to create them just as you want them to be. They will take on the qualities that you ask them to.

Perhaps you want your Nurturing Parents to be gentle, warm, affectionate, protective, easygoing, untroubled, unflappable, attentive, generous, confident, assertive. As you assign them a particular attribute you would like them to have, stop and imagine how they would behave with you if they had that quality. How would your Nurturing Parents show you that they were gentle, attentive, unflappable, and assertive? Imagine yourself in a situation where that quality would be valuable, and see what they do.

Now that you know what your Nurturing Parents look like and have decided what qualities they have, take a few moments to notice what it might feel like to be in their company. Sit with them. See them in your mind's eye. Review each quality one at a time. Imagine yourself in a situation where that quality would be valuable, and see how you feel. Notice how your thoughts, feelings, and sensations shift as your Nurturing Parents respond to the situation.

Give yourself a moment now and ask yourself if there is something about the parents you have created that you would like to change at this point? Is there something about the way they look, or would you like to change one of the qualities you have given them? Do you want to add or subtract a quality? Go ahead and make any changes in their physical appearance or their demeanor. As you learn more about

◇ ◇ ◇

endowing the qualities of your nurturing parents (cont)

them and as you grow and change, the images you have of them and the qualities you ascribe to them also may grow and change.

◇ ◇ ◇

Hanging Out with Your Nurturing Parents

In this part of the meditation, you will have a conversation with your Nurturing Parents. Take your time. When you feel ready, begin to talk to one or both of them. You can tell them anything you want to—something you did today that was fun, something you are looking forward to doing, something you have been thinking about lately. You might want to talk about the room or something in the room. Each time you speak to them, let them respond to you.

How does it feel to listen to them, to hear each one's words and tone of voice? Do you find their voices pleasing? If you do not, you can change them so that they are pleasing to you. You can make them speak slowly or quickly, as you wish. Notice how you feel when you look into their eyes and at their faces. Do you feel safe with them? Do you feel that they are paying close attention to you as you speak? Is there anything that they could be doing or saying that would make you feel even more at ease with them? If there is, have them do it.

Now spend a few quiet moments with your Nurturing Parents. You may want to get up from your chair and move to sit between the two of them. Whether you are sitting between them now or have decided to remain in the chair across from them, feel their wise, loving and protective presence. What words would you use to describe how you are feeling right now? What sensations do you notice in your body? Remember that your Nurturing Parents are here for you. There

◇ ◇ ◇

hanging out with your nurturing parents (cont)

is no place they would rather be than here with you, listening to whatever you have to say, or just sitting quietly with you if you have nothing to say.

◇ ◇ ◇

Calling on your Nurturing Parents will help to make them an integral, functioning part of who you are. The perspective they provide will serve you well. In the realm of emotion, your Nurturing Parents will help you to identify your feelings, honor them, experience them fully, and release them. In the cognitive realm, they will help you to notice your thoughts and beliefs, evaluate them, and put aside those that are not accurate or do not serve you. In the behavioral realm, the Nurturing Parents will help you to participate in all of the decision-making moments in your life with more clarity. They will encourage you to be open to guidance from God/All That Is, to tune in to the subtle messages that are constantly being sent your way. Coincidence, metaphor, insight, and inspiration are all messages and they hold important clues about your "next step" with respect to taking creative action.

This "next step" could relate to any area of your life—work, relationships, where to live, or how to discover and pursue your most heartfelt desires. The Nurturing Parents encourage you to be introspective and reflective, to ask good questions of yourself. What does my dissatisfaction with my job right now mean? Is there a personal issue with one of my co-workers that I need to address? Is there another way of working that would be more satisfying for me? Do I want to consider looking for another position in my current field or do I want to make a career change? Is the relationship I am in right now good for me? Do I feel cherished within it? Does it encourage me to come into my largest

Self? Is it time for me to move to another city? Do I even want to live in the city? Why do I still feel blocked about pursuing my most cherished dreams? Do I feel free to go after any of the opportunities that are open to me or are some too frightening to consider? Why do those possibilities frighten me?

When you are in touch with your Nurturing Parents, your perception of a situation that is emotionally charged or demanding changes; so does your experience within that situation. You see choices where before you may have felt at the mercy of your feelings. You feel confident that you can take on the challenges of the situation where before you may have given in to a sense of hopelessness about your ability to cope. You find that you can stay aware, responsive, and patient, even during the most stressful situations. You can rest in the Interval and wait for the resolution to reveal itself to you.

Each of you have within you the seeds of the Nurturing Parents. If, as a child, you were surrounded by adults who behaved toward you in ways that were tender, supportive, and validating, then the Nurturing Parent aspects of Self will be firmly established within you. If you were not surrounded by such adults, then the Nurturing Parents will not be so obvious or strong. But they can become stronger in all of us. Indeed, one of my primary goals in sharing the theory of the aspects with you is to help you strengthen your internal Nurturing Parents.

In Chapter Five, **Meeting Your Maturing Aspects,** I will introduce you to the three Maturing Aspects that live in you. Each of these archetypal beings have a special relationship to the life of your feelings. These beings or aspects of Self are the Emerald Child, the Suffering Child, and the Critical Detractor Child. Getting to know these three aspects will help you to explore and have a better understanding of your feelings, beliefs, impulses to act, and behaviors.

MEETING YOUR
MATURING ASPECTS

Breathe deeply and gently.

Let your body soften.

See yourself within the space that surrounds you.

Feel yourself within the space that surrounds you.

Who is doing the seeing? Who is doing the feeling?

I n recent years, much has been written about the inner child. This is the little person who lives within those of us who have survived traumatic childhood experiences but still carry unresolved feelings as a result of them. The spectrum of what constitutes emotional trauma is broad. It can include growing up with a parent who is addicted to alcohol or other drugs; coping with separation or divorce; exposure to neglect or abuse (physical, emotional, or sexual); and less extreme, but still deeply felt, experiences of hurt, disappointment, or deprivation. Emotional trauma also extends to include prejudice, poverty, and growing up in the context of war or natural disaster.

In a sense, your inner child lets you know that your grief, rage, or terror related to such experiences is not yet finished. If you are riddled with feelings of worthlessness despite many accomplishments, or find it very difficult to relax and be playful, your inner child may be calling out for help. If you are struggling with addiction or another compulsive behavior, it may be your inner child's way of finding some relief from her pain. If you establish goals for yourself and notice that you consistently sabotage your efforts to achieve them, your inner child may be trying to tell you that some unresolved issues or feelings are preventing her from moving on.

I use a combination of body work, meditation, ritual, and various theories of counseling, to invite the inner child to come out and reveal herself fully. What my students and I have discovered, however, is that there is more than one inner child. Over the years we have identified three inner children. I call them the Maturing Aspects. They are: the Emerald Child, the Suffering Child, and the Critical Detractor Child.

The Emerald Child, present from birth, does not have her origins in emotional trauma. She is looking for a way to participate in life's adventure. She wants to be free to express her playfulness, her creativity, and her optimism. She needs to know that her energy is welcomed, and that you will provide the boundaries which she requires and cannot provide for herself.

When you experience the presence of your Emerald Child you feel unburdened, you breathe more deeply. Your body feels lighter, your posture is more upright, and your walk has a bounce in it. You smile more, and more things strike you as funny. You may even find yourself laughing inappropriately at times. Colors look brighter, food tastes better, and life is infinitely more interesting. When your Emerald Child is present, you are filled with a sense of wonder and well-being.

The Suffering Child, on the other hand, has her origins in emotional trauma. She carries the feelings that are related to traumatic experiences from the past. She becomes established within you as a result of those experiences. She is in search of healing. She wants to let go of the pain that she is carrying and the self-defeating, distorted thoughts that accompany those feelings.

It is not surprising then that the energy of your Suffering Child is weighty and oppressive. When she is present, your step is heavy and it takes extra effort to hold yourself erect. Your face is closed and unanimated. Through her eyes, you see the world in shades of grey, and experience little or no joy in the beauty that is all around you. You rarely smile, and there is little to laugh about. When your Suffering Child is present, you are filled with feelings of anxiety and foreboding.

The Critical Detractor Child also becomes established as a result of traumatic experiences, but her response to those events is very different from the Suffering Child's. This aspect responds to emotional trauma by imitating her abusers. She parents you in the same abusive way. Through her speech, she mimics her abusive, indifferent, undermining, role models.

When the Critical Detractor Child steps up to the microphone, several things can occur. If you have chosen to identify with your Critical Detractor Child you might find yourself adopting a belligerent posture, chest thrust forward, face hard and unyielding. Or you might take on a superior stance, with a haughty look on your face. In either case, your body will tense, and you will defend yourself by cutting yourself off from your feelings. If, when your Critical Detractor Child speaks, your Suffering Child is triggered, you will manifest her energy instead—that of the hopeless victim.

In a sense, the Suffering Child and the Critical Detractor Child are like Siamese twins. Intimately connected to one another, they feed off one another. When the Suffering Child feels that she is unworthy of love, the Critical Detractor Child chimes in and reminds her that she is unlovable. When the Critical Detractor Child says, "you're really ugly," the Suffering Child's feeling of ugliness arise to torment her. Regardless of which child is triggered first, the other always mirrors her response.

Fortunately, the Suffering Child and Critical Detractor Child are as equally inseparable during the healing process. Regardless of which one responds first to the loving overtures of the Nurturing Parents, the other quickly follows along. In truth, each exists only within the shadow of the other.

Getting to know each of the Maturing Aspects of Self in a theoretical way is important. Understanding who they are and where they come from will give you a clear understanding of the role they play in your life. The descriptions of the aspects of Self that follow have been derived from the accounts of men and women I have worked with over the years. As you read these descriptions, try to notice if these

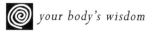

interior beings exist within you. Can you identify with the persona of the Emerald Child, the Suffering Child, and the Critical Detractor Child? Do the feeling states and thought patterns associated with each of these aspects feel familiar to you?

THE THREE MATURING ASPECTS

Even more important than learning who your Maturing Aspects are and where they came from, is learning to recognize them when they make an appearance inside you. Each time you notice that one of your Maturing Aspects is present, you enter a relationship with her as a living part of yourself. You know her as she exists within you. As you read about each aspect, begin to notice what your face, throat, chest, and belly feel like when your Emerald Child's playfulness presses you to stop reading and do something that's more fun. Notice your face, posture, and tone of voice when your Suffering Child makes an appearance. What happens to your eyes, your breath, your energy when you hear the voice of your Critical Detractor Child replaying an old tape of verbal assault. As you read about the Maturing Aspects, remember that I am describing children that already exist within you. Read slowly, stop along the way, and greet each child as she steps forward to meet you.

THE EMERALD CHILD

The Emerald Child is a treasure that lies deep within you, a sparkling jewel that radiates passion, vitality, and fearlessness. Representing boundless possibility and inexhaustible energy, this aspect of Self encourages you to reach for the stars, to settle for nothing less than everything that you imagine and desire. It is the Emerald Child that accounts for the fun-loving, energetic, engaging, and unrestrained way of being that young children so often demonstrate. When we become adults, it is the persistence of our Emerald Child that allows us to be playful, to see goodness in others, to meet each day with happy expectancy, and to look forward to the future.

A magical being, the Emerald Child believes in and communicates freely with sprites, fairies, and angels. She is indomitably curious and delights in learning. Happiest when she has her fingers in many different pies, the Emerald Child is easily bored if she is not surrounded by stimulating activities. This aspect of Self takes great pleasure in herself and in others and finds ways to communicate her joy and enthusiasm wherever she goes. Indeed the Emerald Child is incapable of self-criticism, and criticism from others always comes as a surprise to her. Because she is in touch with her own Godness and perceives that quality in everyone she meets, she can find nothing to reproach in herself or in others. From her point of view, what could there be to criticize in God / All That Is?

The Emerald Child is the embodiment of many fine qualities that inspire you to be fully alive. However, those same qualities can sometimes get you into trouble, especially if they become the dominant energy within a situation or within your life as a whole. The Emerald Child's fearlessness, spontaneity, impatience, and optimism are valuable traits, to be sure, but they can be problematic.

Because she has no fear, the Emerald Child cannot imagine why she should ever hold herself back. She is completely spontaneous and uninhibited. Unpredictable at times, she gives little or no thought to the consequences of her actions and is inclined to act on impulse. The Emerald Child identifies completely with the creative power of God / All That Is. Experiencing this power within herself, she is impatient with the limitations of three-dimensional reality and frequently acts rashly and without forethought. Finally, because the Emerald Child is incapable of negativity of any kind, she sees the world and everyone in it through the eyes of innocence and trust. For this reason, she is not very discriminating and cannot be left on her own when it comes to decision-making.

Since I recently became a grandmother, I now have a whole new area in which to observe the qualities of the Emerald Child. My grandson, Sam, is the personification of the Emerald Child. Wide open to the world, he spends all of his waking hours taking in his environment. He moves quickly and easily from one activity to another, as his curiosity directs him, and delights in each new discovery.

My daughter Wendy and I are fascinated by Sam's total presence and concentration. Completely focused on the object of his attention, he draws us into each moment with him. As we watch him do the simplest things, reaching for a toy or chewing on a bit of food, we become wrapped up in him, mesmerized by his facial expressions and movements. Laughing when something tickles him, crying when he needs to sleep or eat or be comforted, he is totally unselfconscious.

Sam's Emerald Child has been fully celebrated since the day of his birth. I am confident that his parents will be able to provide the unconditional love that will enable him to fully discover himself and his universe. Like all loving parents, they will strive to create a climate that will preserve his spirit nature and his inquisitiveness. He will be free to investigate and explore everything he sees, and the Emerald Child within him will flourish and be available to him throughout his lifetime.

Unfortunately, not all of us are raised in circumstances that nurture the Emerald Child. Despite the intense energy and powerful presence of this aspect of Self, the Emerald Child is not invincible. Because she tends to see only the good in people and is inclined to trust everyone she meets, the Emerald Child frequently makes herself vulnerable to those whose intentions are not always good. If she is repeatedly exposed to indifference or mistreatment, she will take herself away and go into hiding as a means of protection.

Although she is inclined to forgive those who hurt her, the Emerald Child does not forget. Endowed with a strong instinct to survive, she will remain in hiding until she feels that it is safe to come out again. While she is in seclusion, some of her qualities may still be available to you. However, you will not have access to the full force of the gifts which she possesses and her diminished presence will be reflected in your attitudes and behaviors.

Many of us lose access to our Emerald Child when we decide that it is time to "grow up." We mistakenly believe that there is no place for our Emerald Child in our adult world. Years of being ignored, denied, or suppressed diminishes her presence and our ability to experience her. Knowing how you feel about your Emerald Child can help you reconnect with her. If your response to children with an active Emerald Child is to judge them too noisy, too wild, or too silly, it is likely your Emerald Child will feel shy and unwelcome. If you experience delight in their free-spiritedness and desire to join them, it will be easier for you to reconnect to the free-spiritedness within you.

Although your Emerald Child may have withdrawn, she still awaits your call. She awaits your acceptance, your appreciation, and an invitation to participate in your life. You extend this invitation to your Emerald Child by feeling her presence, and by creating opportunities for her to express herself freely.

Encouraging her to express herself freely does not mean that you should start behaving like a child. Remember, you are still the adult in charge, and your Emerald Child needs your guidance. It simply means that you begin to discover what your Emerald Child likes. What foods give her the most pleasure? When she hears that you're going hiking, or swimming, or to a movie, does she get excited? Whose company does she delight in, and who makes her groan when you contemplate spending time with them? When you discover the things that turn your Emerald Child on, do them. Bring your full attention to those activities and allow yourself to feel what she is feeling. Begin to express those feelings in ways that feel comfortable for you.

For those of you who have lost touch with your Emerald Child, feeling her presence may require some practice on your part. You can begin by noticing and appreciating the qualities that happy children exhibit. The next time you pass a playground, or see children in a store or on the street, notice how they behave. Notice the expression in their eyes, and on their faces. Notice the way their bodies move. Notice their energy. Notice their spontaneity. You will discover that they have an amazing gift for turning everything into a game. They find ways to play regardless of whether they're in church, the supermarket, or the playground. They laugh at things adults don't usually think are funny, like someone falling down, or spilling something on themselves. They live in the immediate present; neither the past nor the future holds much interest for them. As you become more familiar with them, invite what you are noticing to awaken in you. The energy of the Emerald Child is lying dormant in you, waiting to be awakened.

When you begin to nurture your Emerald Child, you may become aware of certain thoughts and feelings that oppose this awakening. If left unnoticed, these voices and feelings can deter you from reconnecting with her. These are the voices and feelings of your Suffering Child or Critical Detractor Child. Their very nature is fearful of the possibility of your feeling less inhibited, more creative, and spontaneous. It is difficult and even painful for them when the Emerald Child opens you to experiencing a new sense of wonderment at the magnificent world in which you live. Their efforts will be directed toward maintaining the status quo.

THE SUFFERING CHILD

The Suffering Child is the keeper of feelings that have never been resolved, feelings that are the result of traumatic events in your past. This aspect of Self becomes established when you are exposed to an emotional trauma and do not have access to the attention of caring adults who can help you to recover from that trauma. The Suffering Child becomes even more firmly established each time you experience another trauma and for some reason cannot fully process your feelings related to it. Over time, the feelings of grief, rage, fearfulness, shame, guilt, unworthiness, helplessness, and hopelessness that emerge as a result of these traumatic events increase in strength. The influence these feelings have on your beliefs and behaviors also increases. The Suffering Child aspect who carries these feelings for you becomes more and more weighed down, and her need to get your attention so that she can release her burden becomes more pressing.

The psychological traumas that give rise to the Suffering Child can occur at any stage of growth and development when you are dependent on others for care, whether as an infant, toddler, young child, adolescent, or young adult. The damage that is done by the trauma itself is compounded when the adults you turn to for comfort are unable or unwilling to validate your emotional response to what has happened and assist you in working through your feelings. Indeed, this absence of care in the aftermath of a traumatic experience is at the very heart of what creates the Suffering Child aspect.

It is a tragic irony that the people you are most likely to reach out to after an abusive incident are all too often the ones who perpetrated the abuse. Of course this creates a very painful dilemma for a child or a young person, a profound case of insult being added to injury. It also explains why many of us must wait until we have left home to begin to identify and heal our Suffering Child. Healing can only take place within a safe environment, one in which you trust that you will receive the loving attention you did not get at the time of the trauma itself.

The feelings of hurt, anger, disappointment, loneliness, despair, shame, confusion, grief, guilt, and rage that a child who has been traumatized experiences are quite natural. Likewise it is natural for a child to want to express those feelings and speak about the incident that provoked them (if she is old enough to do so). When the adults to whom this child turns listen to her account of the incident and encourage her display of emotion, then the Suffering Child aspect never becomes established. The child's traumatic experience and her response to it are validated, and so is the child herself. She receives a powerful message affirming her ability and her right to have her feelings and express her emotions. Because she has an opportunity to process her painful experience fully, she learns from it and is strengthened by it. She can then put aside that experience and move on.

On the other hand, if a child who has had a traumatic experience does not have access to a caring adult who can validate her in these ways, that child cannot put her experience behind her. The event becomes unfinished business, and the feelings which rose in response to it remain unresolved by virtue of their not having been fully expressed and lovingly witnessed. At that time, the Suffering Child aspect emerges or becomes strengthened if she is already present. She assumes her role as the keeper of feelings which you could not express and resolve at the time of the traumatic event.

The Suffering Child stores your painful feelings. She also makes it possible for you to come in touch with them at a later time and find the resolution that has been missing. Indeed it is the function of the Suffering Child to carry and display the feelings of fearfulness, unworthiness, helplessness, and hopelessness caused by unresolved traumas. Each time one or more of these feelings arise, it announces its nonclosure and helps you obtain the healing intervention you did not receive in the past. As you will see in the next chapter, your ability to act as your own Nurturing Parents plays a central role in helping the Suffering Child within you to receive that healing.

As the keeper of feelings related to past hurts, the Suffering Child is focused on pain and the expectation of further suffering. With respect to the other aspects, she feels alienated from the Emerald Child, who can so easily experience and express joy. When you call up the qualities of your Nurturing Parents, the Suffering Child may find it difficult to be open to those loving overtures because she does not believe that she deserves such attention. She believes that she deserves to continue suffering. Intimidated by the Critical Detractor Child, her sense of fearfulness, unworthiness, hopelessness, and helplessness are strengthened each time the Critical Detractor Child dispenses her negative comments. Until she receives healing, the Suffering Child is perpetually poised to reexperience the feelings from the original injury that were never sufficiently addressed. She carries with her at all times a store of feelings, like a heavy sack of unfinished business slung over her shoulder. When she is stimulated by a situation that reminds her of the original injury, she reaches down into her sack and pulls out the contents.

As the Suffering Child aspect reviews the feelings and detailed memories thus displayed before her, she travels back into the past, is swept up by the feelings that arose then and becomes disoriented in time. Under this inner aspect's influence, you consciously or unconsciously come in touch with those memories, become overwhelmed by feelings, and lose touch with the present (to varying degrees, of course, depending on the power and scope of the original injury and the extent to which you have begun to heal its effects).

If you become lost in the feelings that are carried by your Suffering Child aspect, you are also likely to become overwhelmed by the sensations that accompany those feelings, sensations that are often physically uncomfortable. You may experience extreme tension, palpitations, nausea, shallow breathing, flushing, sweating, shaking, and other manifestations of stress, just as you probably did at the time of the original injury. When you come under the influence of the Suffering Child aspect, these responses are reactivated. In an instinctive attempt to take care of yourself, you then look for ways to move away from these sensations, just as in the past you sought a way out of the circumstances surrounding the original injury. This natural avoidance reaction accounts for your inclination to fight or take flight when you are under the influence of the Suffering Child aspect. Each of these reactions to your intense feelings and the sensations within them can take a variety of forms.

The urge to fight can manifest as anger held within, but still clearly felt by you and expressed to others: as sarcastic "wit"; as an argumentative nature; as passive-aggressive behavior; as blatantly angry words directed at another person; as physical violence toward another; or through self-destructive acts, which are anger misguidedly directed toward yourself.

Likewise, the urge to flee can be manifested in a host of obvious and not so obvious ways, including an unpremeditated hasty departure (quietly or cursing as you go); running away after making careful, private plans to do so; withdrawing from conversation or other interactions with people around you; avoiding intimate situations as a way of hiding from others; refusing to reveal your true feelings, even in response to tender and direct requests to do so; or retreating into the anesthesia of depression, drug use, abuse, or dependency.

The feelings that you come in touch with when under the influence of a Suffering Child aspect—such as terror, grief, rage, and despair—tend to stimulate specific thoughts and general patterns of thinking that are consistent with each of those feeling states. When you become immersed in terror, you think and somewhere believe that something awful is about to happen. Your mind is more easily attracted to images of harm, punishment, abandonment, or whatever else originally created the terror that you are now revisiting. When you feel intense grief, your thoughts are likewise filled with unhappy memories and the expectation of further sorrow. Under the influence of rage, you tend to see adversaries wherever you look. When you are filled with despair, it is extremely difficult to conceive of solutions to a problem or inter-personal conflict. Indeed, any single intense feeling, or combination of such feelings, can so monopolize your awareness and attention that you find it impossible to think clearly about anything at all.

The Suffering Child also voices the distorted and erroneous thoughts that find fertile soil during or after an emotional trauma. These thoughts usually center around conclusions which the Suffering Child drew long ago concerning the "causative" role she played in the original injury's unfolding. "It must have been my fault," she infers. "I must have deserved it." Based on those thoughts, she goes on to con-clude that she is bad, unlovable, undeserving of rescue or support, etc. In this way, one of the most outstanding characteristics of the Suffering Child—low self-esteem—takes hold and frequently becomes more established as the years go by. When a situation in the present evokes your Suffering Child aspect and you fall under her influence, you tend to slip into the same negative thinking.

With respect to your emotions and other behavioral manifestations, the Suffering Child's impulses to act and the behaviors that you exhibit when under her influence are drawn from a very narrow range of pos-sibilities. Either you find yourself immobilized by terror and grief, or desperately try to contain the hyperactivity beneath your terror and rage. At the grief stricken end of the spectrum, you will probably find it very difficult to act at all. Where rage takes over, you are likely to behave impulsively and in ways that you will later regret.

Coming from a very primitive and survivalist perspective, the Suffering Child aspect inclines you to react rather than respond. You tend to behave impulsively, to "act out" rather than consider possible courses of action and choose the one that will be most beneficial to you. Your actions at such times are seldom considered and "chosen." Instead they are more often knee-jerk reactions to the intense feelings and sensations you are experiencing.

This acting out represents an unconscious effort on your part to relieve yourself of the powerful and painful feelings which the Suffering Child aspect has been carrying on your behalf. When you behave in such a way, you may experience a welcome catharsis, but one that does not contribute to healing the original injury. It is more like steam escaping around the edges of a boiling pot, releasing excess vapor that can no longer be contained. Your actions may escalate the emotional charge within you and in others present, making the situation even more volatile and less amenable to resolution at that time.

Viewed in a larger context, outbursts which signal the presence of a Suffering Child are a necessary first step toward the healing the Suffering Child aspect within you craves. This healing occurs when you identify the original injury, recall the events surrounding the injury itself, and release your emotions in the company of a nurturing adult.

It is important to cultivate this larger point of view about your behaviors and their origins. Summoning the Parent Who Listens and the Parent Who Leads in the midst of a conflict will help you to do that. Without their input, you may fail to recognize that a Suffering Child has come on the scene and are more likely to judge your behavior and the feelings underlying it too harshly. You may then fragment and polarize the situation even further by labeling yourself as "totally crazy" or the people around you as "totally insensitive" for eliciting such feelings and "making you act crazy."

Convinced that she is not entitled to the attention, protection, and affection that children should receive, the Suffering Child aspect discourages you from reaching out to others when you need their help most. With little or no hope that her circumstances will change for the better, this aspect's sense of despair and impotence make it hard for you to see possibility and promise in situations where she has been activated. You then have difficulty in maintaining an open perspective from which to observe the circumstances that evoked her and to interact with the people involved in that scene.

Until your Suffering Child aspect receives the attention she needs, she will continue to influence your behavior. Her process of recovery begins when you become aware of the feelings which she carries. These feelings belong to the children you once were. They are calling out for help, urging you to act on their behalf and enter into a process of exploration and healing. Unrecognized and untreated, these feelings have the potential to sabotage your growth and vitality. On the other hand, they can become your path to salvation if you learn how to engage your Nurturing Parent aspects and apply their skills to promoting the Suffering Child's transformation. When your Suffering Child is liberated, so are you.

Once this transformation occurs, you can relinquish your tendencies to act out of the Suffering Child's space. You become aware of a much broader range of behaviors from which to choose, with respect to your relationships and other aspects of your experience. You can assume a new level of responsibility for the way you express yourself emotionally and are able to bring a new perspective to your past and present intimate relationships. You can let go of what is no longer relevant to your adult life, detach from formerly restrictive patterns of behavior, and respond to each moment with clarity and creativity.

THE CRITICAL DETRACTOR CHILD

The Critical Detractor Child is not as likable a character as the other inner children because her voice is that of the dysfunctional adults she is mimicking. But you have much to gain from interacting with her. Indeed, resolving the issues which she brings will help you to let go of negative, self-defeating beliefs and attitudes, and learn to love yourself unconditionally.

Like the Suffering Child, the Critical Detractor Child becomes established as a result of traumatic events in your past, but she has taken a different route in trying to cope with those traumas. Instead of engaging the feelings of grief and rage that rise, as the Suffering Child does, the Critical Detractor Child suppresses her feelings and creates a kind of perverse alliance with the adults who abused you. She does this in a misguided attempt to protect herself from further abuse. As Robert Firestone writes in his book, *The Fantasy Bond:*

> "The child takes on the characteristics of the punishing parent in order to relieve anxiety and gain some measure of security. In 'identifying with the aggressor,' in this case the parent, the child feels as if some mastery has been gained over stressful situations."[5]

The Critical Detractor Child identifies with your abusers and essentially becomes another version of them, an internalized version. This gives her a modicum of control and turns down the intensity of the pain associated with being mistreated. Then, from within your own head, she imitates the abusive adults you have known. When you hear her voice, whether it is directed at you or at someone else, you are hearing the voices of those adults who abused you.

The dynamic underlying the establishment of this aspect is a form of "if you can't beat 'em, join 'em." In "joining them," the Critical Detractor Child then becomes obliged to torment you in the present in the same way that abusive adults did in the past. When she does this, she evokes or strengthens the stored feelings of fearfulness, unworthiness,

109

helplessness, and hopelessness which your Suffering Child so easily comes in touch with.

A clever and persistent tormentor, the Critical Detractor Child practices a form of psychological abuse on you. From inside your own head, she dispenses messages that are hurtful and invalidating. The dialogue of the Critical Detractor Child is filled with condemnations and warnings, such as:

> "You're so ugly. Why would anyone want to pay any attention to you?"

> "What a wimp you are. You can't even stand up for yourself. You never could!"

> "We know you're not perfect. But for God's sake don't let anyone else see how worthless you are."

> "Don't bother trying. You know it's not going to be good enough."

> "You messed up again, and as usual it's all your fault."

> "You have no future, so you might as well give up."

> "Be careful, you're just going to make another mistake. And then you'll be exposed for the fool that you are."

> "You're too much, tone it down. If you stand out, people won't like you."

> "It was just dumb luck so don't get too big for yourself. Who do you think you are, Albert Einstein?"

> "Don't let anyone see your real feelings, they'll just take advantage of them and hurt you."

"Don't admit that you love sex or everyone will think you're a slut/sex fiend."

"Sex is dirty and you can only do it with bad boys/girls."

"You can't trust him/her, s/he just wants to use you."

The common thread among the caretakers and other influential adults after whom the Critical Detractor Child is modeled was a tendency to speak or behave in ways that had the effect of putting you down. They may have teased you, intimidated you, made fun of you in front of others, discredited your accomplishments, or done any number of things that led you to feel worthless, incompetent, and unlovable. These dysfunctional adults could have included anyone who influenced you during your most impressionable years—parents, grandparents, teachers, coaches, spiritual leaders, even siblings if they were charged with supervising your care. They communicated to you, in word and deed, by overt and subtle means, that you did not deserve to be loved. At best they were unaware and misguided; at worst they were cruel and consciously destructive.

Fashioned after these adults, the Critical Detractor Child sets out to do as they did, to belittle and reproach you. She speaks to you in ways that undermine your sense of worth. She tries to persuade you that goodness in others is not to be found, and that even if it were, you would not be deserving of it. She discourages you from seeking help when you need it and tries to convince you that such a need is proof of your weakness, stupidity, or imperfection. Under her influence, you struggle to function successfully in the world and when you do, you cannot appreciate your achievements. You not only feel at a distance from yourself, but also lose sight of your connection to God/All That Is.

In all of these ways, the Critical Detractor Child undermines you and retraumatizes the Suffering Child within you. By provoking feelings of fear, shame, guilt, and despair, she reminds the Suffering Childthat the world is a dark and dangerous place, fraught with occasions for suffering. When your Critical Detractor Child triggers the intense feelings stored by your Suffering Child, two things may occur. You may find yourself identifying completely with your Suffering Child, or you may fall under the influence of your Critical Detractor Child.

If you are inclined to identify with your Suffering Child, you become overwhelmed by feelings and memories associated with past traumas. Your perspective narrows, and your ability to think clearly about what is currently occurring around you diminishes. Your actions at such times are usually consistent with those of a frightened child who feels threatened, abandoned, vulnerable, and desperate. You may become passive and tend to give up or give in.

If you identify with your Critical Detractor Child, you are likely to act in ways that are mean-spirited, overbearing, disdainful, and judgmental toward yourself and others. You will act aggressively, often behaving like a bully or a know-it-all. At those times, your actions are reflecting the beliefs, attitudes, and behaviors of the dysfunctional adults who parented you.

Your goal with the Critical Detractor Child is to reparent her. On the surface it appears that her only goal is to torment you in the same way that certain adults did, often with the very same words. In everything that she does, the Critical Detractor Child is asking for your help in accessing and healing the feelings that lie beneath her harsh exterior. But this behavior is really a facade.

Reparenting the Critical Detractor Child is done in stages. First you must name her when she is present. Then you must acknowledge her messages, and notice the effects they have on you. Next, you silence the hurtful messages she broadcasts, and replace them with validating self-talk. Repeating this process whenever she appears will eventually convince your Critical Detractor Child that she is deserving of love and attention and that the world can be a very good place indeed. But, your Critical Detractor Child is extremely resistant to change, and you may need to repeat this process thousands of times before you heal this misdirected and needy aspect of Self.

In your attempt to reparent your Critical Detractor Child, you will come in touch with two very formidable obstacles. The first obstacle is her intense fear of the deep grieving that must precede her liberation. She believes that if she re-experiences the pain associated with the original injury, she will die. She also believes that if she feels this pain again she will be unable to maintain her superior pose. She will lose her control over the Suffering Child, be at the mercy of her feelings, and be unable to protect herself from that child's behavior.

The next obstacle you will encounter is her strong sense of loyalty toward the adult(s) she modeled herself after. Her misplaced loyalty is extremely difficult for her to let go of; with it she must also let go of the dream of ever getting what she wants from the adults who mistreated her. She still longs for affection, approval, and protection from those adults, even though she may recognize that she can never obtain that love. She persists in the hope that she can win from her abusers the loving attention which has always been withheld from her. The Critical Detractor Child still balks at saying goodbye to her tormentors even though she knows that only by letting go of her unrealistic anticipation of long-overdue tenderness can she begin her new life.

Robert Firestone writes about the dynamic which underlies our reluctance to transform such an obvious oppressor as the Critical Detractor Child:

> "Emotionally deprived children find it impossible to see the parents' faults; they cannot afford to do that because then their situation would seem genuinely hopeless. To defend against their pain and despair, they see themselves as bad and imagine that by performing, by trying to please, or by doing the right thing, they can get their parents to love them."[6]

113

As children, we are totally dependent on our parents for care; our lives are literally in their hands. We sense this at a very profound level and accordingly endow our caretakers with all the magic and infallibility that we associate with such awesome power. In trying to make sense of the absence or withdrawal of affection, a child will reason that if the adults in charge do not see fit to give her the love that she needs, then she must not deserve that love. Surely such an omission could not be the grown-ups' fault; therefore it must be the child's. The adults could not be wrong in withholding their love from her; therefore she must be doing something to prevent them from offering it. She must be bad, since by definition these magnificent adults represent all that is good.

In order to transform the Critical Detractor Child and assist her on her journey toward recovery, you have to relinquish your fantasy of the bond you would like to have had with your abusive caretakers. You must acknowledge the true poverty of those relationships and mourn the losses that your fantasy hid from you. Only in this way can you heal your Critical Detractor Child and begin to reclaim your sense of worthiness and inherent goodness.

In Chapter Six, **Learning to Parent Yourself,** you will get closer to all your Maturing Aspects. You will learn how your Nurturing Parents interact with them, and you will have an opportunity to interact with them as your Nurturing Parents would.

LEARNING TO
PARENT YOURSELF

Breathe deeply and gently.
Let your body soften.
See yourself within the space that surrounds you.
Feel yourself within the space that surrounds you.
Who is doing the seeing? Who is doing the feeling?

ust as a child looks to his parents for attention and guidance, each of the Maturing Aspects is looking for a certain kind of attention from you. Each wants to be welcomed, heard, understood, and reassured. When you learn to interact with your maturing aspects in these ways, a transformation occurs. Feeling welcomed, the Emerald Child begins to reveal himself. His presence invites you to be more spontaneous and creative. The Suffering Child feels safe and his long-held feelings of fearfulness, unworthiness, helplessness, and hopelessness begin to dissipate. Unburdened of these feelings, you feel less fearful and more hopeful. Knowing there is a wise and loving adult in charge, your Critical Detractor Child can put down the burden of his parenting responsibilities and begin the process of learning to use his talents in more productive ways.

With the help of the Parent Who Listens and the Parent Who Leads, you can attend to all three of the Maturing Aspects and become the parent these inner children need. You can temper your Emerald Child's impatience, focus his boundless energy, and revel in his enthusiasm for life. You can work through and release the feelings of fear and self-doubt that you experience when your Suffering Child appears. You can change the cruel and counter-productive thoughts that you find yourself entertaining as a result of your Critical Detractor Child's presence. You can heal the wounded being who is at the core of your Critical Detractor Child. By behaving as your Nurturing Parents would, you are able to manage the input from these three aspects, make conscious and informed choices, and respond confidently to the situations that evoke them.

The Nurturing Parents offer the most precious and practical gift of showing you how to love and care for yourself with all the tenderness, skill, and steadfastness that the most loving parents possess. In the process of liberating your Emerald Child, and working through the feelings of your Suffering Child and the beliefs of your Critical Detractor Child, you have insights about your feelings, thoughts, motives, intentions, and behaviors. You become more aware of your thoughts and feelings, clearer about what motivates your behavior, and more skillful at observing and participating in the complex dance created by your Maturing Aspects.

As you continue to read, remember that your goal is to strengthen the presence of the Nurturing Parents, and to develop a loving relationship with your Maturing Aspects. Take a few moments to bring to mind the images of the Nurturing Parents you created and to remember the qualities you gave them. As you read about their relationship to the Maturing Aspects, imagine that you are relating to your Maturing Aspects in this way. Notice how seeing through the eyes of your Nurturing Parents affects the way you relate to your Maturing Aspects.

THE ROLE OF THE PARENT WHO LISTENS

The primary goal of the Parent Who Listens is to watch over the three Maturing Aspects and pay attention to the thoughts and feelings that arise in situations where these aspects emerge. The listening parent invites the Emerald Child to display his gifts of playfulness, creativity, and optimism. S/he encourages you to feel his energy throughout your body, and to allow his thinking to become part of your own. S/he keeps a careful eye on his impatience, and prevents him from prompting you to act impulsively and unwisely.

The listening parent's role in relation to the Suffering Child involves a sequence of responses, all of which are aimed at communicating tender and loving acceptance. Each time the Suffering Child emerges, the Parent Who Listens reaches out to him, no matter how he presents himself. Whether the Suffering Child reveals himself as shy and retreating or belligerent and feisty, the listening parent welcomes this tender aspect of Self. S/he says, "Take my hand, climb up onto my lap. Come into my arms and let me comfort you." Softly s/he speaks to him, "I see you, I utterly see you." With these words, s/he lets the Suffering Child know that every feeling, every thought, every inclination, every bit of history which this wounded aspect brings with him is welcome. The Parent Who Listens never disapproves of the Suffering Child's grief, rage, or terror. On the contrary, s/he invites the Suffering Child to reveal all that he has been holding inside.

The listening parent's dialogue with the Suffering Child might sound something like this:

> "Come, my cherished one. I'm listening. Take all the time you need to tell me everything that you have been holding in your heart for so long. What are you feeling in your body? Do your feelings want to come out? Let me hold you while you have your feelings. You will be free of them if you let yourself cry or yell. It is good to express your feelings. Does this situation that you are in now remind you of something that happened in the past? I am here to listen, so you can tell me all about it. I want to hear everything. That is why I am here with you. That is why I will be here whenever you need me. "

The compassion and unconditional love that emanates from the Parent Who Listens makes the Suffering Child feel safe and secure.

In response to gentle but persistent overtures, the Suffering Child begins to pour out his feelings. The Parent Who Listens attends to him in the most therapeutic way; s/he gives the Suffering Child undivided attention and uses words, tone of voice, gaze, and posture to shower this inner being with love. S/he assures the Suffering Child that he can take as much time as he needs. S/he validates every feeling that the Suffering Child exhibits: confusion, grief, guilt, rage, shame, whatever he reveals.

Dialogues between the Parent Who Listens and the Suffering Child can take place in two ways. The first involves you talking to yourself—aloud or silently. The listening parent within you speaks directly to the Suffering Child within you. S/he invites him to breathe deeply and bring his attention to what he is experiencing in your face, your throat, your chest, and your belly. S/he encourages him to describe what he is feeling, and to become intimate with those feelings. The listening parent teaches you how to glean all you can from the information hidden within these feelings and sensations. Protecting you when emotions arise, the listening parent embraces you while you cry or scream.

The second way in which such a dialogue can occur involves someone else acting the part of the Parent Who Listens, drawing out your Suffering Child. This person could be a friend, a counselor, or anyone whom you trust. There are certain advantages to having someone besides you play the part of the Parent Who Listens. When someone else takes on this role, you can devote more of your energy to coming in touch with your Suffering Child. A proxy listening parent may also teach you something new about the behaviors that characterize this archetypal being. You may observe your "other listening parent" using behaviors with your Suffering Child that you had not used before or had not imagined using. These new techniques can be added to those that are already part of your repertoire.

When another person provides the dialogue of the Parent Who Listens and takes on that role for you, you can pay close attention to how you feel in response to that person's interventions. Which verbal and nonverbal behaviors used by your other listening parent make you feel safer, calmer, more cherished? Which behaviors make you feel less safe, less calm, less cherished? Has your proxy listening parent helped you go deeper into yourself, or have doors closed that might otherwise have opened? You can incorporate the information that emerges from answering these questions into your evolving sense of who the listening parent is and how s/he performs. You may also notice that your proxy listening parent has failed to demonstrate the qualities that you were looking for in a particular situation. The omission of a quality or a particular technique can also help you to clarify your sense of who the Parent Who Listens is and the role s/he plays.

Many situations are emotionally charged for you because they are reminiscent of traumatic events from your past. With this in mind, the Parent Who Listens asks the Suffering Child, "Does the situation you are in right now remind you of something that happened in the past?" The presence of the listening parent reassures the Suffering Child that it is safe for him to travel back in time and remember the details of such an event. If the Suffering Child can recall such an event, the listening parent invites him to talk about it. This helps the Suffering Child to release the feelings he carries in relation to the experience.

In the course of opening up to the Parent Who Listens, the Suffering Child asks the questions that are uniquely his: "Why did this happen?" and "Why did this happen to me?" The listening parent reassures the Suffering Child that he did nothing to deserve the mistreatment that evoked the feelings that he carries now. S/he tenderly acknowledges that life is not always fair and that we do not always receive the loving care that we deserve. S/he emphasizes that a child never deserves to be mistreated.

By encouraging the Suffering Child to come in touch with his thoughts, memories, feelings, and sensations, the Parent Who Listens is, of course, inviting you to experience all of those phenomena. By being utterly present, the listening parent creates a safe, protected environment for you and your emotional experience. You can let go of the notion that you must keep your feelings at bay in order to protect yourself. S/he allays your fears of being overpowered by your feelings, or

119

getting lost in them. You learn that you will not die if you allow yourself to experience your feelings.

By witnessing the totality of the Suffering Child's experience, the Parent Who Listens encourages you to be open to all of your thoughts, feelings, and sensations. By attending to the Suffering Child, the listening parent initiates a holistic event, an occasion for you to be exquisitely present in the moment. You can be present to your body and all of its sensations, to your mind and all of your thoughts, to your feelings and your impulse to express yourself emotionally, and to the ways in which you actually do express your emotions. You can be aware of all your impulses to act and your actual behaviors within a situation.

In a very real sense, the Parent Who Listens is midwife to the "I" who emerges once your Suffering Child has had a chance to release his intense feelings. Each time you articulate the feelings that are carried by your Suffering Child, you release some of the emotional energy that is stored within those feelings. Each time, the feelings themselves and the Suffering Child who has been carrying them, occupy a little less space within you. They no longer contribute as much to your sense of who you are. After s/he has helped you to come to this new place, this new sense of Self, the Parent Who Listens celebrates the "I" who has emerged.

By embracing every feature of what is taking place within you, judging none of it, patiently and wholeheartedly welcoming each new detail, each new manifestation of your emerging Self, the Parent Who Listens models for you how to be exquisitely open to Self. S/he shows you how to be completely accepting of who you are at any given moment. Through the experience of being truly seen and treasured by this listening parent, you learn to be present to yourself and to love yourself unconditionally, just as s/he does. You also find it easier to be present to others in that way, to welcome them and behave lovingly toward them.

Whenever the Critical Detractor Child appears, the Parent Who Listens initiates another sequence of responses that is designed to interrupt the abusive remarks put out by this Maturing Aspect and to take care of the needy child who is at the heart of the Critical Detractor Child. First, the listening parent comforts you by negating any hurtful remarks that have been made by your Critical Detractor Child. Then s/he reaches out to your Critical Detractor Child in the same way that s/he reaches out to your Suffering Child. In the same loving voice, s/he welcomes the Critical Detractor Child: "Come to me, come up onto my lap. Put aside your bravado, and let me help you." S/he persuades him to stop his abusive adult act and release the feelings of hurt and rage that all his bluster and venom have been trying to conceal. The listening parent helps the Critical Detractor Child to see that he has much more in common with the Suffering Child than he ever did with the abusive adults whom he has been imitating.

THE ROLE OF THE PARENT WHO LEADS

The primary goal of the Parent Who Leads is to stir you to act, and everything s/he does is designed to prepare you for taking action. The leading parent is aware of the three Maturing Aspects, of course, but s/he relies on the listening parent to attend to them. The Parent Who Leads is aware of your feelings, but s/he does not engage you in relation to them as the Parent Who Listens does. The leading parent observes your emotional state to determine if your Maturing Aspects are influencing your feelings and preventing you from acting or from acting wisely. If s/he judges that your feelings are getting in the way of your taking creative action, the Parent Who Leads refers you back to the Parent Who Listens. The listening parent then helps you to resolve those feelings. When you reach a place of greater clarity, the listening parent hands you back over to the Parent Who Leads. S/he then picks up where s/he left off earlier.

The leading parent's dialogues differ from those of the Parent Who Listens and reflect the difference in their priorities. The listening parent's dialogue is focused on eliciting the feelings and thoughts carried by the Maturing Aspects. In order to extract that information, s/he speaks directly to those three aspects. S/he speaks to your Emerald Child, your Suffering Child, or your Critical Detractor Child as each one appears within a situation. The Parent Who Leads, on the other hand, speaks to *you*, not to your individual aspects. It is you, your *Integrating, Emerging, Adult Self*, not your separate aspects of Self, who will decide on a course of action and who will act. Therefore it is you who has to be in dialogue with the Parent Who Leads. Naturally all of your aspects are present when you have this dialogue with the leading parent, just as they are present in other situations, but the Parent Who Leads addresses them as part of a unified whole. Each time s/he does this, you have an opportunity to experience yourself as that unified whole. You experience yourself as the sum of your parts and as something larger than that. You experience your *Integrating, Emerging, Adult Self.*

The leading parent's strategy for stirring you to act can be broken down into a number of steps. First, s/he helps you to recognize the decision-making moments in your life. Then s/he reminds you that in each of those moments you have a variety of choices before you and s/he encourages you to take your time to investigate them. By helping you to stay calm, s/he then makes it possible for you to distinguish the voices of your Maturing Aspects from that of your Intuitive Self. When you feel the confidence that comes from knowing the choice of your Intuitive Self, the Parent Who Leads stimulates your impulse to act. S/he encourages you to follow through on the choice you made, or s/he turns you back over to the Parent Who Listens for a time so you will become ready to act. After you take some action, the Parent Who Leads helps you to assess the effects of the action you took. Let's take a closer look at each of these steps.

The Parent Who Leads is tuned in to the big and small decisions you face in the course of a day and over the course of your lifetime. Some of these decisions relate to major life choices, such as changing jobs or getting married, while others have to do with the mundane but still important details of day to day life. "How will I start that conversation I have been wanting to have with my son about sex? What should I wear to the party this weekend? Should I tell my mother the truth about my visit to the doctor? Should we continue to rent this apartment or make plans to buy a house? Do I want to go to school in the fall or go off to see the world?"

As you become more familiar with your leading parent aspect, you will be more tuned-in to the decision-making moments in your life. Those moments will begin to stand out, to announce themselves. You will find yourself taking more time to observe the thoughts, feelings, and sensations that arise in the moments before and after you make a decision.

In addition to helping you recognize decision-making moments, the Parent Who Leads also helps you to appreciate the variety of choices that lie before you when you are faced with a decision. This Nurturing Parent's expanded view of all the ways in which you could respond becomes your view. It is as though you are seeing the situation through the eyes of the leading parent.

This expanded way of seeing becomes even more accessible if you relax and come into the Interval whenever you are faced with a decision. As you parade each choice before you, feelings and sensations arise and move through your body. Within the Interval you are able to notice these phenomena and use them to decipher which choices trigger the fears of your Suffering Child or Critical Detractor Child. They tell you which choices enliven your Emerald Child. And when you are at peace in the Interval, your experience of these feelings and sensations tell you when you have reached the choice most advantageous to your Integrating, Emerging, Adult Self—the choice offered up by your Intuitive Self.

Let's stop and take a look at a particular decision-making moment and the choices within it. First, take a deep, gentle breath. Let your body soften. Come into the Interval. See yourself in the center of the space that surrounds you. Now take another deep breath, and imagine that you are in the midst of a conflict with your spouse, lover, friend, or colleague. Here are some of the choices you have with regard to your internal experience of this situation:

- To let all your feelings, sensations and thoughts rise into your awareness or to suppress them;

- To listen for the voices of your Suffering Child, your Critical Detractor Child, your Emerald Child or not;

- To respond to each of these aspects as the Parent Who Listens would, or not;

- If your spouse/lover/friend/colleague takes on the role of the listening parent, to let yourself open up to his or her overtures, or not.

Take another deep breath. Here are some of the choices you have with regard to your outward behavior:

- To stay and work through the conflict or remove yourself from the situation;

- To share what you are thinking or feeling with your spouse/lover/friend/colleague or not;

- To ask of your spouse/lover/friend/colleague whatever would make you feel safe about revealing your thoughts and feelings, or not;

- To simply observe what is taking place and respond at some other time;

- To ask your spouse/lover/friend/colleague for a 'time-out' so you can collect your thoughts and review your feelings outside of the situation itself.

To help you examine the choices you have, the Parent Who Leads asks, *"What is there for you to learn from this situation?"* With this question, s/he is encouraging you to stop and reflect, to consider the possibility that there is more to this decision-making moment than meets the eye. If the feelings you experience within a situation seem familiar, then that situation may be related to an important event from your past.

Perhaps one of your Maturing Aspects is seizing this opportunity to get a message through to you so you will give some attention to that past event and to the feelings and impulses to behave that linger because of it. If you examine that event and the feelings and impulses related to it for just a moment, you may be able to stop yourself from reacting automatically, or from overreacting to your situation.

If the choices you identify or the conflict within a situation seem familiar—as though you have been here before—then a pattern or a central issue may be trying to reveal itself. You may be on the outskirts of an insight experience that could reveal why you repeatedly find yourself in certain kinds of situations, or why you tend to behave as you do in certain situations. Exploring your feelings, sensations, thoughts, and impulses to act within that situation may provide some very useful information and inspire you to respond in a new way. On the other hand, you may conclude that you are looking at a simple, straightforward decision-making moment that has no special significance or symbolism. If you come to that conclusion, then you can simply move on to the next step in the process: tuning in to the voice of your Intuitive Self and learning what is in the best interest of your Integrating, Emerging, Adult Self.

Once the Parent Who Leads has helped you to identify the choices before you, glean all the information you can from them, and discover the desired response, s/he stirs you to move ahead. S/he invites you to ask, *"What wants and needs to happen next?"* With this question, s/he is stimulating you to act decisively on the basis of what you have learned in each of the previous steps.

However, when the Parent Who Leads asks, *"What wants and needs to happen next?"* s/he is also asking a larger and more general question. S/he is prompting you to discover what needs to happen in your life as a whole so that you can continue to grow and learn. S/he is asking, "What needs to happen so that you will be in a position to acquire new and better life skills? What needs to happen to provoke your Suffering Child and your Critical Detractor Child into appearing again, so that you can resolve the remaining feelings and life issues which they carry

125

and become even more integrated and focused? How can you place yourself in situations that will help you to resolve past hurts that are getting in the way of your being fully engaged in creative action, every day, in every arena of your life?"

In a sense the Parent Who Leads is a benevolent trouble-maker. S/he wants you to place yourself in situations that will shake things up and evoke your Maturing Aspects. It is within these situations that you discover your areas of woundedness and can start to heal them. The Parent Who Leads knows that in order for you to grow, in order for you to heal the wounds you carry via your Suffering Child and your Critical Detractor Child, you must go in search of them. You must draw them out by placing yourself in the circumstances that will elicit them. Once these two aspects emerge, then they will get the attention they need. The feelings and beliefs they carry will be dealt with and will no longer rule your behavior. You will become an adult acting out of an adult's point of view. You will move through personal recovery and into creative action.

The Parent Who Leads also encourages you to participate in situations that will challenge any limited view you may hold of yourself. S/he helps you uncover and develop your strengths, reminding you to call upon them when faced with a difficult situation. And s/he helps you discover how resilient you are when things do not go as you wished they would.

After you have taken some action, you can ask yourself the questions that will help you to evaluate the effects of your actions. Here are some questions you might ask after the fact in relation to the hypothetical situation we created above. Has the action I took altered my thoughts, feelings, and sensations? How does it seem to have affected my spouse/lover/friend/colleague? Does he or she seem calmer or more agitated, more open to talking or more reluctant, more tender toward me or more hostile? How have my actions affected the general tone of the situation? Does it seem to be moving toward resolution or has the emotional charge increased? Is this a conflict that looks as though it can be settled rather quickly, or will it take further discussion and a more patient approach to be fully resolved? How will the actions I have taken in this situation influence the course of my life or the life of my spouse/lover/ friend/colleague? With all of these questions, you are asking *"What have I learned from this situation?"*

The specific questions you ask after the fact will be different, of course, in each situation. But they are always in pursuit of revealing and consolidating the insights you have had about the situation and your part in it. How has it changed me? What do I know now about myself and life that I did not know before? How will I use this new knowledge in my day-to-day life? What might get in the way of my using what I have learned?

In all that s/he does, the Parent Who Leads is trying to help you develop your Intuitive Self and find your intuitive voice. This self is the bridge between your physical life and your spiritual life. It is through your intuitive voice that God/All That Is speaks directly to you, revealing the hidden meaning to be found within specific moments in your life. Your Intuitive Self notices and interprets the metaphors and coincidences that present themselves to you each day. The Parent Who Leads urges you to act on the insights you have when you come in touch with your Intuitive Self. The Parent Who Leads encourages you to refine your ability to hear that voice and to use it. S/he helps you integrate the Intuitive Self into who you are.

The Nurturing Parents bring a systematic approach to your experience of situations that evoke your Maturing Aspects. They help you to identify which Maturing Aspects are present. They monitor the extent to which you become caught up in the influence of those aspects. They also stand ready to intervene if you become confused or overwhelmed by the feelings, thoughts, and impulses you experience when your maturing aspects come out.

Naturally your Nurturing Parents' perspective is quite different from the perspectives of the three Maturing Aspects. Whereas each of the Maturing Aspects is totally devoted to her perception of what is occurring in a situation and inclines you to act from that limited perspective, the Nurturing Parents have a comprehensive, panoramic

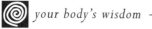

view of what is happening. Like shepherds tending their flock, they are constantly scanning the entire landscape that surrounds a situation so they can locate and track all three of the Maturing Aspects and help you sort out the thoughts, feelings, sensations, and impulses you are having as a result of their influence.

The Heart/felt Interface

A meditation I call the Heart/felt Interface is a wonderful tool for discovering what happens when you integrate the Nurturing Parents into your sense of self. This technique is one of the most powerful processes I know to transform your Suffering Child's feelings of fearfulness, unworthiness, hopelessness, and helplessness—feelings that prevent you from experiencing the joy that life can give. It also transforms the hurtful messages of your Critical Detractor Child into loving and supportive ones. Each of us has our own personal litany of hateful messages that we repeat over and over again in our minds. Hearing them, and discovering the heart/felt messages that negate them is the process by which you heal both your Suffering Child and your Critical Detractor Child.

For various reasons and to various degrees, each of us has learned to ignore the presence of our Emerald Child. The Heart/felt Interface helps you recognize your Emerald Child's feelings and desires. It encourages you to take into account the needs of your Emerald Child when making decisions. Recognizing and valuing your Emerald Child, enables you to reintegrate his playful and life-affirming attitudes into your sense of Self.

The story of a young woman who I will call Fran illustrates how this technique works. Fran was in her early thirties when she came to see me. She had just ended one of several relationships, all of which had followed a similar pattern. The men she was drawn to were loving, affectionate, and sexual. Each relationship began with promise. She felt emotionally safe, intellectually stimulated, and sexually aroused. But as soon as the relationship deepened and became more sexual, she would lose her sexual energy, and the energy that attracted her to these men would begin to wane. Eventually the relationship would end. She became despairing that she would ever be able to maintain a life-long partnership.

We began each session by relaxing, and coming into the Interval. Over time we developed the presence of the Nurturing Parents. After several months of inviting the Nurturing Parents to participate in her life, she began to feel more secure. Her sense of safety told her it was time to examine the issue that originally triggered her visit to me.

On this particular day, she imagined that her Parent Who Listens was sitting with her. First, she pictured the way s/he looks. Then, she moved her attention into the physical area of her heart. Knowing that her heart is the repository of her gentleness and kindness, it was important for her to come in touch with it. She took several long, slow, deep breaths. At the end of each inhalation and exhalation, she held her breath for a count of ten. Holding the breath while paying attention to the heart helped her hear and feel her heart beating. She continued this breathing and holding technique until her heart felt open and was totally within her awareness. Next she reviewed the qualities she had imbued in her listening parent. As she experienced the sensations each quality generated in her, a feeling of warmth and tenderness began emanating from her. Then quietly she began to say to herself, "I love you, Fran," until she began to experience a sense of joy.

Once that was accomplished, Fran then invited her leading parent to approach, and pictured the way s/he looks. Using the same breathing and holding technique, she asked her body to reveal the location of her power center, the place within her that cradled her feelings of self-determination. Slowly her attention was drawn to the area immediately above her pubic bone. At first it felt hollow, as though the whole lower part of her body didn't exist. She began sending long, slow, deep breaths into her pelvis. With each breath, she felt as though her pubic area were filling in, coming alive. This awakening did not arouse her sexually, instead it made her feel grounded, stronger, and more self-assured. Fran then reviewed the qualities of the Parent Who Leads. In the silence at the end of each breath, she experienced the sensations each quality generated throughout her body. Slowly she began repeating the phrase, "I trust you, Fran," repeating it until a feeling of confidence awoke in her. As the qualities of Fran's Nurturing Parents came alive in her, so did her compassion and her sense of personal power.

Once this was accomplished, she began to scan her body. Her attention was immediately drawn to her face. It felt hot with shame. She noticed her breathing had become shallow. She felt as though a hand were over her mouth. Her throat felt constricted, her windpipe narrow, and there was an egg-shaped object stuck between her throat and her chest, preventing her from speaking. Her stomach felt tight, and her thighs were tense and pulled together. Her genitals and anus were constricted and she had a feeling in her chest and belly that made her want to curl up into a small ball and hug herself.

Acting as the Parent Who Listens, I helped Fran hold her focus on these physical phenomena, moving back and forth between them. Suddenly, in her mind, she heard her mother saying, "A woman's body is ugly, especially her genitals. You shouldn't let anyone see your vagina. Good girls don't like sex. They certainly don't talk about it. You're a slut if you want sex. You only have sex when you want to get pregnant." As she listened to these phrases, her physical symptoms became stronger. Continuing to act as the listening parent, I reminded her that she was safe, and encouraged her to remain present to all her sensations.

As soon as Fran heard everything her mother had to say, she put an end to the diatribe. Breathing deeply into her heart, she visualized a vibrant light emanating from it. Slowly she began to feel the warmth of that light. She encouraged the light and the warmth to grow until they enveloped the shameful words and feelings. She held her focus on the sensations related to her feelings, continuing to permeate them with light and warmth until they began to ease and dissipate. Then, she asked her heart what it wanted to say, and waited silently and patiently, listening for its answer.

Invariably, once the heart is brought into this method of self-observation the loving feelings and words that exactly interface the nasty words and feelings present themselves. From her heart rose these interfacing phrases: "It is wonderful to kiss and have sex with another human being. It is a gift from the Universe. It is your gateway to love. It is exciting and pleasurable and God wouldn't have made it so much fun and so compelling if S/he didn't want you to do it. Sex is natural, and if it were simply for the purpose of procreation you would only want to do it when you were fertile. Your vagina is beautiful, and it's natural for a man to want to know all about it."

Fran repeated these new phrases for several minutes to implant them in her consciousness. Moving into her body, she then experienced the feelings and sensations these new messages created. She gave herself time to enjoy each new experience. She then repeated the old phrases and watched the effects they had on her body. She moved back and forth between these two sets of feelings—shame/guilt and excitement/delight—building tension between them. After doing this for some time, she had a flash of insight. She realized that for the past fifteen minutes *she* had been orchestrating the various feelings she was experiencing. She discovered that she was capable of generating whichever feelings she focused on. And it was exquisitely clear that her body responded with the appropriate sensations and body language.

Having discovered this most amazing fact, she then brought her focus back into her pubic area. As soon as she felt grounded she invited the old messages to present themselves one at a time. As each one had its say, she asked her power center what it would like to say. From deep within her came these words: "I'm not a bad person for wanting to have sex. All of my body is beautiful especially my vagina. Sex is natural, I'm supposed to like it. I want to have a loving, sexual relationship, and I'm going to actively pursue one."

These phrases, supported by the presence of her Nurturing Parents, grew directly out of Fran's examination of her old beliefs and feelings. They became her affirmations of freedom and joyfulness. Each time the old phrases or feelings presented themselves, she would interface them with these new ones, and allow her body to experience the sensations and feelings associated with the new affirmations. Affirmations supporting the fullness of life that rise directly out of feelings that diminish life are extremely powerful.

Next, I asked her if there was anything she wanted to say to her mother, the critical detractor who had planted these negative messages in her. First she began to sob, then her anger rose. She raised her fists, and beat the pillows in front of her while screaming: "I hate you for doing this to me. I'll never let you do it to me again. Just because you never enjoyed sex doesn't mean that I can't. I love sex and if you think I'm a bad person then we don't have to see each other any more."

After releasing her pent-up rage at her mother, Fran went back and scanned her body again. She noticed that her face was no longer hot with shame. Her breathing had become fuller and deeper. The egg-shaped object in her throat had diminished considerably. The tension she had felt in her stomach, thighs, genitals, and anus had relaxed. She no longer felt like curling up into a small ball. In fact, she felt more like stretching, singing, and moving.

When Fran started screaming at her mother and released her pent-up rage, the restrictions she had placed upon herself in order to stay loyal to her mother disappeared. No longer afraid to express her own feelings and ideas about sexuality, Fran was now ready to take responsibility for her own sexual life. Her willingness to break with her mother was crucial to her healing process.

Eventually, Fran became so cognizant of the negative words and sensations related to this issue that she was able to address them before they had an opportunity to trigger her old feelings of shame and anger. Each time she interfaced the old litany with her new affirmations, they lost their power over her. Over time they moved into the realm of memory, no longer able to affect her behavior.

As Fran's sexual relationships improved, she was surprised to discover that she had received a totally unexpected gift. When her negative feelings about sex disappeared, so did the hatred she felt toward her mother. She stopped blaming her mother for the sexual attitudes she had passed on to her, and could now accept the fact that her mother had done the best she could. It was not her mother's intention to hurt her. Malice was not her mother's motivation; her behavior was a reflection of her own ignorance and shame. Not only was Fran able to forgive her mother, she began to feel compassion for all the years of joy her mother had missed. She hoped her own recovery might be of some help in releasing her mother from the shame she felt. Returning home as a responsible adult, Fran was able to begin a new relationship with her mother.

Fran's recovery took several years. Her commitment to healing herself through self-love was her greatest ally. She spent many hours suffering the wounds inflicted by her Critical Detractor Child. She persevered in establishing a lasting relationship with her Nurturing Parents. This relationship eventually became the foundation for a new way of being with herself. She used the Heart/felt Interface many thousands of times. Each time she heard the first notes of any self-deprecatory and shaming phrases, she quickly replaced them with supportive and joyful ones. By using the Heart/felt Interface, Fran found an antidote to her sexual shame, and a tool to heal the woundedness of her Suffering Child, and Critical Detractor Child.

In Chapter Seven, **Life Issues and the Persistence of Fearfulness, Unworthiness, Helplessness, and Hopelessness,** you will learn how certain feelings create your life issues. These feelings are carried by your Suffering Child and promoted by your Critical Detractor Child. Using your parenting skills, and the Heart/felt Interface, you can give these two Maturing Aspects the attention they need and transform the feelings they are carrying. Then you not only experience personal recovery but you also become free to contribute to the Universe that which is uniquely yours to give.

LIFE ISSUES AND THE PERSISTENCE OF FEARFULNESS, UNWORTHINESS, HELPLESSNESS, AND HOPELESSNESS

Breathe deeply and gently.

Let your body soften.

See yourself within the space that surrounds you.

Feel yourself within the space that surrounds you.

Who is doing the seeing? Who is doing the feeling?

Any pattern of behavior that hinders a person's vitality, creativity, and sense of worth and possibility is considered a life issue. The feelings and beliefs that motivate those behaviors are part of a life issue, too. Addiction, perfectionism, an exaggerated need for control, the avoidance of responsibility, and relationship problems such as co-dependency and fear of intimacy are some of the life issues I have explored with people over the years.

Of course there are many theories to explain such behaviors and many therapeutic approaches to changing them. In terms of the aspects of Self theory, life issues are created when you act out of the feelings and beliefs that are carried by your Suffering Child and your Critical Detractor Child. Let's take a look at the issues we referred to above in light of these two Maturing Aspects.

Addiction—to food, drugs, work, or sex—reinforces the feelings that are carried by your Suffering Child. By imposing a false euphoria and numbing your authentic feelings, addiction removes the motivation to examine what moves you to use or abuse a substance or an activity. The physical, financial, and social consequences of addiction promote fear and anxiety. The addicted person feels helpless and hopeless because she is indeed out of control. Not being able to control her behavior strengthens the feelings of low self-esteem that may have motivated her to become addicted in the first place. As self-esteem falls, this person's Critical Detractor Child gains an even stronger hold.

Perfectionism also reinforces the Suffering Child's feelings of fearfulness, unworthiness, helplessness, and hopelessness. These feelings rise anew each time you fail to meet the misguided goal of being perfect, a goal that is ultimately unattainable. Each time you fail to reach perfection, your Critical Detractor Child's negative beliefs and attitudes are reinforced. Perfectionism also creates problems by causing you to procrastinate and put off the pursuit of cherished dreams because you believe that you could never achieve the level of accomplishment you have set for yourself.

Closely related to perfectionism is an exaggerated need for control. This life issue represents your attempt to deal with your Suffering Child's reservoir of fearfulness and silence your Critical Detractor's prophecies of doom. When you carry this life issue, you find it very hard to relax and enjoy life's simple pleasures. Your relationships are stunted by the messages you constantly send out to others saying that you do not need anything from anyone. As you become more convinced of these messages, you close yourself off from the gifts you could receive from other people and from the universe.

The flip side of trying to control everything is the avoidance of responsibility. The operative belief within this life issue is that you are incompetent and will certainly fail if you try to pursue a goal. The Suffering Child carries this belief, and the Critical Detractor Child reinforces it. If you carry this life issue, you constantly step aside when asked to take on some responsibility or leadership. In doing so, you manage your performance anxiety, but also remove yourself from the circumstances that would allow you to experience your vitality and creativity, your sense of worth and possibility. Without opportunities to witness and delight in your skills, you become even more convinced that you are incompetent.

Intimate relationships are sure to evoke your Suffering Child, your Critical Detractor Child, and the feelings and beliefs that are carried by each of these aspects. At the heart of the life issue known as fear of intimacy is your fear of rejection. You avoid intimate relationships to protect yourself from someone discovering parts of yourself that you consider bad. You believe that if someone gets to know the real you, they will no longer love you and they will leave you. But of course in the process of protecting yourself from someone else's disapproval, you give up the chance to learn about loving, being loved, and coming to know yourself through another person.

The life issue known as co-dependency revolves around an inability to interact with your Suffering Child and your Critical Detractor Child in healing ways. In a co-dependent relationship, partners unknowingly use each other to maintain patterns of behavior that are maladaptive. The healthy alternative is for each partner to love each other into recognizing their Suffering Child and their Critical Detractor Child, and work together to find ways to give those two aspects the attention they need.

All life issues are proof that you are still strongly under the influence of your Suffering Child and your Critical Detractor Child. Indeed, their influence is so strong that they essentially are making your decisions for you. You are the one who is acting, of course, but your actions are based on the feelings and beliefs that are carried by this dysfunctional pair—intense feelings of fearfulness, unworthiness, helplessness, and hopelessness plus distorted, self-defeating beliefs that arise from such feelings. When you act out of these feelings and beliefs, you create and maintain your life issues.

Obviously life issues cause conflict and unhappiness, but they also contain a gift. That gift is the opportunity to discover—indeed to bring into being—your integrating, emerging, adult Self. This Self becomes more established and more recognizable to you each time you attend to the two aspects of Self at the center of a life issue. When you give your Suffering Child and your Critical Detractor Child what they need, these two have an opportunity to grow and so do you.

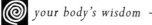

When you listen to your Suffering Child's cry for help, the feelings and beliefs that she carries are transformed. When you silence the negative messages put forth by your Critical Detractor Child, and reparent that aspect in a tender way, the feelings and beliefs that aspect is carrying are also transformed. This transformation then extends to your behavior and your sense of identity. You stop acting out of intense, unresolved feelings and distorted beliefs because those feelings and beliefs have changed. You step out of the personae of your Suffering Child and your Critical Detractor Child because those two aspects have changed. You emerge into your adulthood.

Your emerging adult Self derives the greatest part of her identity from the Nurturing Parents and your Intuitive Self. Your emerging adult Self observes all three Maturing Aspects and interacts with each one without getting caught up in the aspects' feelings, thoughts, and impulses to act. This Self sifts through and then organizes what she observes. She seeks the silent space within herself where she hears the guiding voice of her Intuitive Self offering up the wisdom that resides in her. This Self acts; she does not react on the basis of the feelings, thoughts, or inclinations presented by one of her Maturing Aspects, no matter how intense those phenomena may be. This Self initiates and executes creative action—action that is considered, intentional, and directed by her Intuitive Self. In that moment of choice, your integrated adult Self emerges, reveals herself to you, and becomes more established within you. The energy that moves through you and emanates from you is a reflection of her presence. Your sense of who you are becomes clearer and stronger. You observe your Self emerging—open, compassionate, focused, confident, and purposeful.

ALL LIFE ISSUES STEM FROM ABANDONMENT

Every life issue we can name ultimately stems from some form of abandonment. Indeed, at the core of each life issue is the experience of having somehow been cut off from the protection, understanding, loving attention, and guidance which all children need. The Suffering Child aspect, who becomes established as a result of abandonment experiences, carries feelings of fearfulness, unworthiness, helplessness, and hopelessness. Along with those feelings, she also carries a set of beliefs about herself and the world. Because she was not cherished and celebrated, she believes that she is alone, unlovable, and inept. She believes that the world is a dangerous place, full of people who are uncaring and who cannot be trusted. When you act out of these feelings and beliefs, you create and sustain your life issues.

The experience of abandonment takes many different forms. Some are obvious, others less so. At the far end of a continuum of scenarios is the child who is literally left to fend for herself. One of the most striking examples of this form of abandonment was publicized recently when police in Chicago found a group of ten young children living in an empty apartment building. They had only the clothes on their backs. The floor of their apartment was strewn with the remnants of garbage which they brought home each day after searching nearby streets for food. Through their investigations, police discovered that a group of parents and other relatives had worked together to coordinate the abandonment of these children. These adults gathered up the children, placed them in the apartment, and left them alone, without supervision or protection, for long periods of time.

In our culture we also experience a form of physical abandonment that does not occur in other parts of the world. Here babies are taken away from their mothers, sometimes moments after birth, and placed in a nursery, all for the convenience of the hospital staff who care for newborns. This arrangement deprives a newborn of the warmth and protection of her mother's body and cuts her off from the familiar, comforting sounds that come from her mother's body. At home, we are usually placed in a crib. We sleep alone and when we are not asleep, we may only come in contact with our mother when we are being fed, changed, or bathed. This separation can create a sense of isolation and abandonment, too.

If parents do not hold their child or find other ways to express their affection physically, that child is cut off from her care givers in a very significant way. When a child is placed in the care of people (baby sitters, teachers, or other guardians) who cannot meet her needs for affection, protection, understanding, and gentle care, she is abandoned.

A child deprived of the physical necessities of life—such as food, shelter, clothing, or medical care—is also abandoned. It is important to add that parents who cannot afford to provide these basic needs are not necessarily guilty of neglect. They should be distinguished from parents or other adult care givers who have the financial means to provide such things but choose to withhold them. The child who does not have access to adequate food, shelter, and clothing because her parents could not afford to provide them will still feel abandoned. But working through the feelings associated with her deprivation will take on a different tone if she knows that these basic necessities were not withheld from her; rather they were not available.

A child is abandoned when too many demands are placed on her or when she is not sufficiently challenged. In the case of the former, she finds herself in situations that demand the performance of skills or a level of skill which she has not yet acquired. This child is left to her own designs at a time when her designs are sure to fall short of what her situation requires. As an adult, her feelings of having been abandoned are replaced with a deep sense of inadequacy.

At the other end of the spectrum, failing to provide a child with opportunities to engage in activities that will help her to acquire and practice skills that are age-appropriate is also a form of abandonment. Asking either too much or too little of a child will prevent her from becoming "response-able," the former by overwhelming her and the latter by failing to provide adequate stimulation. Both extremes make the child who is exposed to these circumstances feel as though she has been cut off and set adrift. She will most certainly feel abandoned by her care givers.

Another very painful and damaging experience of abandonment occurs when parents are unable to feel, or express delight and appreciation for who their children are. When children feel they are not cherished, and valued by their parents, they experience a deep feeling of loss, and their own sense of self-worth is severely damaged. When parents do not encourage the budding athlete, artist, musician, dancer, or writer in a child, then that child is deprived of an important source of recognition and validation. She may give up some of her most cherished dreams for lack of her parents' support.

When parents are unable or unwilling to understand the nature of a child's needs and recognize those needs as they arise, that child is effectively abandoned. This inability to relate to the life of a child is very damaging and can be expressed in a variety of ways, in many different arenas. Perhaps parents do not recognize that their child is floundering in school, and they fail to give her the help that she needs with her school work. Maybe they fail to perceive that the child is having difficulty fitting in and making friends, that she needs emotional support and guidance in social situations. Or possibly parents do not recognize the importance of teaching their children how to protect themselves emotionally or physically, or how to recover from such abuse. While working with a young woman struggling with feelings of hopelessness, she came in touch with her Suffering Child who was crying, "I'm here! Doesn't anyone see me? Doesn't anyone hear me? Can't anyone help me?" When children suffer and their suffering goes unnoticed and is not addressed, they come to the conclusion that they are alone in the world.

By providing support and guidance as a child tries to master specific developmental challenges, parents convey that she is important to them, that they cherish her, and that they want to be actively involved in her life. Every effort that a parent makes to communicate these messages confirms a child's sense of worth and loveability. In the presence of such validation, a child feels that she belongs and that she is surrounded by caring people. She does not feel abandoned. Conversely, when these demonstrations of interest and concern are missing, a child may easily conclude that she is of no importance to her parents and therefore of no value to anyone else. Each time she comes to such a conclusion, her sense of deprivation and abandonment is strengthened.

When parents withhold emotional support at important junctures in a child's growth and development, that child is effectively abandoned. For example, if her parents were not comfortable with the topic of sexuality, they probably had difficulty helping her to cope with the physical and emotional changes associated with puberty. Their anxiety and her resulting lack of information could easily cause this child to feel afraid, ashamed, or helpless in the face of newfound and intense sexual energy. In this way a rite of passage that deserves to be celebrated can become yet another experience of abandonment.

If a child is born with or later acquires a physical or mental illness or disability and her parents distance themselves from her because of their discomfort, then once again the child is left to cope on her own. Most children will interpret such behavior as a form of abandonment. Acting out of their own insecurity or embarrassment, parents may even ridicule a child in regard to these conditions. This only adds to the already considerable emotional demands faced by a young person who is trying to adjust to being different from her peers by virtue of an illness or a disability.

Children who have experienced divorce, the death of a parent, or desertion by a parent, often carry a long-term sense of abandonment. In all three cases a child often fears that she will lose her remaining parent and be alone in the world, with no one to love her or care for her. Children who are survivors of death, desertion, or divorce sometimes believe that they caused the absent parent to leave or even to die. In her innocent way, such a child "reasons" that if she were really loveable, her now-missing parent would never have left.

Perhaps the most pervasive form of abandonment is a kind of benign neglect that is acted out by parents whose own Suffering Child and Critical Detractor Child are still strong within them. These parents are essentially loving, and their intentions toward their children are good. They are doing the best that they can, but their best is limited by the persistent feelings and beliefs of their Suffering Child and Critical Detractor Child aspects. Under the weight of those beliefs and feelings, these parents cannot provide the guidance and direction which their children require. These children are left to discover for themselves (or not) the skills they need to develop into secure, creative, and happy adults.

Chronic abuse is probably the most damaging form of abandonment, and the most difficult to overcome. Having been abused themselves, many parents learned to be abusers and are unable to control their own abusive natures. They perpetuate the abuse—physical, psychological, sexual—by continually abusing their children physically, psychologically, and sexually. The emotional atmosphere abusive parents create around their children through their language and actions destroys their will and fills them with despair and self-loathing. Each time a child is abused in any way, she is abandoned.

As children we see our parents as god-like figures. They have all the power, all the resources. Our very lives depend upon them. If they abuse us or seem to not care about us, we may conclude that even God has deserted us. For some people I have worked with, this sense of having been abandoned by God is their most powerful experience of abandonment. Many people who have suffered extreme poverty, illness, prejudice, or natural disasters may also carry intense feelings of having been abandoned by God. Fortunately adults can return to these experiences in a therapeutic context and heal the wounds associated with them. They are able to release their sense of abandonment and restore their sense of connection to the Source.

It is easy to see then how experiences of abandonment can create feelings of fearfulness, unworthiness, hopelessness, and helplessness within a person. In the next section we will explore the way in which these four feeling states can influence the Suffering Child and Critical Detractor Child aspects of Self, and thus affect a person's thinking and behavior. We begin with fearfulness.

FEARFULNESS

For the Suffering Child and Critical Detractor Child who embody fearfulness, life is a constant battle to manage the dread and apprehension that so many situations can evoke in them. Their fear is the filter through which they view every situation. They are frightened by change or the prospect of it. Making decisions, making requests, stating opinions, taking a stand—all of these arouse their fear. Being asked to reveal themselves in any way makes them feel exposed and vulnerable. People scare them most of all. They do not trust them or their motives. They cannot imagine that anyone could have a sincere desire to know or help them. They expect to be hurt if they let people in, yet they crave the closeness that people can provide.

At the underfunctioning end of the behavioral spectrum, these aspects of Self urge you to remain in relationships, living situations, jobs, or other circumstances for the sake of familiarity, even if they are not satisfying. They discourage you from taking risks, even when you have carefully weighed the pros and cons of a plan to act. Better safe than sorry, they warn you. Under their influence, you will want to isolate yourself from others in order to protect yourself. You will be inclined to run away when someone reaches out to you.

At the overfunctioning end of the spectrum, they can move you to become aggressive, overbearing, and belligerent. You may find yourself taking over in conflict situations, or in projects that are meant to be cooperative, in an effort to hide your fearfulness from yourself and others. If your fearful Suffering Child and Critical Detractor Child aspects of Self feel threatened—emotionally or physically—you may react by becoming hostile or abusive.

UNWORTHINESS

The Suffering Child and Critical Detractor Child who embody unworthiness are filled with shame, guilt, and self-loathing. Their shame is pervasive and goes to the heart of these tender aspects. They see themselves as fundamentally flawed and unloveable. They may even believe that they do not deserve to live. They cannot imagine that your thoughts, your feelings, or your desires are of any interest to anyone. They do not believe that you deserve to be treated with warmth and tenderness, nor do they feel that you deserve to experience happiness, love, or success. Those things are for others.

The guilt that these aspects of Self carry begins to form when a child assumes responsibility for the unhappiness within her family. This guilt grows as that child observes that the members of her family continue to be unhappy despite her best efforts to solve all their problems. She believes that she can and should improve the quality of their lives and she struggles with her belief that they would be happy if only she could figure out what to do differently. Her guilt grows, of course, if her parents actively blame her for the problems they encounter in their lives.

At the underfunctioning end of the behavioral spectrum, the Suffering Child and Critical Detractor Child who embody unworthiness urge you to keep a low profile in order to avoid drawing attention to yourself. Under their influence, you hold back from activities that could bring positive energy into your life. You shy away from relationships that are loving or seek out those that lack warmth or that are blatantly abusive. You become withdrawn and are reluctant to communicate your thoughts, opinions, or desires. You have difficulty taking pleasure in your achievements or discussing them with other people. To others you may seem aloof and superior, but what is really operating behind that facade is an overwhelming insecurity.

At the overfunctioning end, these aspects can move you to seek out high profile positions in the hope of finally obtaining the validation you crave. You behave in ways that make you the center of attention, all in an attempt to defend against feeling unimportant. You frequently exhaust yourself doing for others, in the hope that if you work hard enough, you will be rewarded with the love and attention you so desperately desire. You may be addicted to perfectionism. If so, you experience an uncomfortable mixture of anxiety and shame each time you fail to live up to your own expectations or those of others. To be less than perfect is dangerous, since the slightest mistake can quickly destroy whatever tenuous hold you have on your sense of competence and self-worth. After all, no one could possibly love or respect you if you made a mistake or revealed that you do not know everything.

HELPLESSNESS

The Suffering Child and Critical Detractor Child who embody helplessness have little or no sense of their competence. They see themselves as defenseless victims who cannot direct their own life (with any measure of success) and therefore need others to do that for them.

Helplessness takes hold in children who experience either neglect or overprotection. In the case of neglect, there is no one there to appreciate a child's strengths and skills. She is playing to an empty house, so she gets no feedback about her competence and no special attention in areas where her skills are lagging. In the case of overprotection, there are no (or too few) opportunities for a child to meet and master life's challenges. This child never gets to test herself because her parents insist on doing everything for her. This means that she never gets to experience the thrill of mastery or the confidence that goes along with it. Understandably, this child concludes that she is incapable of fending for herself.

Perhaps more closely related to neglect is a certain form of invalidation that will cause a child to feel helpless. If parents notice a child's accomplishments but judge them by the same standards they use to measure their own, that child will surely feel that she always falls short of the mark. In a similar zone of invalidating our achievements, parents may criticize a child when she does not perform perfectly.

At the underfunctioning end of the behavioral spectrum, these aspects of Self will influence you to give up and become passive whenever you are in the company of people who seem to be self-assured. If you are faced with choices or the need to take some action, these children will encourage you to look for someone who will make those choices for you or act on your behalf. You may give yourself over completely to that person, relinquishing all of your decisions to him or her.

At the overfunctioning end of the behavioral spectrum, you may actively, often obsessively, manipulate others to do for you what you are certain you cannot do for yourself. In those situations you may end up resenting these caretakers for their attempts to give you what you wanted, despite both your having chosen them and their putting forth their best efforts to please you. You may find yourself accusing them of being domineering and keeping you from achieving your potential. Or you may become angry and feel betrayed if they fail to care for you in exactly the way you wish them to—a sort of pass-it-along perfectionism.

HOPELESSNESS

The operative belief for the Suffering Child and Critical Detractor Child who embody hopelessness is that no matter how hard they try, they will never be able to achieve their dreams. The only reward for trying will be crushing disappointment. The underlying feelings which these forlorn aspects carry are despair, discouragement, powerlessness, and defeat.

Hopelessness can take hold in a child in several ways. Infants who are left alone crying in their cribs for long periods of time, who are not fed when they are hungry or changed when they are soiled, get the message that they cannot get what they need. Older children and adolescents who make their needs known but are met with parental indifference will also conclude that it is useless to articulate their needs. Understandably, these children come to believe that they have no power to affect their own lives.

For some children, hopelessness sets in because of a pattern of promises made but never kept. If a parent holds out promises of love, attention, support, or pleasure but does not follow through, a child will understandably conclude that expecting the good things in life is an exercise in futility. In the course of exploring his feelings of hopelessness, one young man I worked with recounted, "My father was always promising that he would teach me to play ball, take me to a baseball game, explain some homework to me, or buy me something that I wanted. But when it came down to it, he would get mad at me for something, and then use that as an excuse to bail out." Through his behavior, this father established and nurtured the hopeless Suffering Child and Critical Detractor Child within his own son.

When you fall under the influence of this Suffering Child and Critical Detractor Child, their dark point of view becomes your own, and your behavior reflects that view. At the underfunctioning end of the behavioral spectrum, you withdraw from verbalizing and pursuing your desires. With no expectation of getting what you want, you hold yourself back from articulating your goals and dreams. You are reluctant to invest your time, money, love, or other energies in working toward cherished goals. You tend to expect the worst in every situation. Convinced that things cannot change for the better, you are not motivated to try to shape the outcome of a situation. You give up.

At the overfunctioning end you do just the opposite, insisting that anything and everything is possible, setting goals that are grandiose and frequently unrealistic. Pursuing your goals, you work obsessively, without stopping to reevaluate the wisdom of your behavior. In this way you set yourself up for the kind of disappointment that confirms these aspects' central belief, that only fools and masochists try to pursue their dreams. It is better to protect yourself by relinquishing them altogether.

The four feelings of fearfulness, unworthiness, helplessness, and hopelessness can combine in many different ways within a situation or over the course of a longer period of time in your life. Noticing these feelings is the first step in exploring them. Experiencing and describing the sensations that accompany these feelings tells you even more. Distinguishing the differences between the sensations that rise and move through your body when you feel fearful, unworthy, helpless, or hopeless is also extremely valuable. It is also helpful to recognize the various thoughts that run through your mind when you come in touch with these four feeling states. Knowing who is activating your feelings and coloring your thoughts makes it possible for you to dialogue with the Suffering Child or the Critical Detractor Child.

It can also be helpful to ask yourself, "What is my earliest memory of feeling fearful/unworthy/helpless/hopeless? What were the circumstances surrounding that experience?" The answers to these questions can help you to identify events from your past that may have established chronic feelings of fearfulness, unworthiness, helplessness, or hopelessness.

The more you explore the roots of these four feeling states and weed out those roots, the less power they will have over the decisions and choices you make. As the Maturing Aspects who carry these feelings get the attention they need, you will no longer feel drawn to act out the feelings they carry. You will notice the feelings they bring to an experience, but those feelings will no longer be at the center of your experience. Instead they will become one of a number of features that you observe and respond to within a situation.

MISTRUST OF BENEFICIAL CIRCUMSTANCES

In addition to producing the four feeling states we have just examined, abandonment experiences also can lead to the phenomenon known as "mistrust of beneficial circumstances." The person who carries this form of mistrust becomes very uncomfortable in the presence of good fortune. Her Suffering Child tells her, "This abundance/pleasure/ happiness is not real. It cannot be real. You cannot trust this situation. Get away as quickly as you can, or else." Her Critical Detractor Child warns her, "This abundance/pleasure/ happiness might be real for someone else, but not for you. You do not deserve this positive experience. You'd better get away before someone catches you in the wrong place at the wrong time."

Feelings of unworthiness foster the belief that we do not deserve to be surrounded by positive conditions, that we have no right to expect them. Feelings of helplessness convince us that there is nothing we can do to ensure that we will have a happy, successful life. And the sense of hopelessness that many survivors of abandonment embody strengthens the belief that their lives can never really change for the better.

How is it that a person could be uncomfortable when things are going well, and why is this phenomenon so common? There are several theories to account for the way in which beneficial circumstances, or "good times," can become a stimulus for mistrust. The first theory is derived from the way in which we come into the world. After floating in the warm, protected environment of the womb for the first nine to ten months of life, we experience a sudden and drastic change in our circumstances when we are born. Viewed from this perspective, birth can be seen as our first and perhaps most profound experience of bliss followed by loss. At birth the comfortable, protected world that we once knew is gone; we find ourselves separated from all that was familiar and secure.

Obviously we cannot know in a definitive way if some newborns come into the world believing that bliss will always be followed by pain and loss. They do not possess the cognitive skills to perceive the birth experience in this way, nor do they have the language skills with which to describe their perceptions, whatever those may be. Still, I believe that as a result of the birth experience, all of us come into the world with a vague but persistent expectation that contentment will be followed by loss.

A more literal and behavioral approach to understanding mistrust of beneficial circumstances has to do with the realistic expectation of pain that is established in children who are chronically abused. Children who are physically, emotionally, or sexually abused learn that good times are inevitably followed by some form of pain. In between their abusive experiences, these children may enjoy periods of relative peace and contentment. However, that contentment can suddenly be replaced by chaos, confusion, and emotional and physical pain, often for no apparent reason.

There is no way for these children to know when the next episode of abuse will occur, so they become increasingly uncomfortable as the gap between the last abusive incident and the anticipated next one grows. Instead of feeling more at ease when things are going well, these children become more tense if things continue to go well. They may even long for a traumatic incident in order to relieve the anxiety that accompanies their expectation of further, but unscheduled, abuse. Of course this longing does not mean that they want to be beaten, belittled, or sexually violated. It only means that they long for an end to their fear of what will happen next and when. This is a particularly ugly version of "waiting for the other shoe to drop" syndrome.

A client of mine who had been frequently abused as a child, physically and verbally, found it very difficult as an adult to rejoice in times of good fortune. Whenever things were going well in her life, her Suffering Child would become anxious and hypervigilant. In response to that anxiety, this woman was always looking over her shoulder, literally and figuratively, in an effort to protect herself from the harm which she believed was just around the corner. One of the first steps toward resolving her mistrust of beneficial circumstances was to offer her Maturing Aspects the opportunity to tell their story. This allowed the woman to express her grief and rage and receive the comfort that had not been available to her as a child.

Another theory concerning the origin of mistrust of beneficial circumstances comes from Drs. Gay and Kathlyn Hendricks, authors of *Conscious Loving*. The Hendricks look at this phenomenon from a somewhat larger perspective, one that takes into account the evolution of our species. They write:

> "Human beings have been suffering and struggling for millions of years; we are highly skilled at handling negative energy. We believe that at this time in evolution our species is actually creating new channels in ourselves for experiencing positive energy. How to feel good naturally, without chemical assistance is a new task in evolution...."[7]

In the context of a single lifetime, it is also true that some of us are very skilled at dealing with negative energy. This is certainly true for adult survivors of childhood abuse or neglect. Those who do not pursue some process of recovery concerning these experiences may continue to feel more comfortable with negative energy (or "non-beneficial circumstances") simply because that energy and those circumstances are more familiar to them.

The person who is accustomed to negative energy may experience the physical sensations that accompany joy, warmth, tenderness, and other positive feelings as uncomfortable and unpleasant—even frightening. In an effort to stay within a comfortable, familiar range of physical sensation and emotional experience, this person may avoid or sabotage situations that could generate positive energy. By shunning beneficial circumstances, she feels better because she has stopped the flow of uncomfortable sensations, but she also cuts herself off from many positive experiences. She does not let herself experience the bounty which the Universe holds out to all of us. This is a very big price to pay for the restoration of familiar and more comfortable sensations.

Closely related to mistrust of beneficial circumstances is a phenomenon which Drs. Gay and Kathlyn Hendricks refer to as the "upper limits problem." This phenomenon works in the following way: you've just had a wonderful day; you feel great. You made an excellent presentation at work. Someone you've been wanting to get to know better just invited you to the theater. Your bathroom scale says you're three pounds lighter than last week.

"Suddenly your mind is full of worry thoughts, everything from the condition of the world to the condition of your carpets. Why right now, when you were feeling so good? The culprit is the 'upper limits problem.'

Due to our past conditioning, we all have a limit on how much positive energy we can tolerate. Go past this limit and an alarm goes off in your unconscious mind. If you do not rest at this point, allowing yourself time to integrate the energy, your unconscious mind will find a way to stop the flow of positive energy. Its strategies can be very primitive: arguments, illness, accidents. It is far better to become adept at noticing when your limit has been exceeded, so that you can consciously find a way to integrate the energy rather than leave the task to your unconscious. "[8]

One symptom that I have found to be universal in those who suffer from the "upper limits problem" is an inability to accept praise. Many people who carry chronic feelings of fearfulness and unworthiness report a strong physical discomfort whenever I praise them. I myself used to experience discomfort when people praised me. It took many years for me to overcome this uneasiness, and occasionally it still arises, especially in areas where I have not yet owned my success or where I fear that I will not be able to meet the expectations implied by a compliment.

Whenever you have difficulty hearing or accepting praise, this is a sure sign that your Suffering Child or Critical Detractor Child is present. These aspects feel unworthy of praise and become uneasy when it is bestowed on you. At such times you can help these aspects to articulate and release their feelings of unworthiness. You can do this by simply listening to them, patiently and lovingly. At the same time, you acknowledge what they believe and feel, while communicating complete confidence that they can let go of those thoughts and feelings and come in touch with how precious and deserving of all good things they truly are.

THE COMPONENTS OF A LIFE ISSUE

When you act out of some combination of the feeling states I have been describing, you create and maintain your life issues. Each life issue scenario has an emotional, physical, cognitive, and behavioral component. Let's take a look at each of these.

The emotional component of a life issue scenario consists of the feelings you are experiencing. These feelings are carried by your Suffering Child and strengthened by your Critical Detractor Child. They can range in intensity from mild to overwhelming.

When you are in the midst of a life issue scenario, you perceive your situation through the eyes of your Suffering Child and your

Critical Detractor Child. In a particular moment you will come in touch with the feelings that are carried by the aspect which you are identifying with most strongly. If you are identifying most strongly with your Suffering Child, you will feel some assortment of fearfulness, unworthiness, helplessness, and hopelessness. You may find yourself whining, cringing, or simply shutting down. If you are identifying most strongly with your Critical Detractor Child, you will feel harshly judgmental toward yourself or someone else present. You may find yourself hard, disdainful, or haughty. Often you will experience some combination of the feelings that are carried by these two aspects. This is because your Suffering Child rather quickly draws out your Critical Detractor Child, and vice versa. So you might feel helpless and harshly critical of someone else present, or fearful and disapproving of yourself.

The physical component of a life issue scenario is to be found within the sensations that accompany your feelings. When you relax and come into the Interval, you become very aware of the details of your physical experience. You notice the sensations that are part of your feeling experience—heat, cold, tightness, trembling, emptiness, heaviness, pulsing, tingling. These sensations and many others can be felt anywhere in your body as an accompaniment to your feelings, and they precede your emotional expression.

The cognitive component of a life issue scenario is revealed through your thoughts, your self-talk, and the ease or difficulty with which you can think clearly and creatively in the midst of such a situation. Predictably, the thoughts and self-talk that arise within a life issue scenario are closely linked to the predominating feeling. If your Suffering Child is feeling fearful, your thoughts will run toward, "Something awful is about to happen. I'm in danger." Your Critical Detractor Child will jump on the bandwagon and say, "You got too big for yourself again. You're in big trouble here." If your Suffering Child is feeling helpless, your thoughts will be a variation on the theme of, "I can't do this. I'm not strong enough, smart enough, etc." And your Critical Detractor Child will again confirm all of that.

If your Suffering Child is feeling hopeless, your thoughts and self-talk will tell you, "This situation is never going to get better. Why bother trying to deal with it?" Your Critical Detractor Child will agree that you do not have what it takes to deal with this situation effectively. If your Suffering Child is feeling unworthy, your thoughts will run toward, "I'm no good. Nobody loves me. I don't deserve...(fill in the blank)." That which you feel unworthy of could be anything that would bring you happiness or success—a job, a relationship, the chance to be playful, the pursuit of a cherished dream. Your Critical Detractor Child will try to convince you that if you pursue any of these dreams you will only end up with crushing disappointment.

At such times your thoughts and self-talk tend toward sweeping generalizations and are filled with "always/never/no one ever" kinds of statements. These statements reflect the grief and despair that are carried by the Suffering Child and the discouragement and defeatism put forth by your Critical Detractor Child. Some examples are:

- "It has always been this way for me."
- "How come this always happens to me?"
- "No matter how hard I try, nothing ever seems to change."
- "No matter how many people are around me, I always feel alone."
- "I give and give, but no one ever gives anything to me."
- "No matter how hard I work, it never seems to be good enough."
- "Everyone else seems to be able to find a loving partner, so how come I always attract someone who's angry?"

The difficulty of thinking clearly that most people experience in the midst of a life issue scenario is in part caused by the intense feelings they are having. Quite simply, it is very hard to concentrate when you are overwhelmed by your feelings. Under the influence of your

Suffering Child, you are filled with pain and discomfort due to your feelings of fearfulness, unworthiness, helplessness, and hopelessness. The intensity of those feelings and their negative effect on your thinking becomes even stronger when your Critical Detractor Child emerges.

This difficulty in concentrating and the confusion that often goes with it is also a function of the internal tug of war that takes place within a life issue scenario between your Suffering Child and your Critical Detractor Child at one end and your emerging adult Self at the other. The first two are pulling you in the direction of "intense feelings/uncomfortable memories/distorted thinking/denial/impulsiveness/reactivity," while your adult Self wants to take a breath, slow down, and attend to your Suffering Child and your Critical Detractor Child so you can really digest your feelings. Then you can settle into the Interval, communicate with your Intuitive Self, and learn how best to respond to your situation.

Your Suffering Child and your Critical Detractor Child tend to get caught up in the spiraling energy within a life issue scenario, while your adult Self steps back and looks at how to turn that scenario into a learning experience with a positive outcome. Your adult Self wants to find a way to process and defuse your intense feelings so you can act out of a more aware, less distressed space—one that takes feelings into account but is not ruled by them.

The behavioral component of a life issue scenario includes the decisions you make and the actions you take. Within such a scenario, your decision-making and your behavior are strongly influenced by the presence of your Suffering Child and your Critical Detractor Child. Whenever the thoughts and feelings they carry become the basis for your decision-making, your actions tend to be impulsive and unwise. On the other hand, when you act out of your adult Self, you take time to review your thoughts and feelings before you make a move. Then your actions are not impulsive and are much more likely to have a good outcome.

The behavior you exhibit while under the influence of your Suffering Child and Critical Detractor Child falls into one of two categories: passive and underfunctioning, or aggressive and overfunctioning. At the underfunctioning end of the behavioral spectrum, you opt to play it safe and participate in life as little as possible. You tend to be passive, to pull back, and to keep your wishes, needs, and opinions to yourself. You may even choose denial as your defense. If you are aware of your feelings, you will probably discount them and choose not to explore them further on your own or share them with others. If you can imagine a course of action that might influence the outcome of the situation in your favor, you probably will not act. You do all of these things in an attempt to protect yourself from experiencing even more intense feelings of fearfulness, unworthiness, helplessness, and hopelessness.

At the aggressive, overfunctioning end of the spectrum you tend to bully people or try to make decisions for them. You like being the center of attention and paint yourself as the expert. Your actions are saying, "Look at me! I can do anything (or at least do it better than you)!" When you operate at this end of the behavioral spectrum, you feel superior and in control. You convince yourself that you can meet and master any challenge. Those feelings are much more comfortable than fearfulness, unworthiness, helplessness, or hopelessness. In the overfunctioning realm of behavior, you also tend to take on too much responsibility and arrange your life so that you are constantly on the go. Staying busy is a rather effective way to distract yourself from uncomfortable thoughts and feelings, but it is not a healthy long-term strategy for coping with the thoughts and feelings stored by your Suffering Child and Critical Detractor Child.

In the next section we will try to bring to life the theory related to life issues. We look at one woman's experience with two rather common issues—perfectionism and the need to control. As you read through Annie's story, see if you can recognize the emotional, physical, cognitive, and behavioral components of these two issues. See if you can recognize the moments in the story when Annie comes under the influence of her Suffering Child, her Critical Detractor Child, or her Emerald Child. At what points do you think she is acting out of the personae of those aspects? By contrast, at what points do you think she is acting out of her emerging, adult Self?

ANNIE'S STORY

Annie is the adult child of an alcoholic. The oldest of five children, she grew up in an atmosphere that was filled with chaos and crisis because of her father's addiction and abusive behavior. When he drank, he was totally out of control. He was psychologically and physically abusive, and no one felt safe around him. At a very early age, Annie took on the role of protector in her family. She was constantly on her guard, watching out for her brothers and sisters and her mother, trying to keep them out of trouble with her father or extricate them from it. Annie also took on the role of counselor to her father. She spent many late evenings sitting in the kitchen talking with him, trying to convince him to give up drinking. But she was never successful, and for that she not only felt disappointed but also ineffectual. She believed that she should have been able to get him to stop. She remembered thinking to herself, "I love him. I'm smart. I'm determined. I want him to stop drinking more than anything in the world. So I should be able to get him to quit, right?"

These childhood experiences led to the formation of two life issues—perfectionism and control. The first evolved as a result of her efforts to please her father and thereby motivate him to stop drinking. "If I am very good at everything I do, then he will be proud of me and stop," she reasoned. At school, in sports, in everything she did, Annie set very high standards for herself and would become very upset if she did not live up to those expectations.

Annie's control issue grew out of her need for safety, a need which every child has, of course, but one that is thwarted on a regular basis for children who live with an addicted parent. The unpredictability, the lack of boundaries, and role confusion (Annie was parenting and her father was being irresponsibly child-like) that permeated Annie's house created tremendous stress for everyone. To compensate for all of that and provide herself with some sense of security, Annie focused on controlling every aspect of her environment that was not related to her father.

These two life issues followed Annie right on into her adulthood and played themselves out in her home life and at work. At home she expected two hundred percent of herself. The house had to be spotless at all times. She never took time out for herself, but made herself available to her husband and children whenever they needed her. She was Super Wife and Super Mom—and she was exhausted! At work she had the same high expectations of herself. She was a production manager at a publishing house, and her motto was "No mistakes allowed."

It was shortly after a bizarre experience at her office that Annie and I met and began to work together. Part of her job involved supervising the staff who read over a magazine's galley proofs to correct any errors before the final copy went on to the printer. The staff who performed this job had an excellent reputation. In the entire year that Annie had worked there, only one typo had gotten past these people. But for that entire year, Annie had put in many extra hours "proofing the proofers." Just before the magazine was to go to the printer, she would sneak into the office, at night or on a weekend, to read over everything that her staff had already reviewed. She did this in an effort to prevent the dreaded possibility that a typo would slip through and appear in the published magazine. She was terrified that such a thing might happen. If it did, it would only confirm what she had been desperately trying to hide all her life: that she was ineffective and worthless, just as her father had so often told her and just as she herself had come to believe. "If I were really smart," she had told herself so many times, "I would have figured out a way to make him stop drinking. We would have been happy back then and he would not have died so young."

One night when she sneaked into the office to perform her proofing ritual, a curious thing happened. Within moments of getting down to work she noticed a strange sensation in her right shoulder. A combination of itching and aching, this sensation extended up and over her shoulder and into her back. She rubbed the muscles there in an effort to make the sensations go away, but they only grew stronger. Chalking these sensations up to the occupational hazards of prolonged desk work, she tried to focus on her work but was unable to do so. The sensations and her irritation at them were just too strong.

In frustration, Annie began to speak directly to the sensations. "Okay," she said out loud, "just what is this all about?" She put her left hand up onto her shoulder and began to rub it. "What is going on in there? I'm too young to have arthritis, or maybe I'm not. Great, that's all I need right now. Give me a break!" The sensations became even more intense despite her rubbing, so she stood up and began to walk around the room as she continued to converse with what was happening in her body.

"I can't deal with this now! I don't have the time! Enough is enough!" she yelled. "If you can't leave, then do me the favor of moving to some other part of my body?"

Suddenly a voice in her head answered, "But if I move, I won't have as good a view. Sitting up here I can see everything that you're doing. I can keep my eye on you. You're bound to make a mistake sooner or later."

Annie was shocked, but before she had time to ask the voice "Who are you?" she realized whose voice it was. Right down to the choice of words and their inflection, it was the voice of her father. The fact that he had been dead for six years in no way diminished his presence. Annie felt terrified, not just because of the memories that were flooding in, but also because this was the first time in her life that she had experienced someone else's voice speaking through her thoughts. "Great," she thought, "now on top of everything else, I'm nuts."

When we met, Annie recounted this experience to me. In the course of our work together we explored her need for control, her addiction to perfection, and the feelings of fearfulness and unworthiness that lay beneath both of those life issues. She realized that she had been carrying these two feelings around with her and acting out of them for most of her life. Over a period of several months, Annie learned how to use the Heart/felt Interface to silence the harsh remarks of her Critical Detractor Child and then reparent that aspect, who bore a striking resemblance to her father. She learned how to take care of her Suffering Child, the one who was so afraid of being caught in a mistake. She assimilated the Nurturing Parents and learned how to parent herself and her Maturing Aspects. Annie was on the way to becoming an integrated adult.

Over time she became more willing to share the responsibilities of running the household with her husband and children. No longer convinced that her self-worth hinged on getting the dishes done right after supper or keeping the house in perfect order, she became more relaxed and playful. She learned to enjoy letting her husband and children help with the chores, even if those chores were not done exactly as she would have done them. She also came to realize that parenting is a difficult challenge and that making mistakes is part of the package. The fact that she made them did not brand her as unloving or inept. It simply confirmed that she was human and fallible. She realized that she could make mistakes without her world falling apart.

The same insights that allowed her to change her behavior at home also made it possible for her to change her behavior at work. She was able to let go of her trips into the office to duplicate her proofers' work. A typographical error would occasionally slip by them, but Annie was no longer afraid that such a mistake would become a public proclamation of her incompetence. It was just a mistake, not the end of the world, not a comprehensive statement about her, and certainly no cause for intense feelings of humiliation. When these errors did occur, she would simply meet with her proofers and calmly discuss how they could perform their jobs with more accuracy in the future.

There are many stories like Annie's and each one is sacred, a unique account of the way in which people are influenced in their day-to-day lives by their Suffering Child, their Critical Detractor Child, and the feelings and beliefs that are carried by these two aspects. Honoring these stories is the first step in transforming the life issues that are contained within them. Through that transformative process you, too, can explore the feelings and reevaluate the thoughts that are carried by your Suffering Child and your Critical Detractor Child. When you change these underlying feelings and thoughts, your behavior also changes. You begin to consistently place yourself in situations where your vitality and creativity will be welcomed and celebrated. You actively pursue possibilities that you may not even have recognized before.

In Chapter Eight, **Identifying and Transforming Your Life Issues,** we outline the steps that will help you to identify your life issues. Then we look at the process of transforming those issues and the behaviors related to them. Within that process, the feelings of fearfulness, unworthiness, helplessness, and hopelessness that your Suffering Child and Critical Detractor Child carry also are transformed. You emerge from that process an integrated adult, ready to claim all the treasures of adulthood.

CHAPTER EIGHT

IDENTIFYING AND TRANSFORMING YOUR LIFE ISSUES

Breathe deeply and gently.
Let your body soften.
See yourself within the space that surrounds you.
Feel yourself within the space that surrounds you.
Who is doing the seeing? Who is doing the feeling?

t is important to remember that any situation you repeatedly find yourself in that hinders your vitality, creativity, and sense of worth and possibility is considered a life issue. Life issues are the result of behaviors prompted by chronic feelings of fearfulness, unworthiness, helplessness, and hopelessness. For instance, if you continually find yourself attracted to a particular kind of person, and regardless of how the relationship begins, you always end up being abused or abandoned, you are caught in a life issue. This life issue may be a repetition of the relationship you had with your parents. By continually placing yourself in this situation, your Suffering Child may be attempting to find some resolution to those childhood experiences. Or, your Critical Detractor Child may be desperately trying to confirm his feelings of unworthiness, in his attempt to hold onto the fantasy bond he has with his abusive or neglectful parents. Moving beyond your self-limiting beliefs and behaviors requires that you learn to identify your life issues and find ways to transform them.

All of the tools I have outlined in the book so far are put to use in the process of identifying and transforming a life issue. Relaxing and coming into the Interval makes it easier for you to notice the pheno-mena that are part of a life issue—your thoughts, feelings, sensations, impulses to act, and actual behaviors. When you are relaxed and rest-ing in the Interval, you are much more open to the clues that can help you to identify a life issue. You also find it easier to participate in the process by which that issue is gradually transformed. Knowing the aspects of Self helps you to tune in to your thoughts, feelings, and impulses to act when you are in a life issue scenario. Finally, learning to parent yourself makes it easier for you to give the inner children who emerge during a life issue scenario the attention they need.

You identify a life issue by paying close attention to situations that are emotionally charged and especially demanding or challenging for you. Each time you find yourself in such a situation, try to pay attention to these five areas: your thoughts, your feelings, your body sensations, your behavior, and the nature of the situation itself. If you collect information about these five areas each time you find yourself in a tense or difficult situation, you will eventually be able to name the life issue that is operating.

Identifying a life issue is a bit like becoming your own private detective. Each time you find yourself in a situation that is emotionally turbulent, take a deep breath and put on your "detective hat." You can know that a situation is emotionally stressful if you feel agitated, dis-tracted, impatient, frustrated, or shut down. Imagine that you have been hired to observe and collect information about each of the areas we listed above: thoughts, feelings, sensations, behaviors, and the nature of the situation that is emotionally charged. It does not matter which of these five areas of inquiry you are drawn to first, that area becomes your starting point, your "way in" to collecting the information you need to name the life issue that is operating.

As you become more experienced in your detective role, you may notice that one of these five areas usually gets your attention first. Some of you will notice your thoughts first, collect some information about that area, and from there go on to collect some information about your feelings, sensations, behavior, and the nature of the situation that is stressing you out. Some of you will notice your feelings first, gather some information about that area, and from there go on to collect information about the other four areas. Some of you will notice sensations first and go on from there. Some will notice behavior first and go on from there. Some will be drawn to the details of the situation itself and go on from there.

It does not matter where you start or in what order you investigate each of these five areas. However, you should be thorough. Each time you find yourself in a situation that is charged in some way, try to collect at least one piece of information about each of the five areas. Ask yourself, in whatever order you wish:

- What kinds of thoughts am I having?
- What feelings am I having?
- What sensations do I notice in my body?
- How am I behaving?
- Do I notice a theme within this situation? What is it?
- Does this situation or any detail within it remind me of other situations that have been stressful for me?

You can also ask others to help you identify your life issues. People whom you trust and who know you well—a spouse or lover, a friend, a sibling, or some other member of your family—often have some very useful insights about your habits, behaviors, or ways of looking at the world that they feel limit your creativity or general happiness. Their observations in these areas can help you to name a life issue and begin to get a sense of how to transform it. You also may want to seek out a professional counselor, therapist, or spiritual advisor to help you identify and begin transforming your life issues.

Transforming a life issue involves working through your feelings of fearfulness, unworthiness, helplessness, and hopelessness. You work through these feelings by inviting the aspects who carry and promote them to come out and tell you everything they can about these feelings. If you listen carefully, you discover what your Suffering Child is feeling and thinking. You notice how his presence colors your perception of a situation and your response to it. By listening, you also discover the thoughts and feelings that your Critical Detractor Child is provoking in you. You see how his presence inclines you to respond in certain ways.

The information you collect by paying attention to your Suffering Child and your Critical Detractor Child becomes part of an insight experience. That insight allows you to behave in new ways. You stop acting out of your feelings of fearfulness, unworthiness, helplessness, and hopelessness because those feelings have been processed and released. Instead of acting from some combination of your Suffering Child and your Critical Detractor Child, you respond to life issues from the strength of your emerging adult Self.

Transforming a life issue does take some time and practice. It is important to be patient with yourself and with the process of learning how to respond to an intense situation in a new way. Your behavior will not change overnight, but it will change. As you collect more information about the five areas we discussed earlier and patiently process that information, you will definitely have insights about what motivates your behavior within a life issue scenario. Those insights will make it possible for you to practice new behaviors and integrate them into your adult Self.

As you work at transforming a life issue, you will notice yourself passing through several stages. In the earliest stage, you do not realize that a life issue has come up until you step out of the scenario in which it was operating. In this stage you notice after the fact that your thoughts, your feelings, and your behavior within a situation were all saying, "This is a life issue scenario." But noticing after the fact is still very useful. It will help you to notice that you are in a life issue scenario at an earlier point the next time that issue plays itself out.

In the next stage, you recognize that you are in a life issue scenario while it is still going on, but you are unable to behave in a new way. Your awareness of the situation, along with your thoughts, your feelings, and your sensations, tell you that you are in a life issue scenario, but your old way of responding still comes out. In this stage you are still acting out of some combination of your Suffering Child and your Critical Detractor Child, but you know that is what you are doing. You are still reacting rather than choosing a new response, but you are aware of your behavior. Your skills are definitely growing. Being able to recognize that you are in a life issue scenario while it is going on is real progress. And being this aware of everything that leads up to your reaction makes it possible to move on to the next stage.

In the final stage, you quickly recognize that you are in a life issue scenario and you are able to respond in a new and very deliberately chosen way. At this stage you are doing a number of things with a high level of skill. You are noticing your thoughts, feelings, sensations, and impulses and you are able to make a choice about your behavior. You can see yourself moving up to the point where you could respond in an old way and you are able to catch yourself before you react impulsively. Instead of reacting, you choose a new response, act, and then observe how the situation proceeds when you act from your adult Self.

In every stage of learning to transform a life issue, it is important to be patient with yourself. This is especially important in the first two stages. Do not beat up on yourself if you notice that you are not yet able to respond to certain situations in the ways you would like to. Instead remind yourself that your awareness and your skills are growing, and that the next time you find yourself in a life issue scenario you will catch yourself sooner. You may need to have this dialogue with yourself hundreds of times before you get to the point where you can perform all of the functions that a life issue scenario demands. But each of these dialogues represents you parenting yourself in a loving way.

In the next section we present some steps that you can take to promote the process of identifying and transforming a life issue. All of these steps will help you identify life issues and then strengthen the qualities that we associate with the Nurturing Parents and the Intuitive Self so that you can choose new ways of responding to a life issue scenario.

IDENTIFYING AND TRANSFORMING YOUR LIFE ISSUES

Practice noticing your thoughts, feelings, and sensations in a particular moment. Practice relaxing. Practice coming into the Interval.

The key to identifying and transforming a life issue is learning to notice your thoughts, feelings, and sensations. It is through your awareness of these phenomena that you will recognize which situations or life choices are emotionally charged and especially difficult or stressful for you. A heightened emotional charge is your body's way of telling you that a life issue is at work. We each react differently to emotionally charged situations. In an effort to disengage from the charge, you may deaden your feelings and go numb; or, if you tend to become agitated in the face of an intense situation, you may act out as a way of dissipating the energy within the charge. Many people combine both responses by engaging in addictive behaviors and at the same time numbing themselves by over-eating or taking drugs. Becoming aware of *how* you react to emotionally charged situations is the first step in changing your old patterns and replacing them with behaviors that support your vitality, creativity, and your sense of worth and possibility.

Once you have recognized a habitual response to an emotionally charged situation, it is important that you stop, relax, and enter the Interval. This will allow you to become aware of your feelings, thoughts, and sensations. It also will help you to detect the presence of your Suffering Child and your Critical Detractor Child. Since these two aspects of Self are at the heart of a life issue, their presence tells you that a life issue is being played out. As you interact with each of these two aspects, you will be able to name the life issue that is operating and begin to transform it.

Develop an intimate, loving relationship with your Suffering Child and your Critical Detractor Child. Get to know them and practice having conversations with both of them, as your Nurturing Parents would. Remember to stand firm when your Critical Detractor Child tries to deliver her hurtful messages, or when your Suffering Child wants to collapse.

The best way to develop a loving relationship with these two maturing aspects is to imagine that you are the Nurturing Parents. When your Suffering Child and your Critical Detractor Child emerge in a situation, take a deep breath and imagine that you have all the patience, tenderness, warmth, and compassion that the Parent Who Listens has. Then extend those qualities toward your Suffering Child and your Critical Detractor Child after you have reminded this aspect that his hurtful messages are no longer acceptable and will not be permitted.

By listening to your thoughts, feelings, and sensations, you will get to know your Suffering Child and your Critical Detractor Child. When you notice that you are having feelings such as fearfulness, unworthiness, helplessness, hopelessness, grief, guilt, and shame, then you know that your Suffering Child is present. If you notice any of those feelings, there is a very good chance that your Critical Detractor Child is present, too. Listen in and see if you can hear the voice of someone putting you down, criticizing you, or discouraging you from going after what you want. That is the voice of your Critical Detractor Child.

Help your Suffering Child and your Critical Detractor Child to open up and reveal themselves so you can collect information about the thoughts and feelings they are carrying with respect to a life issue. Give them all the time they need to share their feelings, their thoughts, their memories. Respond to them as the Listening Parent would. Tell them that you will hold them while they talk or cry or rage. Give them the loving attention they need, the attention that was missing when the trauma first occurred.

Make the commitment to know yourself fully.

What exactly do I mean by "knowing yourself fully?" It is to welcome whatever you discover when you look within yourself. To know yourself fully, all you need to do is relax, come into the Interval, and be open to the variety of thoughts, feelings, and sensations that rise into

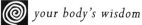

your consciousness. Knowing yourself fully means that nothing which enters your sphere of awareness is turned away.

When you promise to know yourself fully, the process of identifying and transforming a life issue moves right along. This is because you are very open to noticing the details that will help you to name an issue and transform it.

This attitude is essential to any process of self-awareness and growth, but it is not always an easy one to maintain. I have found that a clear statement of intent such as, "Regardless of how difficult or painful it may be, I am committed to seeing all aspects of myself through eyes filled with compassion and forgiveness," is a powerful tool for sustaining the resolve that is needed to pursue the goal of getting to know ourselves. When I make such a statement, out loud or in writing, God/All That Is supports me in a variety of ways. I begin to meet people who are on a similar path. We talk, share insights, and cheer each other on. I find books or films that relate to an area I am currently investigating and I feel even more encouraged to continue my explorations.

Promise that you will receive all you learn about yourself with compassion, acceptance, and forgiveness.

It is essential that you come to the process of identifying and transforming your life issues with a nonjudgmental attitude toward yourself. This is what will make it safe for your feelings, thoughts, and memories to surface so that you can name the issue that is operating and begin to transform it. This is also what will make it safe for your Suffering Child and your Critical Detractor Child to reveal themselves. The easier it is for them to come out and have dialogues with you, the easier it will be for you to name the life issue which they are carrying and which is causing you to act out.

Learning how to act as the Parent Who Listens will help you to extend acceptance and compassion toward yourself. Parenting yourself in a loving way as you explore a life issue will also help you to deal with any fears that arise. Many of us are afraid of what we may find if we begin to explore our feelings. What if the feelings I tap into in the course of exploring a life issue are uncomfortable? What if I come in touch with painful memories from my childhood? What if I come in touch with some feeling, belief, or memory that makes me feel bad about myself or about something I once did? Because all of these things are possible, it is very important to promise that you will receive and hold whatever you discover with an accepting and forgiving heart.

Create a safe and supportive environment in which you can experience your feelings and express the full range of your emotions.

The Nurturing Parents are the key to creating a space where you feel safe to explore and express your feelings. By inviting the Suffering Child and the Critical Detractor Child to share their thoughts and feelings, the Parent Who Listens makes it safe for them to come out. While encouraging the Suffering Child to express all his emotions, s/he comforts him in the midst of his grief, rage, and terror. The listening parent is always available, so the Suffering Child never feels that he is alone with his feelings.

When the Critical Detractor Child reveals himself, the Parent Who Listens first stops him from repeating his litany of abusive remarks, ensuring that the Suffering Child will not be attacked while he is revealing his feelings. S/he then invites the Critical Detractor Child to express the thoughts and feelings that underlie his harsh words.

The Parent Who Leads is confident in the ability of the Parent Who Listens to tend the Suffering Child and the Critical Detractor Child. The leading parent is also confident that you will discover what action needs to be taken in regard to your feelings. Together, the Nurturing Parents let you know that you will be watched over while you are having your feelings and that the best course of action will be revealed because you let yourself experience your feelings.

Over the years I have listened to many people describe what it is like for them to come in touch with intense feelings. Images like "being run over by a train," "falling into a well," "being lost in a dark forest," or "running down a long corridor as though I was being chased" were often part of their descriptions. Phrases like these point out the fear that many of us have about coming in touch with our feelings. But one of the most powerful metaphors to describe this fear came not from a student's account, but from a true story told to me by a friend.

The story concerned a couple who were caught in a typhoon while sailing in the South Pacific. Both of these people were experienced sailors, but they were suddenly overwhelmed by a storm that had changed course. Frightened that they would be swept overboard and separated, they put on life jackets and tied themselves to one another with a rope. A giant wave crashed over the deck, sending both of them over the side and into the water. They rose to the surface together and were frantically trying to console each other when suddenly another wave pulled both of them under the water. After a few moments, the husband rose to the surface alone; his wife did not come up. She was never found and was, of course, presumed dead.

When I heard this story, I was deeply moved and for some days afterward found myself wondering what the last moments of this woman's life must have been like. I would fantasize and imagine myself in her place. I envisioned myself thrashing about in terror during the long moments of being pulled under by powerful waves. In that instant I knew that there was nothing I could do. I would not be able to resurface in time to take a breath; death was happening. As soon as I recognized that, the following question rose into my thoughts: "Do you want your last moments of life to be spent in this way—thrashing about, lost in terror— or do you want to be aware of the entire experience as you pass from this realm to the next?" I believe this question came from my Nurturing Parents and Intuitive Self. They were telling me, "We are here with you. Let us in to this experience. Let us walk through it with you."

Those imagined final moments and the question that emerged from that scenario became a kind of meditation for me. I found myself returning to the question whenever I was in a situation that felt emotionally overwhelming. Few of us will end up in the ocean, but we will find ourselves in heavy emotional seas. At such times, your tendency might be to struggle and thrash about, or go numb, but if you move past those tendencies, you can ask yourself, "Do I want to spend these moments thrashing about and closed off from my feelings, or do I want to be aware of my entire experience?" If you can remember to ask this question in the midst of an emotionally charged situation—the very kind of situation that a life issue can produce—then you can change the way you experience that situation and each moment within it. You can focus on your body and soften around the physical discomfort you are experiencing. You can breathe deeply into your discomfort and relax. You can come into the Interval and be completely available to your feelings and sensations without becoming overwhelmed by them. You feel safe to go deeper, to feel even more, to experience all of the detail within your feelings.

Feeling safe to experience your feelings is the first piece of this step. The next is feeling free to express your emotions and release the energy within your feelings. Emotional expression can consist of talking, sobbing, shaking, shouting, and different forms of movement. What circumstances make you feel that you have permission to express your emotions in these ways? What kinds of situations make you feel safe to show your feelings, verbally and/or physically? Think about what you would need from another person and from your surroundings in order to feel free to express your emotions. Then think about how you could create those circumstances. Give some thought to how you could ask another person to provide the circumstances and the support that you would need to express the full range of your emotions.

Keep in mind that it is rarely a good idea to vent your feelings with the person who has actually provoked them. Instead it can be very useful to separate yourself from someone who has pushed your feeling buttons. Go into another room where you have the freedom to kick, scream, curse, or sob. After you have released your emotions, take a deep breath, come into the Interval, and examine the thoughts, feelings, and sensations that are moving within you. You may discover that your intense response has little to do with the person and the incident that triggered your emotions. Eventually you may come to thank the person who provoked your reaction because he or she has helped you to come in touch with a reservoir of feelings related to some other unresolved incident. Your awareness of those incidents brings you one step closer to transforming the life issue connected with them.

Acknowledge that you are capable of understanding your feelings and deciding how to respond to them.

The key to taking responsibility for your feelings and your actions lies in acknowledging that you are capable of doing just that. When you open your heart and mind to your Suffering Child and your Critical Detractor Child, and pay attention to these aspects in the most loving way, you become deeply aware of what you are feeling. That awareness allows you to make choices about how you experience, express, and share your feelings. The ability to make choices is the essence of "response-ability" with respect to your feelings and your actions.

Many of us have been given the message that people cause each other's feelings and the actions that emerge from them. Statements such as, "Because of you I had to give up my career and that's why I'm so depressed" or "It's your fault I hit you, you made me very angry" or "I was mean to you because you hurt my feelings" reinforce that message. But the fact that we influence each other's feelings and actions does not mean that we cause them. With respect to our feelings and our behavior, "the buck stops here"; that is to say, it is up to each of us to try to understand and own our feelings, the way in which we express them, and the actions we take in response to them. That challenge becomes more attractive and more manageable when we treat ourselves and our aspects of Self as the Nurturing Parents would—with patience, understanding, and compassion for all of our feelings, their origins, and our efforts to express and release them. The firmness that we express when addressing the negative input from the Critical Detractor Child is also an expression of our love and understanding. It is a demonstration of what is sometimes referred to as tough love.

We can accept the responsibility to understand our feelings in an oppressive, militaristic way—"You had better understand your feelings and the actions related to them, or else!"—and create all sorts of pressure on ourselves to "straighten up and fly right!" Or we can remove the pressure and the performance anxiety that is implied for some in the phrase "taking responsibility" and take a more relaxed approach. We can view "taking responsibility" for our feelings as a gentle invitation to get to know our feelings and the aspects of Self who embody them.

Many of us still carry and act out of the repressed feelings of our Suffering Child and Critical Detractor Child. The rage, grief, and terror that are carried by those aspects naturally intensify your emotional responses to certain situations. But when you invite those aspects to tell the story behind their feelings and receive their story in the loving, compassionate way of the Nurturing Parents, you understand your feelings and sensations in a new and much more useful way. This understanding allows you to finally release feelings that have been stored up. Then they no longer have the power they once did to compel you to behave in defensive or aggressive ways in certain situations. Your choices with respect to how you behave, even in the most challenging situations, increase tremendously.

Expand your capacity to experience more and more joyful energy.

You can do this by coming in touch with your Emerald Child. That aspect of Self will become more and more available to you as you pay attention to your Suffering Child and your Critical Detractor Child. When you release the feelings carried by them and transform their beliefs and attitudes, then your Emerald Child feels safe to come out. This happy aspect of Self delights in life's simple pleasures and is completely uninhibited about showing his excitement and enthusiasm.

When you come in touch with your Emerald Child, you can re-integrate him into your emerging adult Self. You will be able to participate in an experience as he would. You will notice the heightened feelings you have when you take in the sight and smell of a beautiful flower, watch the sun set, or stand in the rain on a warm summer day. You will notice how wonderful it feels to share a moment of success with a friend. If you allow the feelings and sensations to be found within

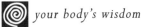

such experiences to go deep into your mind and your heart, your Emerald Child will come alive in you. Then you will find that your ability to experience and express joy will grow and keep on growing.

Create a vivid, textured "feeling sense" of how you would like your life to be.

Every situation you participate in is an energetic experience. The feelings, thoughts, and impulses to act that you experience in any given moment radiate energy. You perceive this energy inside your body as sensation and all around you as "emotional atmosphere." Together your internal experience of sensations and your impression of the energy surrounding you constitutes the "feeling sense" of a situation.

When you feel happy, safe, engaged, appreciated, and fulfilled, you notice certain internal sensations. You also have an impression of the energy that surrounds you and others present. This energy is generated to a great extent by the feeling content of the situation. When you feel unhappy, insecure, bored, unappreciated, and dissatisfied, the feeling sense of that situation will be quite different in terms of your body sensations and the energy that you perceive around you. All experiences have a certain feeling sense or energetic signature about them, and each of these experiences is unique.

You can start collecting information about the phenomenon of a feeling sense by noticing the sensations that move through your body then you are in various situations. Notice the thoughts, feelings, and sensations that move through you when you are filled with vitality and feel creative, and entitled to great possibilities. Notice the emotional energy that surrounds you in situations where you experience these same things. The feeling sense that you experience within and around you in situations that make you feel good about yourself is the feeling sense that you will want to look for and encourage in your everyday life. This is the energy that you will notice more and more as you work at identifying and transforming your life issues.

When you name the things that you want in your life—challenging work, adventure, aesthetically pleasing surroundings, supportive friends, a loving partner—try to find the words that describe the feeling sense you would also like to have in your life. Such words might be: stimulating, warm, relaxed, joyful, passionate, secure, light-hearted, playful. Let this feeling sense become part of the palette with which you paint a vivid, textured picture of the life you want to live.

Pay attention to your body language.

Learning to notice the body language that accompanies your feelings, sensations, and thoughts can help you to name a life issue and do the work of transforming it. There are many features to body language—posture, facial expression, tone of voice, eye contact, moving closer to or farther away from someone, or turning toward or away from a person with whom you are interacting. Maintaining an awareness of these and other features of your body language will help you to stay centered in your body. The more centered you are, the easier it will be to relax and notice your thoughts, your feelings, and the sensations that move throughout your body.

Often your body language contains your most spontaneous and authentic emotional response to what is happening around you. Knowing this can help you to label your feelings and a life issue related to them. If your shoulders suddenly roll forward and your chest caves in, these could be signs that you are feeling bored, frightened, hopeless, or just very relaxed. If you are conversing with someone who is recounting a joyful moment and you notice that your smile seems frozen, the rest of your face becomes stiff, and you have difficulty maintaining eyecontact, then you may be experiencing jealousy, sadness, or boredom. If you are speaking with someone and begin to notice a whining quality to your voice, you may want to ask something of that person but feel reluctant to do so for some reason.

Your body language can clue you in to the presence of your Maturing Aspects and help you decide which one is influencing you the most. When you come under the influence of your Suffering Child, your body language will communicate the fearfulness, unworthiness, helplessness, and hopelessness which this aspect carries. When you come under the influence of your Critical Detractor Child, your body language will communicate the arrogance, disdain, vindictiveness, and harsh judgment which that aspect carries. The emotional atmosphere created by these feelings can provoke similar feelings in other people present, increasing the sense of conflict within a situation and making it harder to come to resolution.

When you are first learning how to observe and interpret your body language, it is important to resist the temptation to edit your body's messages. Try to stay open to all of your observations. It will be easier to do this if you bring to your observing the energy of the Parent Who Listens. Reminding you to be totally accepting of all the body/mind phenomena you observe, s/he will encourage you to notice every detail of your body language without judging or eliminating certain observations. If you do not keep your Listening Parent in mind as you observe, you might be inclined to suppress or change your facial expression, your tone of voice, or your posture so as not to reveal a part of yourself that you judge as unacceptable. You may not want your body to communicate to someone else that you are feeling helpless or vindictive, or you may not want to admit to yourself that you are capable of such feelings.

Later on you can start to experiment with intentionally shifting features of your body language. There are several steps to this process. First, observe your body language and use your observations to determine which of your maturing aspects is present. Is your body language announcing that your Suffering Child has emerged? Is it telling you that your Critical Detractor Child is present? Then shift one or more features of your body language so that you can move out of the emotional and cognitive space that belongs to your Critical Detractor Child or your Suffering Child and into the emotional and cognitive space that belongs to your adult Self.

Your goal in intentionally shifting features of your body language is to change the emotional atmosphere within a situation. Notice what happens to the situation you are in when you adopt the body language that feels consistent with the image you have of your adult Self. Notice what happens when you bring your attention into the eyes of your adult Self and look out at your surroundings through those eyes. Does the nature of your thoughts or feelings change? How do your thoughts change when you consciously alter your posture, your tone of voice, your facial expression, or the distance between you and another person? How do your feelings shift when you consciously alter any of those body language features?

Changing any single feature of your body language can have a profound effect on a situation. By altering your posture, facial expression, or voice as you are paying attention to your thoughts, feelings, and sensations, you will see those thoughts, feelings, and sensations from a different and very revealing perspective. You will learn something about them and about the connection between body and mind. By consciously shifting your body language, you can change the emotional atmosphere in which you are having the thoughts and feelings associated with a life issue. This shift in body language will influence the way you articulate your thoughts and feelings, and it will affect the way you express your emotions. Changing your tone of voice, facial expression, and posture in the midst of a life issue scenario can help to promote a happier outcome between you and the person you are dealing with.

Let's try to bring this theory into the realm of practice. Pretend that you are in a situation that has stimulated feelings of unworthiness or hopelessness. You applied for a job that you wanted very much, but the interview went badly. As you are recounting the details of the interview with a friend, you notice that you are huddled up in the corner of the sofa, your knees pulled tightly together, your arms hugging your chest. As you are speaking, you keep looking away from your friend. The muscles under the skin of your face feel loose and slack. Your face feels like a mask. You wonder if there is any expression on your face at all. Your voice is low and complaining.

Become this person. See yourself as we have described him. Actually sit on your own sofa and adopt his posture, his facial expression, his tone of voice. Feel the emotional atmosphere within this situation. Feel who you have become. As you continue to talk about the job interview and how badly you felt during and after it, begin to change your body language. Let the muscles of your thighs soften and your knees separate. Is there a shift in the emotional atmosphere? Drop your arms and let them rest lightly in your lap. Is there a shift in the emotional atmosphere? Stand up and begin to walk around as you continue talking. Speak in a louder voice. Has the emotional energy shifted? Stop speaking for a moment and move all of the muscles in your face. Open your mouth wide. Frown and release. Purse your lips and release. Bring an accepting smile to your mouth and eyes. Now continue the role-playing and see how your thoughts, feelings, and sensations have shifted. Return to the sofa and sit down. What is your body language saying now? What is the emotional atmosphere of this moment?

Identify the life issue that you want to change.

To name a life issue, you can use any of the approaches I outlined at the beginning of this chapter. Just knowing that you want to identify a life issue will cause the information you need to rise into your consciousness. It may come immediately or it may take hours, days, weeks, or months to become available. In quiet moments and in the midst of activity, you will start to receive the information you need to identify one or more life issues. Try to be patient and remember that behaving toward yourself and your aspects as your Nurturing Parents would will make it easier for you to receive information about a life issue.

Identify the behaviors that are creating and maintaining the life issue you have named. These are the behaviors you will find yourself dropping or altering as you move through the process of transforming the life issue you have named.

Let's say that the life issue you identify is compulsive spending. This issue is creating many different problems for you—anxiety because there is never enough money to pay your bills on time, a feeling of being out of control, embarrassment that your friends will find out about your addiction to spending, the realistic fear that soon you will not be able to make your mortgage payments and could lose your house, a feeling of urgency that is spreading to other areas of your life besides money.

List the behaviors that are maintaining your overspending—not keeping a running balance in your checkbook, refusing to set up a monthly budget and sticking to it, buying things on impulse that you do not need, accepting invitations through the mail to set up new credit card accounts. This experience will also provide you with a list of things that you can start to do differently. Changing even one of these behaviors will contribute to the overall process of transforming that issue.

Make a list of new behaviors that could bring you closer to the life you really want. What feelings and thoughts arise when you imagine yourself behaving in these new ways?

Transforming a life issue does not happen overnight. This transformation is accomplished over time and through many small steps. For any life issue that you can name, there are many ways in which small changes in your behavior can have very positive effects. In the example we cited above—compulsive spending—you could set up a budget, reward yourself for not buying on impulse (as long as the reward does not involve spending!), or join a support group of people working on the same issue. The most important behavior you can institute, however, is to sit down and have a conversation with your Suffering Child each time you feel compelled to spend money.

If the life issue you are trying to transform is fear of intimacy, you can try in small ways to invite people into your life and share yourself with them. Each positive experience in this area will incline you to reach out again. If the issue you want to change has to do with being too controlling, you could try delegating pieces of a project to someone else (at work or at home) and letting go of the outcome.

When you behave in a new way in relation to a life issue or simply imagine yourself doing that, the thoughts, feelings, and sensations that rise in a real or an imagined situation will provide some useful information. These thoughts, feelings, and sensations can tell you something about your resistance to change. Most of us resist change to some degree, even when that change is something we desire and set out to accomplish. One way to deal with your resistance to change is to move into the Interval and come in touch with your Intuitive Self. In the presence of your Intuitive Self, you become the Quiet Observer of the thoughts, feelings, and sensations that say, "It's too hard, I can't change," "Why bother?" or "Things are fine just the way they are." When you are the Quiet Observer, you know that you can notice your discouraging thoughts and feelings without giving in to them. You can remind yourself that having such thoughts and feelings does not mean that you cannot act. You do not have to stay stuck in a pattern of behavior that is limiting.

The thoughts and feelings that arise when you behave in new ways, or imagine yourself behaving in new ways, provide the opportunity to dialogue with your Suffering Child and your Critical Detractor Child. These dialogues allow you to identify and work through the feelings of fearfulness, unworthiness, helplessness, and hopelessness which these two aspects carry and promote. As you work through those feelings, you begin to feel confident, deserving, capable, and optimistic, and your behavior starts to reflect those feelings.

Be open to change and find ways to get support for the changes you make.

As you go through the process of identifying and transforming a life issue, you will probably be drawn to rearrange certain aspects of your life—a living situation, a relationship, a job, a leisure, or community activity. The desire to make changes is a natural consequence of the insights you have when you work through and release the feelings at the heart of a life issue. As your Suffering Child and your Critical Detractor Child heal, your Nurturing Parents, your Emerald Child, and your Intuitive Self become stronger within you. Increasingly you see the world through their eyes, and your actions reflect that change in perspective.

Even when we are inspired to make changes in our lives, we may experience some resistance to doing things differently. Treat that resistance in the same way you would treat the feelings that your Suffering

Child or your Critical Detractor Child would present: invite it to reveal itself, explore it, notice the thoughts that are part of it, notice the sensations in your body as you come in touch with it. Embrace your resistance so that you can move past it.

As your resistance melts, you will want to look for different ways to motivate yourself to go forward. One of the ways I sustain my resolve to follow through with changes is to periodically review my life and my plans for the future. I take note of the circumstances in my life that bring a smile to my face and give me a sense of fulfillment. I allow myself to fully experience that joy. I congratulate myself on the ways in which I have shaped my life so that I can experience joy. I listen to the thoughts that support my happiness and success. I rest in the emotional atmosphere created by these thoughts and feelings. I examine them and become familiar with them.

Then, I give equal attention to the circumstances in my life that cause me to frown and feel unfulfilled. I examine my feelings of discontent. I listen to the thoughts that support this limitation. I rest in the emotional atmosphere created by these thoughts and feelings. I become familiar with them. I try to imagine what my life would look and feel like in one, five, ten, and fifteen years if I could not change the circumstances that are restricting me.

Then I imagine what my life will feel like if I succeed at making those changes. I place the vision of change, with its promise, on my right and the vision of no change, with its lost opportunities, on my left. I rest in the emotional atmosphere created by each possibility. I move back and forth between the two, allowing the tension between them to build. Experiencing the feelings and sensations associated with no change and no growth is usually all the encouragement I need to move ahead and make the choices that will let me be my biggest, most authentic Self. You too may want to use this technique whenever you experience some resistance to the changes that quite naturally grow out of the process of transforming a life issue.

It is not easy to change old, established patterns of behavior, so the more support you find for your new behaviors, the better. One way, of course, is to invite other people into your process of change—your spouse or lover, a friend, a sibling, a counselor or therapist. If these people were involved in helping you identify behaviors that you wanted to change, then they are in a very good position to support the changes that you do make.

Of course there are other ways to get support for the changes you are making. Meeting regularly with a group of people who are working on the same issue you are is another excellent way to get positive reinforcement for changes in your behavior. Hearing others' stories can stimulate insight into why you behave in certain ways and provide the motivation to do things differently. In general, spending time with people who want to live an examined life, people who are curious and open to change, will support your efforts to grow and change. Spending time with people who model the attributes of the Nurturing Parents also will promote your efforts to transform a life issue. Through the gifts of their friendship and support you can know yourself more deeply and make the changes that will transform your self-defeating behaviors into healthy ones.

A TRANSFORMATIVE EXPERIENCE

For many years I have been exploring a life issue that became established when I was very young. That issue is a reluctance to ask for help. For many years I was so afraid to ask for help from others that I was almost phobic about it. The very idea of asking stimulated a whole collection of uncomfortable body sensations that made me want to run away and hide.

This issue became established when I was very young. As a child I had always felt that my needs were secondary to those of my parents. They were preoccupied with each other and with their business, and each time I turned to them for help or attention of any kind I felt guilty and ashamed. I felt that I was placing a burden on them and making a nuisance of myself. Whenever I reached out to them, I ended up feeling disappointed, hurt, unloved, and more alone than I had felt before I went to them.

To avoid the painful feelings that rose when I even imagined asking my parents for help with something, I developed an air of never needing anything from them, or from anyone for that matter. At a very young age, I decided that if I was going to be left on my own to solve my own problems and negotiate the challenges of the world, then I would become very good at that. And I began to communicate to my parents and everyone else that I could take care of things all by myself, thank you very much.

There were strong feelings of fearfulness, unworthiness, and hopelessness lying just beneath my fierce independence—fear about taking the chance to reach out for help, a sense of vulnerability each time I contemplated trying, a sense of shame that I needed help and could not take care of it myself, a sense that I must not deserve anyone's help if my own parents had been unwilling to give it, and a sense of despair that anything could ever change around this issue. Somewhere—in the heart of my Suffering Child—I believed that it would always be this way. I carried that belief and the behaviors that stemmed from it into my adult years.

As an adult, I noticed that my reluctance to ask for help came up often, as did the agitation and anxiety that would crop up when I found myself wanting to ask for some kind of assistance or support. Predictably, this issue most often revealed itself in the context of my intimate relationships—with my husband and, after we were divorced, with my lovers, and with my close friends. I wanted to believe that the people I was close to would welcome the chance to help me when I needed it, but I was always afraid to ask for fear they would turn away, as my parents had done. Then I would not only suffer a sense of rejection, but I would also have to revisit the grief and sense of abandonment that rose whenever I recalled my parents' behavior toward me.

As the mother of five children, keeper of a large and busy house, and a professional, I had more than a few opportunities to notice my discomfort about asking for help. Sometimes, though, my need for help outweighed my discomfort over asking. Then I would ask my husband or my children to lend a hand with the household chores. Of course, I was too frightened to ask those friends who would gladly have given me whatever I asked for. The uneasy feelings associated with the asking never subsided. Each occasion to reach out was extremely uncomfortable for me, emotionally and physically.

Outside of my family, I was attracting into my life people who were reluctant to give of themselves or incapable of doing that. In every sphere of my life, I was creating an environment that constantly reaffirmed my long-held beliefs that help was not available and that I had better be able to take care of myself.

Finally, during an especially difficult time in my life, I decided to look for professional help in exploring this issue. I found it with a therapist, Dr. Steve Stein. In the context of that relationship, I felt free to acknowledge that I needed people but was afraid to let them know that. Together Dr. Stein and I explored the childhood events that gave rise to this life issue and the beliefs and behaviors that were maintaining it.

Through his kindness, generosity, and skill as a therapist, Dr. Stein showed me that I was worthy of loving attention from others. He behaved as Nurturing Parents would and taught me how to behave toward myself in those ways, too. We explored my feelings of fear and unworthiness. I began to trust that I could ask others for help and get what I needed. I also began to feel confident that if I asked for what I wanted and did not get it, I would not fall apart. The world began to look like a very different place indeed.

Major changes took place as I continued to explore this issue in therapy and on my own. I decided to leave my marriage and moved into an apartment where I lived alone for the first time in my life. I changed my profession and began to study massage and body/mind therapies. Each of these changes brought more caring people into my life and gave me opportunities to explore the feelings and behaviors that had been feeding my fearfulness, my compulsion to be independent, and my reluctance to reach out to people for help.

Most life issues are established in childhood, and we begin to become aware of them and work through them as adults. The process of understanding and transforming these issues is a gradual one. It is punctuated by large and small insights that make us see ourselves in different ways and allow us to behave in new ways. We "try on" new behaviors as a way of "trying on" our new sense of who we are and who we are becoming.

For me this new awareness of Self took the form of realizing that I was worthy of attention and support from others. I also realized that I did not have to do everything alone, no matter how competent I was. As my therapist helped me to work through my grief about not having received loving attention from my parents and my fears about looking for it from others, I became bolder about letting others in to the small circle I had created for myself. I began to expand this circle and fill it with people who were naturally generous and loving. I was reaching out more and I was doing that with people who were likely to delight in giving me just what I was looking for. Increasingly I was setting myself up for success and finding it.

However, success at transforming a life issue does not mean that such an issue stops presenting itself. The feelings of fearfulness, unworthiness, helplessness, and hopelessness that underlie all of our life issues can be reactivated in many different situations. The fact that those feelings are reactivated does not mean that we have failed at transforming the issue associated with them. It simply means that the process of transformation is still taking place, at more subtle levels.

Each time we deal with a life issue scenario, it is like peeling back the layers of an onion. As we peel back one layer and then another, we come to the heart of transforming that particular issue. Within the process of examining an issue repeatedly, from different angles and in response to slightly different stimuli, we become more skillful at noticing that we are in a life issue scenario, at naming the issue, and at entering into a dialogue with our Suffering Child and our Critical Detractor Child to explore the details of the issue. We also become more skillful at naming the feelings and thoughts that run through us in such a scenario, at noticing the body sensations that also run through us, and at expressing the emotions related to our feelings.

Finally, as we become more skillful at dealing with these scenarios, we recognize and opt for new ways of behaving in response to such situations. We take more risks with the people who are with us when these scenarios unfold and we are generally rewarded for doing so. We may not get the exact outcome we hoped for, but we always emerge with new information, fresh insights, and a sense of direction as to what we want and what needs to happen next.

The following experience, which took place a few years ago, demonstrates the way in which a life issue can continue to present itself so that we refine our understanding of its place in our lives and its impact on us. While visiting my lover, Stu, one weekend, I awoke with a terrible pain in my back and hip. Without even realizing I had done it, I immediately moved into my self-protective mode of behavior. Determined not to let Stu know that anything was wrong, I made my way into the bathroom as gracefully as I could and downed a pain killer and a muscle relaxer.

As the morning progressed, so did the pain, and the pills no longer gave me any relief. I spent the next several hours lost in old patterns of thoughts and feelings, going back and forth in my mind—should I tell him what's going on with me?...no, don't tell him...leave...stay. I debated with myself about my choices. I could tell him about the pain and leave, or I could just announce that I was heading home without telling him why. I could make up some other excuse and keep my physical problems to myself. That way I would not have to risk finding out that he could not or would not give me what I needed just then.

When I heard myself contemplating leaving without saying why, I understood for the first time that day how lost I had become in the thoughts and feelings of my Suffering Child. For several hours I had completely forgotten all that I had learned over the years about this life issue of mine, and had reverted back to very old patterns of thinking and behavior. I had forgotten to call on my Nurturing Parents and Intuitive Self for support and guidance. I had allowed my Suffering Child and my Critical Detractor Child to take over.

Knowing I needed to make a decision about what to do, I created the circumstances best suited for introspection. I found a quiet room where I could relax, practice conscious breathing, and come into the Interval. I imagined my Nurturing Parents being right there with me. I explored all of my thoughts, feelings, and sensations, and opened to the presence of my Intuitive Self.

I invited my Suffering Child and my Critical Detractor Child to reveal themselves. First my Suffering Child presented her point of view. All of her old feelings of unworthiness and the fear of being disappointed moved through me. I could feel a heaviness on my chest and tears in my eyes as I recalled moments in my past when I had desperately needed someone and no one was there. Making her position very clear, my Suffering Child said, "I don't trust Stu. He's going to hurt you. I want to go home."

In the background I could hear the voice of my Critical Detractor Child whispering, "She's right, you can't trust anyone to be there for you. Why would anyone care enough about you to put themselves out to make you comfortable or happy?" Each statement increased my feelings of agitation. I could barely stay seated in the chair. I wanted to get up and run away.

This time I remembered to turn toward my Nurturing Parents. I invited them to engage in a dialogue with my inner children. They reminded me to take long, slow, deep breaths, remain calm, and listen. Then, my listening parent gathered my inner children to her and said, "My little ones, I know you're afraid to trust. I know you're afraid you'll be hurt and disappointed again. I know you believe that you do not deserve to be taken care of, but you need Stu now and it's all right to ask for what you need. You're a kind and generous person. You deserve to be loved and cared for."

I sat quietly for a few moments taking this all in and allowed my body to integrate all the feelings I was having. I breathed into the sensations that were rising, and waited until they subsided and I felt calm and centered. Next, I heard the voice of my leading parent. S/he said, "We do not know if Stu can be relied upon. The questions are: Are you ready to risk finding out who he is and what kind of a relationship you have? Is this a relationship in which you can be vulnerable or not? Can you ask for help and get what you need? Does he know how to be nurturing and does he want to extend that energy to you?"

Entering the stillness, silence, and emptiness of the Interval I wondered what would happen if I went home and never found out if I could depend on Stu in a situation like this one. Would I let myself continue to get close to him if I was not sure I could trust him? I waited patiently for the answer to come. The word "No" floated up from deep within me. "If you cannot be vulnerable with him, you will not be able to get close to him. You will never become intimate with him."

Next, I tried to imagine what might happen if I took the risk of asking for his help and he was unable to care for me. Would I be all right or would I feel devastated? Once again I waited for the voice of my Intuitive Self to speak. "You will be disappointed and all your old feelings of abandonment will rise, but you have learned much about this issue and you will survive and go on." After hearing these words, a deep sigh moved through me, as I experienced the truth of this statement.

I continued, "If he could not care for me in this kind of situation, was he the kind of man with whom I wanted to be in a relationship?" The answer rose, "No, he would not be. You want to be with someone who is able to lovingly care for you when you need him to." Then I let myself imagine what it might feel like if I chose to trust him and discovered that he was someone I could rely on in times of need. Would I then allow myself to stay and take in his nurturing love? Without reservation, a deep and resounding "Yes" rose into my consciousness.

As I came to the end of my inquiry, I heard my leading parent ask, "What do you want to do now Renee?" And I answered, "I will take the risk and draw Stu into my decision-making process. I will ask for his help. It is better to find out who he is than to go on thinking he is someone he is not. If he cannot be there for me, then it is best to know that now." As these last words rose into my mind, a deep, confirming breath moved through me.

Mustering all of my courage, I told him about the physical pain I was having. I shared my fears about needing him and my concern that he might be unwilling or unable to take care of me. As he sat there quietly listening to me, I observed his face and body language for clues as to what he was thinking and feeling. I focused my attention on the emotional atmosphere created by the exchange. I noticed that when he responded, he averted his eyes. He could not maintain eye contact with me. His words were reassuring, but his body language communicated reluctance. He was leaning away from me, as though he had withdrawn ever so slightly. I wondered if I was simply projecting my uneasiness onto him or if what I was noticing was a sign of his discomfort with our situation.

Once again I was faced with a moment of choice. Do I ignore what I am sensing or address it with him? My Suffering Child and my Critical Detractor Child said, "See, I told you so, let's go home." But I decided to persist and to explore my observations about his response. Ultimately I knew that my happiness was at stake. Pursuing this issue with Stu would reveal whether or not he was a man capable of loving me in the way that I had come to believe I deserved. I told him that I sensed he was uncomfortable and asked if he could tell me what he was feeling. He welcomed my question and the opportunity to discover his true feelings. As soon as he went inside himself, he came in touch with the discomfort I had sensed in him. He realized that he was afraid of my being sick and of my needing him. We talked for a while about those fears and their origins.

Stu had his own life issues, too, of course. One of them was avoiding being needed by anyone. We were perfect for each other in the sense that each of us had the mirror image of the other's life issue. I was afraid to ask for help, and he was afraid of being in a situation where he would be asked for it. This conflict had to come out sooner or later. Our related issues were destined to collide at some time, and the time had come.

Stu spoke about how he had avoided being needed by anyone since the death of his wife fifteen years earlier and that of his daughter five years after that. He talked about how helpless he had felt in the face of their deaths. The sense of there being nothing he could do to save either of them had awakened powerful, painful memories of being told by his parents all through his childhood that he was incompetent and that he could nothing right.

In the years since the deaths of his wife and daughter, Stu had carefully stayed away from situations in which anyone needed him. If he was never asked to meet someone else's needs, then he would never have to feel helpless or incompetent with someone he loved. Indeed, part of his initial attraction to me had been my take-charge, independent attitude. My "I can take care of myself" persona had immediately put him at ease. It led him to believe that I would never need him, but that he could need me and get those needs met. For him, I was "safe" as an intimate partner. He had no way of knowing, of course, that I was involved in a process of transforming that persona, of rearranging my sense of my Self and the way in which I presented myself to other people.

But what about now, when I needed some attention and could not be so independent because of my back? He admitted that the situation frightened him and awakened other feelings too—grief and anger over the loss of his wife and daughter, and anger at his parents for their criticisms of him and their failure to let him know that they loved him just for who he was.

We talked for several hours, each of us taking turns acting as Nurturing Parents for the other. Together we decided that I should stay. We cared enough about each other and our relationship to try and move through our uncomfortable feelings and stay open with each other as we did that. He promised that he would try and give me what I needed, and I promised that I would try to let in whatever he offered. He ran a bath for me, made dinner, and we had a picnic in bed. Each of us had taken a major step in transforming a life issue, and we felt much closer to each other for having done that.

Of course, every situation in which you attempt to identify and transform a life issue will be unique. The thoughts that rise within a particular life issue scenario will be unique to that situation, as will the feelings, the body sensations, your impulses to act, and your actual behaviors. The same life issue will reveal itself in slightly different ways each time it emerges. Over time, though, you will begin to notice patterns in your thinking, your feelings, and your behaviors with respect to a specific life issue. You will become an expert on yourself, your Suffering Child, and your Critical Detractor Child. Your expertise and your increasing familiarity with all the signs and features of a life issue will enable you to choose your responses within a life issue scenario. You will be the one in charge. You will experience yourself moving into your adulthood.

In Chapter Nine, **Silent Listening/Intuitive Response,** I present a technique that supports the process of transforming a life issue. This technique shows you how to observe and actively participate in the experience of insight. By listening to your thoughts and feelings as you notice your body sensations, you hear the voice of your Intuitive Self and know just how to respond to a situation.

SILENT LISTENING/ INTUITIVE RESPONSE

Breathe deeply and gently.
Let your body soften.
See yourself within the space that surrounds you.
Feel yourself within the space that surrounds you.
Who is doing the seeing? Who is doing the feeling?

I n this chapter we look at a technique that incorporates all of the skills you have learned so far. That technique is called Silent Listening/Intuitive Response (SL/IR). When you practice SL/IR, you exercise your ability to relax and come into the Interval. You listen to your thoughts, your feelings, and the sensations that rise with your feelings. You dialogue with your Maturing Aspects, your Nurturing Parents, and your Intuitive Self and emerge into your adulthood. From that space, you parent yourself and your maturing aspects in the most loving way.

When you practice Silent Listening/Intuitive Response, you take in everything that is occurring inside of you and around you. As you process all that information you hear the voice of your Intuitive Self. That voice guides you to respond, to take the action that is most beneficial.

Just as its name implies, Silent Listening/Intuitive Response consists of two movements—listening silently and responding intuitively. In preparation for the first movement, you relax and come into the Interval. There you give yourself over to the stillness at the center of all movement. You hear the silence that surrounds all sound. And you see yourself within the emptiness that envelops all form. You become centered in your body and you listen—to your thoughts, your feelings, your sensations, and your impulses to act. When you listen to all of these things and pay special attention to the shifts in sensation that occur as you are listening, you also will hear the voice of your Intuitive Self. That voice guides you toward a response that will enhance your vitality, creativity, and sense of worth and possibility.

Sensation and your awareness of body sensations are important components of Silent Listening/Intuitive Response because they are important components of the insight experience. By paying very close attention to your sensations, you learn to recognize your intuitive voice. From that voice rises insight. The premise that physical sensation is a central feature of insight was pioneered by Dr. Eugene Gendlin. In his book entitled *Focusing*, Dr. Gendlin teaches that each time you have an insight it is accompanied by the physical experience he calls the "felt shift." The "felt shift"—or "shift in sensation" as I will refer to it in SL/IR—occurs each time an authentic piece of information rises up into your conscious mind. As new information becomes available, you quite literally experience it as a change or shift in body sensation. This shift is extremely subtle, and you must give it your fullest attention if you are to recognize it when it occurs. This shift announces and confirms the phenomenon of insight, and that is why it is such an important piece of the overall insight experience.

The physical shift in sensation that occurs during an insight experience accompanies the cognitive component of insight, in which your perception of a situation and your thoughts about it are rearranged. When this cognitive shift occurs, you experience a revelation—or "aha!"—about yourself, a life choice you are facing, or a life issue scenario. Suddenly you see your situation in a new way. You see yourself within that situation in a new way, too. It is as though someone has turned on a light, and that light allows you to see your thoughts, your feelings, your impulses to react, and the solution to your dilemma very clearly.

The shift in sensation that accompanies the insight experience is confirmation that the guidance you have received is coming from your

Intuitive Self. This shift leaves you with a deep sense of the correctness of what you have heard. Your tension dissipates, your confusion evaporates. You feel confident in the action you are about to take. Although a part of you may still be drawn to react in an old patterned way, the confidence you feel in the aftermath of an insight experience helps you to follow through on the advice of your Intuitive Self.

Of course there are many situations in which you might want to tap into your intuition and be guided by your Intuitive Self. But we will focus on using Silent Listening / Intuitive Response in situations where you are dealing with a life issue or where you are called upon to make a life choice. Let's look at each of these two categories in more detail.

In the last chapter we said that there are three stages in which you could find yourself dealing with a life issue. In the first, you do not realize that you have been involved in a life issue scenario until it is over. In the second, you recognize that you are in a life issue scenario while it is going on, but you find yourself responding to it in the same old ways. In the third, you realize that you are in a situation related to a life issue and you are able to respond in a new way.

Let's add a fourth stage to this list. Here you find yourself on the outskirts of a situation that looks and feels as though it could become a full-blown life issue scenario. Something about the nature of your feelings, your sensations, your thoughts, and your impulses to behave in a particular way tells you that you could be drawn into the thoughts and feelings of your Suffering Child and your Critical Detractor Child. You sense that you could be swept away by those thoughts and feelings so you begin to pay very close attention and exercise all of your Nurturing Parent skills.

In this realm of learning to deal with a life issue, you are actually practicing a kind of preventive coping. The situation is still a life issue scenario, but it is one that you are managing from the very start. You will be able to look back on it as simply a situation that might have provoked your Suffering Child and your Critical Detractor Child, a situation that might have been filled with intense feelings and confusing thoughts, a situation in which you might have acted out of those feelings and thoughts, but instead you were able to intentionally move in a very different direction.

You can use Silent Listening/Intuitive Response at each of these four stages of dealing with a life issue: after a life issue scenario, in order to look back on it and learn; in the midst of a scenario when you are not yet able to respond in a new way; in the midst of a scenario when you can respond in a new way; and in the moments when you sense that you could be drawn into a scenario but want to avoid that.

Silent Listening/Intuitive Response is also very useful when you are faced with a life choice. If you are faced with an important decision concerning your job, your family, a relationship, a geographical move, or the spiritual sphere of your life, to name just a few possibilities, then taking time out to practice SL/IR can lend some clarity. You can use the technique to explore your thoughts and feelings about the choices before you. You can use it to dialogue with your inner children and to examine how their thoughts, feelings, and beliefs might influence your inclination to go one way or the other. You can use it to tap into the wisdom of your Intuitive Self. This Self knows what action is in your best interest.

Whether you are dealing with a life choice or a life issue, the technique of Silent Listening/Intuitive Response can be very helpful. Both categories have a level of stress associated with them, though in some ways dealing with a life issue is usually more stressful. In a life issue scenario, your maturing aspects are louder and more intrusive, and you are generally under some pressure to make some immediate decisions. The presence of your Maturing Aspects makes that decision-making process more challenging, to be sure. In a life choice situation, on the other hand, your Maturing Aspects are usually not so loud. They may get stimulated, of course, if they perceive a threat within the choices you are considering. But in general, it is easier to access and act from your integrating, emerging adult Self when you are in a life choice situation than when you are dealing with a life issue.

The emphasis Silent Listening/Intuitive Response places on the awareness of sensation and shifts in sensation make it a unique tool for problem-solving and decision-making. Most of us, if asked, would characterize the process of decision-making as a purely mental activity. We seldom notice the way in which our sensations participate in this activity, and it is even more unusual for us to invite our sensations to participate in our decision-making. But SL/IR shows you how to attend to your sensations and use them in a decision-making situation.

Of course it is not unusual for us to experience sensations and changes in sensation while confronting a life issue or a life choice. Life issue scenarios and important life choices cause intense feelings in most of us—even those of us who have learned to parent our inner children. But if we do not know how to make use of our awareness of sensation, we tend to set that information aside. In situations that are intense, we may try to avoid experiencing our sensations as a way of dampening the feelings that accompany them. If your sensations are uncomfortable—and as accompaniments to feelings of anxiety, grief, rage, or terror they often are—it comes as no surprise that you would try to move away from them. In a sort of reflex action, you try to push down or put aside these unpleasant sensations in order to find some relief from the emotional and physical discomfort within them. You may also believe that these sensations and the feelings that accompany them will actually get in the way of your making a clear decision.

By practicing Silent Listening/Intuitive Response, you will come to recognize your sensations as valuable tools. Helping you to stay relaxed and centered in your body, SL/IR enables you to tolerate sensations that are intense or uncomfortable. You learn how to sit with these sensations long enough to discover the gifts which they contain. By remaining present to your sensations you are able to identify your feelings and your thoughts, notice the presence of your Maturing Aspects, name your life issues, and receive the guidance of your Intuitive Self.

You can see why Silent Listening/Intuitive Response is so useful in situations that are emotionally charged, confusing, or complex. These are the most demanding times because your Suffering Child and your Critical Detractor Child are most likely to emerge. In some situations it can be difficult to resist becoming totally immersed in the persona of your Suffering Child. The more intense the feelings which she carries are and the more effective your Critical Detractor Child is at reinforcing those feelings, the more likely you are to identify completely with your Suffering Child.

Understandably, when these two Maturing Aspects are strongly present, you can become lost in your feelings and sensations and find it harder to respond from your integrating/emerging, adult Self. You can feel very confused about how to respond to your circumstances and the people around you. Should you become more involved or hold back? Should you speak out or be quiet? Do you want to share your opinions and feelings with other people present? How much should you share? Do you want to act? What are your choices? Which course of action is the best one to take? What is likely to happen if you act in this way? What is likely to happen if I respond in this other way? Out of frustration and uncertainty, you may shut down and become very passive, or you may lash out and behave in an impulsive, aggressive way.

Certainly you need to let your Suffering Child and your Critical Detractor Child be seen and heard, and they must employ you to do that. Only in this way can you identify your life issues and eventually transform them. But you also need to maintain a sense of your integrating, emerging, adult Self while these two aspects are using you to reveal those issues and themselves. You need to be reminded that your Suffering Child and her companion are aspects of a moment and do not define you. Silent Listening/Intuitive Response helps you to interact with your Suffering Child and your Critical Detractor Child and to be fully present to each of them while not losing your larger sense of Self or disconnecting from your intuitive voice. You do not have to give yourself over completely to the intense thoughts and feelings that these two bring with them. By using SL/IR to manage the thoughts and feelings of these two Maturing Aspects, you can think clearly and respond creatively to the circumstances that have elicited them.

The entire process of Silent Listening/Intuitive Response takes place within the Interval, and that is what confers the air of patience and receptivity that is so present when you practice SL/IR. A number of things occur within the Interval to promote the insight you are seeking. The Interval attracts your thoughts, memories, feelings, sensations, and impulses to act because it is a place of stillness, silence, and emptiness. The quiet energy within that stillness, silence, and emptiness acts like a magnet for your unresolved issues. Furthermore, when you are in the Interval, it is easier to recognize the shifts in sensation that accompany insight. The Interval also provides a restful place where you can linger while your choices as to how you could behave outwardly reveal themselves.

It is useful to keep in mind that the Suffering Child is somewhat fearful of the Interval. The stillness within the Interval draws out the intense and uncomfortable feelings that this aspect of Self carries. This means that when you come into the Interval in a situation where your Suffering Child is present, she is likely to become agitated. Her instinct will be to withdraw from the Interval as a way of disconnecting from her agitation, and you will feel that inclination rather strongly. But her discomfort becomes an opportunity for you to parent her lovingly. In trying to convince her to stay in the Interval and move through her discomfort, you are parenting yourself in a loving way, too. In communicating to your Suffering Child that she is not alone, that she will get through this uneasy period and that you will be with her the whole time, you are learning to talk yourself through a rough spot.

Ultimately the Interval is a detoxifying and liberating experience for your Suffering Child and for you, too, of course. The Interval invites your painful feelings to arise so that they may be experienced, explored, witnessed, integrated, and released. At that point, you are in a much better position to hear your intuitive voice and respond to your situation in ways that will promote its resolution. If you know that your Suffering Child is likely to become uncomfortable when you are in the Interval, then you are prepared to give her the support and encouragement she needs to stay in that space as you move toward the insight and resolution that will eventually calm her down.

The insight that comes when you stick with your sensations and let them speak to you enhances your ability to engage in creative action. You are in a much better position to act wisely and creatively after you have had some insight into the forces that are shaping your thoughts, your feelings, and your inclinations to act. On the other side of insight you are less likely to act impulsively. You are also less likely to act out your feelings of fearfulness, unworthiness, helplessness, and hopelessness because you have attended to the two aspects who carry and promote those feelings.

PRACTICING SILENT LISTENING/ INTUITIVE RESPONSE

One of the advantages of Silent Listening/Intuitive Response is that you can practice it without the help of another person. However, while you are first learning how to use this technique, it can be useful to have someone read the steps aloud for you as you walk through them. Inviting another person into your learning process assures you of partners with whom you can practice and review the technique. It also gives the people who work with you access to a tool that will be as helpful to them as it is to you.

Reading through the condensed and detailed versions of the steps will also be helpful. In this way you can begin to get a sense of the shape of the overall process. You will notice as you read through the steps that almost every one directs you to listen for a shift in the sensations you are experiencing in your body. This "listening in to the body" helps you to stay grounded and centered in your body. It helps you to remain in the Interval. Listening in to the body also encourages you to notice the shift in sensation that occurs just before or just after you have an insight about yourself, your situation, or another person present.

Before I move on to the next section in which I outline the steps themselves, I have a suggestion about the best way for you to practice

SL/IR. In the beginning, try to practice SL/IR outside of situations that are emotionally charged or complex. For example, you are asked to volunteer your time for a worthy cause. You feel ambivalent, and don't want to be coerced by feelings of guilt or shame. You can use SL/IR to move through the feelings of your Critical Detractor Child, or Suffering Child and discover the action most beneficial to your emerging adult Self. By practicing SL/IR during less stressful situations you will have an opportunity to become familiar with the steps and the shape of the process before you step into a situation that is more demanding. At the next level of difficulty, try to recall a recent situation in which you were dealing with intense feelings or a difficult decision. Return to that situation and use Silent Listening/Intuitive Response to review the thoughts and feelings that arise as you recall the situation. At the next level, take your awareness of the technique into an actual situation and see how many of the steps you can walk through within that situation. You will feel more confident about the process of SL/IR and your skill as a practitioner if you can gradually move through a hierarchy of learning situations that progresses from very simple and not so demanding to more complex and demanding situations.

I recommend that you set aside some time each day or several times each week to practice SL/IR just as you would practice another form of meditation. Find a quiet place in your home, use some conscious breathing exercises to become relaxed, read through the steps, and then bring your attention to the sensations that rise and move through your body. Some people have found it useful to keep a journal of their SL/IR practice sessions. In these journals they make notes of the feelings, memories, and insights that emerge while they are using SL/IR. Other clients keep drawing paper and pens or paints nearby so they can visually document their experiences with SL/IR.

Let's move on now to the actual steps of Silent Listening/ Intuitive Response. In the next section we have included two versions of the steps: a condensed overview, and then a more detailed version. After the outline of the steps is a story about a woman who used SL/IR to explore the feelings that she came in touch with one evening.

THE STEPS OF SILENT LISTENING/ INTUITIVE RESPONSE

AN OVERVIEW

Step 1   Relax and come into the Interval. Awaken the Parent Who Listens and the Parent Who Leads within you. Come in touch with their nurturing energy.

Step 2   Begin to pay attention to your thoughts, feelings, and sensations as they rise into your awareness. Review all of them as though they were part of a parade.

Step 3   Focus your attention on your sensations. Describe them, to yourself or to someone else present, in as much detail as you can.

Step 4   Notice your sensations and the feelings and thoughts that go along with them. Based on what you are noticing about these thoughts, feelings, and sensations, try to determine if one or more of your Maturing Aspects is present, and if so, which one(s)?

   —Breathe in, breathe out, rest. Listen in to your body and see if you experience a shift in sensation. At this moment you are listening for the voice of your Intuitive Self.

Step 5   Attend to the Maturing Aspects who are present. If your Emerald Child and your Suffering Child are present, welcome them. Encourage them to reveal their thoughts, feelings, and beliefs. Listen carefully to what they have to say. If your Critical Detractor Child is present, first silence his negative self-talk, and then attend to him in the same loving way you would the Suffering Child and Emerald Child. Become familiar with any sensations that rise as you dialogue with your inner children. Express whatever emotions rise.

—Breathe in, breathe out, rest. Listen in to your body and see if you experience a shift in sensation. At this moment you are listening for the voice of your Intuitive Self.

Step 6   After you have expressed your emotions, tune in to your body once again. Notice the sensations that remain. Speak directly to your sensations and ask them, "What are you feeling? What do you want to tell me about the situation I am in right now?" In a very relaxed and quiet way, wait patiently for the answers to arise.

—Breathe in, breathe out, rest. Do not attempt to answer the questions, simply listen in to your body and see if you experience a shift in sensation. At this moment you are listening for the voice of your Intuitive Self.

When that voice speaks to you, it will give you some insight about your situation. Sit quietly with this insight for a moment. Notice any further shifts in sensation as you sit quietly with this new insight. Repeat the process until you feel it is complete.

Step 7   Focus once again on your sensations. Ask yourself, "What choices do I have? Do I have choices as to how to feel or think about this situation? If so, what are they? Do I have choices about the beliefs, or needs that will motivate my behavior? If so, what are they? What choices do I have in regard to my behavior? And finally, what choices do I have in regard to the outcome of this situation?"

—Breathe in, breathe out, rest. Do not attempt to answer the question, simply listen in to your body and see if you experience a shift in sensation. At this moment you are listening for the voice of your Intuitive Self.

Now focus your attention on the sensations that remain. Ask yourself, "What wants and needs to happen next? What is my next step?"

—*Breathe in, breathe out, rest. Do not attempt to answer the questions, simply listen in to your body and see if you experience a shift in sensation. At this moment you are listening for the voice of your Intuitive Self.*

Step 8   If you receive an answer as to what action is required, act and notice the effects of your actions on yourself, other people present, and the situation.

—*Breathe in, breathe out, rest. Listen in to your body and see if you experience a shift in sensation. At this moment you are listening for the voice of your Intuitive Self.*

Step 9   Ask yourself, "What have I learned from this experience?"

—*Breathe in, breathe out, rest. Do not attempt to answer the question, simply listen in to your body and see if you experience a shift in sensation. At this moment you are listening for the voice of your Intuitive Self.*

Step 10   Remind yourself that everything you have learned has been fully integrated into who you are and how you will experience your thoughts and feelings from now on.

Remind yourself that everything you have learned is available to you whenever you call upon it.

Take a deep, cleansing breath. Hold it for a moment, then exhale. Repeat this breath several times.

THE STEPS OF SILENT LISTENING/ INTUITIVE RESPONSE IN DETAIL

Step 1
Relax and come into the Interval. Awaken the Parent Who Listens and the Parent Who Leads within you. Come in touch with their nurturing energy.

To come into the Interval, take a slow, soft, deep breath and notice the coolness in your nostrils as you inhale. Hold the breath for a moment and notice the quiet, motionless space at the end of the inhalation. Now let the breath out and notice the feeling of warmth in your nostrils as you exhale. Notice the quiet, empty space at the end of your exhalation. Soften into this space, allowing it to lengthen. Calmly wait for the next impulse to breathe. Watch the breath enter, and rest in the space between breaths. As you do, begin to listen into the silence between the breaths. Bring your attention to your eyes and become aware of what they are seeing. Feel yourself centered within your body, and then within the space that surrounds you.

Now, as you continue to breathe in and out, reach out to the Nurturing Parents within you. Bring the Parent Who Listens and the Parent Who Leads into the silence within you. Feel their presence awaken there, and come in touch with their nurturing energy.

Step 2
Begin to pay attention to your thoughts, feelings, and sensations as they rise into your awareness. Review all of them as though they were part of a parade.

Imagine that you are standing on the sidelines watching a parade go by. This parade is made up of your thoughts, feelings, and sensations. As you watch, you let each feeling, sensation, and thought pass by. Then you notice the next thought, the next feeling, the next sensation, and so on. Remember, if you pay too much attention to a particular piece of the parade as it passes, you will hold up the progress of the parade. Just watch and acknowledge each feeling, sensation, and thought as it passes. If you go off with a particular thought, sensation, or feeling, you will no longer be watching and your experience will be limited to the particular piece that has taken you away. If that should happen, remind yourself to return your attention to the breath and the space at the end of the exhalation, and begin observing the parade once again. Begin to notice any connections between your thoughts, feelings, and sensations.

—*Breathe in, breathe out, rest. Listen in to your body and see if you experience a shift in sensation. At this moment you are listening for the voice of your Intuitive Self.*

Step 3
Focus your attention on your sensations. Describe them, to yourself or to someone else present, in as much detail as you can.

What sensations do you notice? What do they feel like? Where do you feel them? You can experience many different kinds of sensations in any part of your body—heat, cold, queasiness, tightness, fluttering, emptiness, heaviness, tingling, and many more. As you examine your sensations, allow yourself just a little more time than feels comfortable for you to do this. Some of the sensations you notice will be accompanied by images. You may visualize an object taking shape somewhere within your body. These objects may transform into another image or move to another part of your body.

Describe whatever sensations or images you are having to yourself or to another person present. In your descriptions, try to include information about the location, texture, density, size, intensity, temperature, color, and sound of these sensations. Be open to whatever you notice, and remember that your feelings and sensations will reveal themselves to you more readily if you look and listen through the eyes and heart of your Nurturing Parents.

—*Breathe in, breathe out, rest. Listen in to your body and see if you experience a shift in sensation. At this moment you are listening for the voice of your Intuitive Self.*

Step 4
Notice your sensations and the feelings and thoughts that go along with them. Based on what you are noticing about these thoughts, feelings, and sensations, try to determine if one or more of your Maturing Aspects is present, and, if so, which ones?

Paying attention to your sensations and the thoughts and feelings that accompany them can help you to identify which of the three Maturing Aspects are present. If your Emerald Child is present, you will experience the feelings that she carries—enthusiasm, playfulness, curiosity, optimism, and joyful anticipation.

If your Suffering Child is present, you will notice intense feelings such as shame, fearfulness, unworthiness, helplessness, and hopelessness.

If your Suffering Child is present, then your Critical Detractor Child is probably present, too. When she is around, your thoughts and attitudes will be offensive, critical, or aggressive,

If you cannot identify the presence of any of your Maturing Aspects, skip the next step and move on to Step 6.

—Breathe in, breathe out, rest. Listen in to your body and see if you experience a shift in sensation. At this moment you are listening for the voice of your Intuitive Self.

Step 5
Attend to the Maturing Aspects who are present. If your Emerald Child and your Suffering Child are present, welcome them. Encourage them to reveal their thoughts, feelings, and beliefs. Listen carefully to what they have to say. If your Critical Detractor Child is present, first silence her negative self-talk, and then attend to her in the same loving way you would the Suffering Child and Emerald Child. Become familiar with any sensations that rise as you dialogue with your inner children. Express whatever emotions rise.

If your Emerald Child, is present, ask her to come closer. If your Suffering Child is present, invite her to sit next to you. Make them feel safe and welcome. If your Critical Detractor Child is present, you will want to do several things. First, silence her negative messages. Then invite the Parent Who Listens to help you replace those negative messages with more positive ones. Finally, with the help of the listening parent, attend to your Critical Detractor Child in the same way that you would your Suffering Child. Ask these three children what they have to tell you, what they know. While you are doing this, your Critical Detractor Child may try again to send out her hurtful remarks. Simply silence her once more and then attend to her in a nurturing way.

As you attend to each of the three Maturing Aspects, notice the sensations that rise. Allow yourself to express any emotions triggered by these sensations. You may feel like laughing, jumping up and down, crying, screaming, or hitting pillows.

—*Breathe in, breathe out, rest. Listen in to your body and see if you experience a shift in sensation. At this moment you are listening for the voice of your Intuitive Self.*

Step 6

After you have expressed your emotions, tune in to your body once again. Notice the sensations that remain. Speak directly to your sensations and ask them, "What are you feeling? What do you want to tell me about the situation I am in right now?" In a very relaxed and quiet way, wait patiently for the answers to arise.

When that voice speaks to you, it will give you some insight about your situation. Sit quietly with this insight for a moment. Notice any further shifts in sensation as you sit quietly with this new insight. Repeat the process until you feel it is complete.

The answers to these two questions will come in the form of words or images and will be accompanied by a shift in your body sensations. This shift confirms the validity of your observations. This experience will give you an insight—an "aha!"—about yourself and your situation. The shift in sensation is an essential part of your insight experience. Answers to either of these questions that are not accompanied by this shift in sensation are incomplete or incorrect. Those answers will feel like a "minding," a purely mental event, rather than a complete body/mind response. You may have several of these mindings before an answer that is accompanied by a shift in sensation comes. Just continue to breathe in and out slowly and listen patiently for the insight answer. If the shift and the insight still do not come, stop at this point and come back to SL/IR later on. If the shift and the insight do come, go on to the next step.

—Breathe in, breathe out, rest. Do not attempt to answer the questions, simply listen in to your body and see if you experience a shift in sensation. At this moment you are listening for the voice of your Intuitive Self.

Step 7

Focus once again on your sensations. Ask yourself, "What choices do I have? Do I have choices as to how to feel or think about this situation? If so, what are they? Do I have choices about the beliefs, or needs that will motivate my behavior? If so, what are they? What choices do I have in regard to my behavior? And finally, what choices do I have in regard to the outcome of this situation?"

When you ask these questions, you are seeking the guidance of you Intuitive Self. Each time you ask a particular question, a number of choices may rise into your mind. Rest quietly with each choice. Notice any shifts in sensation as you do this. Become familiar with each shift in sensation. The sensations will help you distinguish between the voices of your Maturing Aspects and the voice of your Intuitive Self. When you reach the choice of your Intuitive Self, you will feel a shift that brings a sense of relief, a release of any tension you have been carrying as a result of the issue you are examining. This clear shift of sensation and the freedom you feel after it confirms the correctness of that choice.

—Breathe in, breathe out, rest. Do not attempt to answer the question, simply listen in to your body and see if you experience a shift in sensation. At this moment you are listening for the voice of your Intuitive Self.

Now focus your attention on the sensations that remain. Ask yourself, "What wants and needs to happen next? What is my next step?" When you ask these questions, you are aligning yourself with the

energy of the Parent Who Leads and asking your Intuitive Self to come through and advise you about each aspect of your situation. You are seeking guidance as to the thoughts and feelings to maintain, the beliefs and attitudes to cultivate, and the behaviors to exhibit. By asking your Intuitive Self for guidance, you are seeking a resolution to your situation that will be both creative and harmonious. You are insuring, to the best of your ability, that your action furthers the highest interests of everyone concerned–you are looking to achieve a win-win situation.

When answers rise and are accompanied by a clear shift in sensation, a shift that gives you a feeling of resolve, move on to the next step. If you do not experience the shift, it may be because your Maturing Aspects need more attention before you can move into the realm of action. Invite the Parent Who Listens to help you give more time and attention to your inner children. Another shift in sensation will tell you that the feelings your inner children are carrying right now have been resolved. Then you will feel ready to go on to the next step.

If you do not experience a shift, you can choose not to act at all or you can put SL/IR aside for now and come back to it later on. The absence of the shift does not mean that you have done anything wrong or that the process has not been helpful. It simply may not be time to act.

—*Breathe in, breathe out, rest. Do not attempt to answer the questions, simply listen in to your body and see if you experience a shift in sensation. At this moment you are listening for the voice of your Intuitive Self.*

Step 8

If you receive an answer as to what action is required, act and notice the effects of your actions on yourself, other people present, and the situation.

While you are taking the action you chose, try to stay aware of your thoughts, feelings, and sensations and notice any shifts in those three phenomena. You can do this if you stay in the Interval while you are acting. By breathing in and out slowly and resting in the space that occurs at the end of inhalation and at the end of exhalation, you will be able to come into the Interval and act from that space. You will notice that actions which emerge from the Interval have a very different quality from actions that do not. When you act from the Interval space, you feel very relaxed, perceptive, and confident. You will also notice that the energy associated with those qualities permeates your situation and has an observable influence on other people present.

After you take some action, pretend once again that you are on the sidelines of a parade. Observe the effects of your actions on yourself, others present, and the situation itself as though they were part of that parade.

—Breathe in, breathe out, rest. Listen in to your body and see if you experience a shift in sensation. At this moment you are listening for the voice of your Intuitive Self.

Step 9
Ask yourself, "What have I learned from this experience?"

What have I learned about my Suffering Child? My Critical Detractor Child? My Emerald Child? My Nurturing Parents? What have I learned about my resistance to change? Was I able to identify a specific event from my past that deserves a closer look? What new information do I have about myself and others who were present in this situation or who are somehow connected to it? Did I learn something that will allow me to behave differently if a situation like this one comes up again? What have I learned about my relationship with the Universe? Am I a more responsible person as a result of this experience? Am I a more compassionate person as a result of this experience? Has my sense of oneness with God / All That Is increased? Did I learn anything about myself or my life that I want to share with someone close to me? What have I learned about practicing the technique of Silent Listening / Intuitive Response?

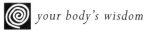

—Breathe in, breathe out, rest. Do not attempt to answer the question, simply listen in to your body and see if you experience a shift in sensation. At this moment you are listening for the voice of your Intuitive Self.

Step 10

Remind yourself that everything you have learned has been integrated into your thoughts, feelings, and sensations.

Remind yourself that this information is available to you whenever you call upon it.

Take a deep, cleansing breath. Hold it for a moment, then exhale. Repeat this breath several times.

SILENT LISTENING/ INTUITIVE RESPONSE IN ACTION

It is 10 p.m. For the past hour Sonia has been going into her cupboards and refrigerator every fifteen minutes, looking for something to eat. But after snacking on cookies, potato chips, cheese, and some chicken, she still feels hungry. As she starts to make her way into the kitchen one more time, she pauses and wonders if what she has been experiencing and responding to with food is really hunger. Her stomach is full, yet the sensations that she thought were hunger continue.

In recent years Sonia has discovered that "unconscious eating" usually is a sign that something is bothering her. Tonight, however, she does not have a clue as to what that might be. She decides to take some time out and use the technique of Silent Listening/ Intuitive Response to find out what is going on.

She walks into the living room and settles into her favorite chair. Sinking down into it, she closes her eyes and begins to breathe softly and deeply. She rests in the spaces at the end of each breath, allowing the spaces to lengthen. After a few moments Sonia feels her muscles start to relax all through her body. For the first time all day, she feels as though she is standing perfectly still, her body and mind at rest.

From this quiet and restful place, she creates a mental picture of her Nurturing Parents. She sees them entering the room, moving toward her, and sitting down next to her. She feels their presence strongly. Their essence, their qualities, begin to affect the emotional atmosphere that surrounds her, and that puts her even more at ease.

Taking another deep breath, Sonia begins to notice her thoughts, her feelings, and the sensations in her body: I need to have the car inspected before the end of the week…those library books on the hall table are overdue…have to buy cat food the next time I go to the store…how come there's never enough time to do all the things I want to do?…I wish I'd gone swimming after work today…I feel anxious and stressed out…it's hard for me to sit still right now, even though it feels good…I want to get up and pace around the room…there is a churning, gripping sensation in my belly…I have a tightness in my throat and chest…my head aches where my jawbone comes up under my ears…my shoulders and upper arms feel heavy.

Suddenly she remembers that she has a meeting with her boss tomorrow. Just as suddenly it feels as though someone has turned up the volume on the sensations she is experiencing. Everything that she was noticing in her stomach, her throat, her jaw, and her arms has become more intense. This shift in sensation confirms for Sonia that the upcoming meeting is indeed the issue that is disturbing her.

"I guess I'm anxious about this meeting," she self-talks. "Maybe that's why I've been eating so much." She feels a subtle shift within the sensations she is experiencing. This shift confirms her deductions.

Someone at work has been stealing supplies from the computer room. Since Sonia's job includes keeping an inventory of supplies, her boss has invited her to meet with him so they can discuss the thefts and make some plans about how to deal with them.

Sonia begins to explore her body sensations in more detail. She sends her breath into the area around her stomach. When she does this, she becomes aware of a small, hard ball in her belly, about the size of a baseball, pushing against her navel. Moving up from this ball is an area about two inches wide that is vibrating. This vibration travels from her navel all the way up into her throat where she can feel another hard ball about the size of a golf ball. She is finding it hard to swallow and her breathing has become more shallow. The sensations of gripping and churning in her belly make her want to go back to the kitchen for something else to eat. But she controls that urge and instead takes a deep breath, holds it for a moment, then releases it slowly. She reminds herself that her Nurturing Parents are with her. She returns to experiencing her sensations.

"These feelings and sensations are so familiar to me," she self-talks. "Is there something about this evening or the way I am feeling right now that reminds me of some event from the past?" At first nothing comes to her. Her Parent Who Listens reminds her to be patient. She takes a deep breath, quiets herself again, and listens. Then suddenly she sees a classroom and a little girl being reprimanded by her teacher. In a flash of recognition, Sonia realizes that the little girl is her. The teacher is accusing Sonia of having stolen another student's lunch. Little Sonia looks frightened and embarrassed as she tries desperately to convince the teacher of her innocence, but the teacher does not believe her. She continues to yell at Sonia and insist that she is the thief, despite the fact that she cannot find the missing lunch among Sonia's belongings or inside her desk.

The scenario continues to unfold, as though Sonia were watching a movie. She sees herself going home from school later that day with a note from her teacher. Her parents become very upset when they read it. Sonia insists to them that she did not steal anything, but they are not concerned with Sonia's guilt or innocence or her need to be comforted. Instead, they are worried about their own image.

"How could you do this to us?" her mother asks. "Your teacher must think that we're awful parents to have raised a child who would steal from one of her own classmates!"

To relieve their rage at her for placing them in such an embarrassing position, Sonia's parents punish her by canceling a birthday slumber party she had been planning for months. They also insist that she go to the teacher and apologize for stealing the lunch.

Sonia screams at them, "It's not fair! I didn't do it! I don't know why, but the teacher just doesn't like me, that's why she's blaming me! I hate school!" She begins to cry, but neither of her parents reaches out to comfort her.

Remembering all of this, Sonia wants to jump up from her chair, go into the kitchen, get a bowl of ice cream, and be done with these uncomfortable recollections. But instead, she takes a deep breath and asks herself, "What would the Parent Who Listens do in this situation?" She quiets herself once again, and patiently waits, listening for her Nurturing Parent's response. Soon the Nurturing Parent speaks: "What are you feeling? Describe the memories you are having." She feels as though she is being held, and hears, "Tell me all about what happened. I am interested in the whole story. What happened that day? What was it like for you?"

Sonia recalls and then describes out loud how her father yelled at her. "You'd better stop crying," he said, "or I'll give you something to cry about." Sonia screamed back at him, "I hate you!" He slapped her face, grabbed her arm, dragged her into her room, and locked the door. The images of this experience begin to fade and as they do, Sonia bursts into tears.

It is obvious to Sonia that the Suffering Child within her still carries many intense feelings related to that day: the pain of being attacked by her teacher; of being humiliated in front of her classmates; of not being believed by her teacher or her parents; rage over being punished by her parents and forced to admit to something she did not do; intense fear that her father would hit her or keep her locked in her room forever. Sonia also recognizes the voice of her Critical Detractor Child, telling her that the whole incident was her fault. "If the teacher doesn't like you it must be your fault. You deserve to be mistreated this way. You should be ashamed for what happened and for yelling at your father the way you did," she says.

"I felt so alone," Sonia says out loud to herself. She takes another deep breath and reminds herself that she is not alone now. Her

Nurturing Parents have been right here with her as she revisited this painful event from her past and the feelings associated with it. She has been aware of their loving, supportive energy. She feels completely surrounded by it, embraced by it and by them. She feels safe to continue examining her feelings and the body sensations that accompany them.

She notices that the hard ball in her belly is still there, but the edges of the ball are not so well-defined now. The ball is pressing down toward her bowels instead of up toward her belly. Her entire chest is filling up with a humming sensation. The hard ball that she felt in her throat earlier is still there, too. When she swallows, she can feel it there. In fact, she has to swallow harder to get around it. The ache in her jawbone and the churning and gripping in her belly are still there, too, but they are not as strong as they were before.

Focusing on the sensations, she asks, "What are these sensations trying to tell me?" Suddenly the sensations change again. The hard ball in her throat opens up and out of it comes a hand that reaches up to cover her chin and mouth. Sonia finds this image very interesting and thinks to herself, "I have always been reluctant to speak up for myself. I'm afraid that people won't really listen or that I'll be punished for saying what I believe."

Sonia speaks directly to the sensations and asks them, "Am I afraid that my boss somehow holds me responsible for the thefts at work? Is this why I am feeling anxious about tomorrow's meeting?"

Once again she silences herself and listens. The sensations shift once more in answer to her question, letting her know that the insight she just had is correct. Now it is much easier to swallow, and the image of the hand over her mouth has faded away. Suddenly she starts to cry and then to sob. In her mind's eye, Sonia moves closer to the Parent Who Listens and settles into her gentle embrace. The grownup Sonia becomes the little girl Sonia who was mistreated that day. The listening parent holds her sweetly and encourages her to speak and cry her tears, reminding her that she did nothing wrong, that she has nothing to be ashamed of. The Parent Who Listens insists that it was not Sonia who was wrong but her parents—for not believing their daughter, for not taking the time to listen patiently and lovingly to her side of the story. The listening parent reminds Sonia that the little girl she was then deserved to be loved and trusted, and that the woman she is now also deserves that.

The Parent Who Listens encourages Sonia to cry for as long as she needs to. When her tears finally come to an end, Sonia feels anger rising. If her parents were in the room right now, she would tell them, "I am not a liar or a thief. You should have known that. You were supposed to protect me and support me. Instead you abandoned me when I needed you most and shamed me for something I didn't even do! And for the last twenty years I have been afraid to stick up for myself. I've been afraid people won't believe me when I tell them something. I've believed that people will attack me and wrongly accuse me of something, and that my friends won't back me up if someone does attack me."

The listening parent acknowledges Sonia's anger and her indignation by responding, "Yes, they should have been there for you. It is not right that they were not. You should not have been treated in that way."

Now Sonia can breathe more easily. She gives herself a few moments to take in what she has learned about herself and this experience from her past. Then she brings her attention once more to the sensations in her body. She notices that it is no longer difficult to swallow, that the hard balls in her throat and belly have disappeared. Her stomach has calmed down; there is no more churning and gripping there. And there is a warm feeling spreading all through her chest.

Now Sonia hears the voice of her Parent Who Leads. "What is your next step?" s/he says. "What do you need to do to take care of yourself? What are your choices in that area?"

Once again she silences herself and listens. A message rises, advising her to think about tomorrow's meeting with her boss. She realizes that she will feel more relaxed and confident if she makes a plan about how she wants to participate in the meeting. Another message rises, reminding Sonia that her boss is a reasonable person, that her fear about the meeting with him was exaggerated because of the conclusions her little girl self had come to over this "theft" experience in her past. There is very little possibility that he will behave toward her as her parents did around the incident at school. And besides, now that she has recalled that experience and worked through some of her feelings and beliefs about it, she will not be dragging those feelings and beliefs into the meeting with her. She can deal with this situation in a constructive, rather than destructive, manner.

She remembers that in the years since the experience at school there have been many occasions in which she was able to speak out despite her fears of not being heard or appreciated. "I am a survivor and a powerful woman," she thinks to herself.

Now Sonia feels more confident about her ability to participate in tomorrow's meeting. She can see herself sitting down with her boss, listening carefully to the discussion, and contributing to it in a relaxed and articulate way. She will visualize her Nurturing Parents sitting there with her, appreciating her intelligence, her communication skills, her ability to be at ease in a group. If she begins to feel uncomfortable at any time, she will invite them to help her get through that.

"What have I learned from this experience?" Sonia asks herself. "How can I use what I have learned to move into my highest Self?"

Sonia becomes very quiet inside and patiently waits for the answers to rise. She hears her integrating/emerging adult Self say, "I am no longer a small child, filled with despair because my parents love their self-image more than they love me. I am no longer alone. I now have Nurturing Parents within me who know me, love me, value me, guide me, and protect me. I am no longer a small child who accepts her parents negative view of herself. I now know that I'm a good person, worthy of love and trust. I now know about my fear of being wrongly accused, and I can take care of myself when it rises. Having learned all of this about myself, I feel more secure, generous, compassionate, and loving toward others. I will be very careful during tomorrow's meeting, and make sure no one is falsely accused."

Sonia thanks both of her Nurturing Parents for helping her tonight. Then she takes several deep, cleansing breaths, gets up from her chair, and prepares to go to bed.

Silent Listening/Intuitive Response is an excellent tool for coming to know yourself and for coming into your most powerful and creative Self. This technique can help you to explore your past. It shows you how to participate in the present with greater awareness. And by helping you to clarify your feelings, beliefs, and goals, SL/IR brings you closer to the future you envision.

In the realm of creative action, Silent Listening/Intuitive Response teaches you how to take the time to come in touch with your Intuitive Self. By increasing your ability to hear the voice of your Intuitive Self, SL/IR also helps you to discover the choices that resonate with your integrating/emerging adult Self. The success that you experience each time you act on the voice of your Intuitive Self increases your confidence in your ability to know and do what is in your highest interest. You become more assertive so that when you do act, your actions are powerful and persuasive.

You can be sure that your Intuitive Self and your awareness of that voice will grow stronger each time you practice Silent Listening/ Intuitive Response. But this process will develop slowly. You can support it by being very patient with yourself. When I first began to practice SL/IR, I noticed that days might pass before I came to some clarity about the feelings I was exploring through this technique. But as I became more experienced with the process, it took less time for me to have an insight about what had stimulated my feelings. I was becoming more tuned in to my intuitive voice.

Eventually the space between recognizing a feeling and having an insight that guided me toward a particular action diminished. I call this phenomenon "closing the gap." As you practice Silent Listening/Intuitive Response, you too will notice your "gap time" decreasing. This diminishing space between a feeling rising and your ability to take an appropriate action with regard to that feeling is a sign that your Intuitive Self is becoming stronger.

221

Over time I discovered that there were three factors which influenced the speed with which I could identify my feelings, understand why they had risen in a certain situation, and choose the best response to that situation. These factors were the severity of the original wound I was exploring, how young I was when the trauma occurred, and the strength of the beliefs that had been created as a result of that trauma. Naturally these factors also influenced the degree to which my Suffering Child and my Critical Detractor Child would be evoked in that situation.

When you are able to listen silently to the voices and the underlying needs of your Suffering Child and your Critical Detractor Child and respond intuitively to your circumstances, you create the environment that lets your Emerald Child feel free to come out. You then have access to the positive qualities which she carries—playfulness, enthusiasm, joyfulness, and spontaneity. As all three of your Maturing Aspects receive the attention they need, your adult Self emerges. This Self has acknowledged, worked through, and recovered from the wounds of his or her past and integrated the gifts and lessons within those experiences. This Self is ready to claim all of the treasures of adulthood and contribute to the Universe that which is uniquely his or hers to give.

In Chapter Ten, the final chapter, **You Are the Universe Creating Itself,** we look at the ways in which each of us co-create the world in which we live. By observing our thoughts, our feelings, and our sensations, we learn how to truly take charge of our impulses to react to the situations we find ourselves in. We are able to appreciate, learn from, and work with whatever happens in our day-to-day lives. In that way we make our unique contribution to the world, and we become responsible conscious co-creators of the Universe.

YOU ARE THE UNIVERSE CREATING ITSELF

Breathe deeply and gently.
Let your body soften.
See yourself within the space that surrounds you.
Feel yourself within the space that surrounds you.
Who is doing the seeing? Who is doing the feeling?

ach of us is continually creating, recreating, and co-creating the Universe. Atoms in the atomic body of God / All that Is, we are energetic beings endowed with free will, radiating our "beingness" into the Universe, changing it as we change energetically from instant to instant. Regardless of the presence or absence of conscious intention, who we are, what we think, feel, sense, believe, and do, has an undeniable effect upon the entire Universe in which we all exist. Our health, our joyousness, our grief, our rage, and our behavior stream forth from us, in the form of energy waves, affecting every other atom in this limitless body.

Stop for just a moment. Take a slow, soft, deep, breath. Begin to notice your thoughts as they pass. Notice the sensations that move through your throat, chest, and belly. Don't fall into self-talk; remain the observer and notice how nothing stays the same from one instant to the next. As these phenomena change, your internal energetic expression, and your biochemical makeup change with them. Because you are a particle within the body of God / All That Is, the shifts and changes that occur within you affect the whole of which you are a part.

And of course the reverse is also true, each shift and change that occurs within the whole has its affect upon you.

Using an individual cell within our body as a microcosmic metaphor for our relationship with the Universe, we can see that any energetic or chemical change in the structure of a single cell existing within us affects a change within our entire organism. As one cell changes, a wave of change begins. All the cells surrounding it must readjust themselves in some way, creating a new relationship to this changing cell. Using an individual human Self within the Universe as a macrocosmic metaphor, we can see that any change occurring within that Self, regardless of its nature, must also effect a change within the entire body of the Universe. Our very existence, our very breath, has a profound and lasting effect upon the "universe," upon God/All That Is.

Each of us, along with everything else in existence comprise the "universe." We are one infinite, unfathomable organism, creating and re-creating itself. Nothing is separate or isolated. We are one with planets and silence, black holes and orchids, comets and fleas, parallel realities and glaciers, sentience and earthquakes, moons and emotions, and the ability to create something out of nothing. We are an integral component of creation expressing itself, from swirling galaxies to the smallest particle in existence, constantly moving, affecting, and transforming the universe, God/All That Is.

When you experience yourself as one with all of creation, you realize that whatever is happening in any part of the organism is happening in you. The result of this evolutionary leap in consciousness is a new sense of responsibility to and for the universe. You honor this responsibility by knowing who you are and how you are affecting any part of the universe from instant to instant. As your awareness of yourself deepens, you are able to intuit your effect on the universe, and choose behaviors that reflect this response-ability.

What has prevented us from experiencing our oneness with all of creation? The degree to which we feel isolated and fragmented within ourselves determines the degree to which we feel at one with all that exists in the universe. The more we are able to lovingly embrace all of who we are, the more connected we feel to all that exists. Throughout *Your Body's Wisdom*, you have been learning how to continually integrate all aspects of yourself into a unified whole. Once you master this process of integration, your feelings of isolation and fragmentation evaporate, and your inter-connectedness with God/All That Is becomes apparent; you find yourself ready to embrace your role as co-creator of the Universe.

If you stop and take a slow, deep, breath…if you let your body soften…if you look inward and feel yourself grounded within your body…if you look out through your eyes and see yourself centered within the space that surrounds you…if you quiet the mind and become very still and listen, then you will hear the voice of your Intuitive Self. You will hear the voice of God/All That Is reaching out to you, through you, inviting you to see yourself in all your fullness, in all your power. You will hear that voice calling you to be completely present to yourself and to the moment. You will hear that voice calling you to find within each moment an opportunity to shape the situation you find yourself in. As you shape each moment, you shape your life. You affect the lives of those you interact with, and you shape the world in which you live.

Does this sound too grand, too impossible a role for you to take up? It is not, I assure you. It is a role which each of you already has. Your happy challenge is to accept the role and use it with conscious intention for the common good. I believe that we are here to contribute to the Universe that which is uniquely ours to give by serving one another in some way. One way we can make those contributions is in the context of our jobs, as artist, doctor, cab driver, nurse, secretary, waiter, chef, parent, writer, farmer, teacher, film maker…the list is endless. Perhaps the most important contribution you make, however, is not what you accomplish in your chosen field, but the effect that you have on the thoughts, feelings, and behaviors of others.

While you are being a cabby, a chef, a parent, or a waiter, do you create an atmosphere that enhances and supports awareness and growth? Are your motives, intentions, and behaviors reflective of the Nurturing Parents or the Critical Detractor Child? Do you put people at ease or make them feel anxious? Do people walk away from an interaction with you feeling valued and empowered or unappreciated and diminished? Noticing how you affect your world is the first step in becoming a conscious co-creator.

Discovering who you are and noticing what you contribute to your world is an ongoing process that always begins with being quietly grounded within yourself. When you are completely conscious of yourself, looking through your own eyes, you can quietly, patiently experience everything that is taking place inside you. As you rest there, you can also look outward and notice what is happening around you. You can take in your surroundings—the images, tones, sounds, and impressions that are constantly shifting and changing. You can observe other people and your interactions with them while getting a sense of the emotional energy generated by the entire gestalt. When you are grounded within yourself and centered within your universe, you are completely present to everything that is happening inside of you and all around you.

Through the act of remaining grounded within yourself as all of these things are taking place, you create a moment that is whole and holy. A human being in the process of evolution, you are also the force at the center of that evolution, orchestrating your growth even as you participate in it. Each time you acquire some new piece of information, you integrate that information into what you already know and you essentially recreate yourself.

At each moment you are more aware of yourself and your surroundings than you were in the previous moment. And in the next moment you are even more aware, even more fully formed. You come to appreciate all of your selves, each you that emerges from moment to moment. You learn from each of those selves and you learn how to work with each of them as they emerge in the context of your day to day life. And all along, you are reintegrating these selves and emerging into your adult Self.

The integrating, emerging adult Self acts out of a place that is both profoundly still and exquisitely energized. He is constantly drawn to an understanding of Self that is both more complex and yet simpler, more elusive and yet more available to him. Knowing that he is being guided in every moment by forces whose every intention toward him is good, kind, and life-giving, he feels one with his Universe. He feels supported in his efforts to explore his Self, the meaning of his existence, and his relationship to God/All That Is.

The concept of the integrating, emerging adult is really quite simple, although the process, at times appears very complex. Each of us is incessantly in the process of integrating and emerging. We are continually integrating and reorganizing every aspect of ourselves as we are revealed to ourselves. Aware of the ways in which we are different from others, and aware of the ways in which we are different from the Self we once were, we are constantly becoming, constantly emerging.

The process of integrating and emerging into this self-aware being is unique for each of us, of course. And it takes place regardless of whether we reflect on it or try to move it along through such activities as therapy, reading, or meditation. Someone who cannot read or does not meditate or lives in a culture where the notion of therapy does not even exist, is just as involved in the process of integrating and emerging into their adult Self as the person who has access to books, meditation, or therapy, and who actively pursues them. The point is that the process of evolution is one in which all of us are engaged, all the time, in a way that is consistent with our culture, our resources, and our inclinations. Via different routes, we all come to the same place—the awakened Self.

Within the process of emerging into adulthood, you consistently move toward greater awareness and acceptance of Self. With awareness and acceptance there is no need to deny any feature of who you are, or who you have been in the past. There is no need to deny any possibility in terms of who you might become. Everything that you were, are, and can be contributes to your life and to the lives of the people around you. Everything that you were, are, and can be is contained within the awareness of your emerging adult Self and held there in the most loving way.

In *Your Body's Wisdom* I have presented one way of looking at the parts that make up this whole which we call Self. Those parts are the interior beings you have come to know as the aspects of Self—the Emerald Child, the Suffering Child, the Critical Detractor Child, the Parent Who Listens, the Parent Who Leads, and the Intuitive Self. By getting to know each of these six aspects as they exist within you, you come to know your emerging adult Self. By looking for these six aspects in different situations, you get to know your Self even better. You discover the thoughts and feelings that are motivating your behavior. You discover that in avery profound way you are a product of those thoughts and feelings. You also discover that you can shape your experience of those thoughts and feelings.

By observing your thoughts, feelings, sensations, impulses to behave, and actual behaviors, you can identify which of your aspects of Self are present. When you do this—with the help of tools such as conscious breathing, relaxation, meditation, the Interval, and Silent Listening/Intuitive Response—you are revealed to yourself. In a sense you meet yourself and create a new Self; a wiser, more informed and aware Self, a Self who has a deeper understanding of where you have come from and how that has helped to make you who you are right now.

Each time you walk through this process, you re-integrate the parts that make up the whole. Then you see yourself in a new light and you are drawn to behave in new ways. You hold a clear intention about treating yourself and others with compassion and understanding. You become more and more drawn to the belief that you are co-creating the Universe. You become more and more drawn to the behaviors that help you to shape your world in ways that support the healing of all beings. You have a growing sense that your actions are not just for shaping your own life but for contributing to the larger sphere of all life, all energies.

The more you practice this process of integration—and it does take practice—the more you realize that emerging into your adult Self involves a very particular rearrangement of your inner aspects. The term "integration" has a slightly different meaning with respect to each of the six aspects of Self:

1. To integrate the **Nurturing Parents** is to consistently, over time, strengthen their presence and qualities within you. To integrate the **Parent Who Listens** is to lovingly embrace your maturing aspects whenever they appear, regardless of how they present themselves

2. To integrate the **Parent Who Leads** is to remember to ask the questions: "What can I learn from this experience?" and "what needs and wants to happen next?" Each time you call upon them, your success will depend upon the consciousness and expertise their presence and development permit. Fortunately their presence becomes stronger and their skills more refined each time you call upon them to help you parent your Maturing Aspects. The more you call upon them, the greater their influence grows. As they become more firmly established within you, you are able to relate to and interact with the Maturing Aspects in increasingly positive ways.

3. To integrate the **Emerald Child** is to revive his many fine qualities within you while also providing the element of supervision that he requires. His naiveté makes him unsuitable as a primary moving force in your life—that role belongs to your emerging adult Self—but you certainly want to incorporate his essence into your sense of Self.

4. To integrate the **Suffering Child** is to identify events and issues from your past that continue to have a limiting effect on you. By integrating your Suffering Child, you actually facilitate a grieving process in relation to each unresolved hurt stored by him. Your grieving allows your Suffering Child to release his burden of stored feelings and memories. Having unburdened himself, you can now bring closure to these painful events from your past.

5. To integrate the **Critical Detractor Child** is to reparent him by exchanging his unsupportive and pessimistic language for a more supportive and positive one. By facilitating this transformation, you take away his power to make you feel unworthy, unlovable, or incompetent. This aspect of Self must be transformed if you are to come into your fullest, most realized, and most powerful Self.

6. To integrate the **Intuitive Self** is to discover that quiet place centered deep within you where you communicate with God/All That Is. By remembering to continually return to this still, empty place with your questions and your need for guidance and direction, you open a line

of communication between your emerging adult Self and your Intuitive Self. When you learn to quiet your mind and patiently listen into the silence that surrounds the voice of your Intuitive Self, you hear that voice speaking to you. By acting on the guidance you receive, you complete the circuit.

Within this new arrangement, the Suffering Child and the Critical Detractor Child become less demanding of your time and energy because they are being healed. As these two heal and transform, they move into the background and your Nurturing Parents, your Emerald Child, and your Intuitive Self come to the fore.

Of course moving into the background does not mean that your Suffering Child and your Critical Detractor Child disappear from your life. They still come out in certain situations. But over time you will find that the way you experience and deal with these two aspects changes. For one thing, their appearances become less frequent and less intense. When they do appear, you are less likely to become engulfed by the thoughts and feelings they carry. And if you do become lost in their energies at certain times, you will not be lost for long. You will find that you can get through the feelings and thoughts which these two bring to a situation much more quickly than you once could.

After all, you have been practicing dealing with each of these Maturing Aspects. You know how to talk to them and to process what they bring before you. You have watched yourself deal with them and respond gracefully despite their presence. You have noticed that the desired behavior you once had to call up with effort now occurs more easily and naturally. You have also noticed that when you make an error in judgment and behave unwisely, you learn from your mistake and discover a way to correct it. In all of these ways, your confidence in your ability to care for yourself and create the life you want has been growing stronger.

As you integrate your six aspects into your consciousness, you embrace a new identity and embark on a new set of experiences. In a sense you recover from the discouraging and stifling influence of the unresolved feelings and self-defeating beliefs your Maturing Aspects carried. Your sense of who you are changes. The way in which you can be present to all kinds of situations changes dramatically. You can direct more of your energy out into the world because the internal demands made by your Maturing Aspects have decreased. The nature of your interactions with others reflect their diminished presence also.

Your Partnership with Your Emerald Child

Your adult Self is a being in whom each of the six aspects has found his or her 'proper' place. Your Nurturing Parents and your Intuitive Self have moved onto center stage. Your Suffering Child and your Critical Detractor Child have moved into the background and are less prominent in your day to day life. Your Emerald Child now has room to come forward and begin to participate in a very active partnership with you.

When you integrate your Emerald Child into your emerging adult Self, his qualities become available to you. You experience his trust, curiosity, spontaneity, enthusiasm, confidence, and creativity. Your thoughts, your feelings, your behaviors, and the life you create reflect his energy. All of your senses come alive. This wondrous aspect of yourself contributes a point of view that enhances every facet of your life. Life is exciting, and you feel passionate about it. Life is more joyful, more meaningful, more valuable.

You and your Emerald Child work in very complementary ways. Leaping over fearful life chasms means nothing to your Emerald Child. When he is present, you experience the freedom that action requires, but first you grab hold of his hand and you decide whether you should leap or find some other way across. The rush of excitement you feel when your Emerald Child sees a mountain he wants to climb becomes part of your decision-making process as you consider climbing this particular mountain. Your Emerald Child is inclined to throw caution to the wind and do the wild dance all night. Your emerging adult Self might choose to do just that, while moderating it slightly to suit tomorrow's responsibilities.

Wanting two ice cream cones, one for each hand, is something your Emerald Child wouldn't think twice about, but your need to watch your weight or your health might cause you to restrain him a bit, while still enjoying a tasty treat. When your Emerald Child stirs your need to be caressed and petted, you invite affectionate people into your life so that need can be met. In touch with your Emerald Child, you may experience a strong desire to feel sand between your toes and spend hours collecting shells. You may realize that your life does not reflect a healthy balance between work and play, and off you go to the beach. When the heart of your Emerald Child awakens a craving in you to experience the majesty of God's presence, you may realize that absence and find a mountain top upon which to sit and watch the sun set.

In the beginning, before we are wounded and the world becomes a fearful place, the qualities of our Emerald Child are fully available to us. We are fearless, flexible, spontaneous, creative, curious, and above all, enthusiastic and confident. These qualities are the result of our innate understanding that we are one with all of creation and that we embody the very same qualities found in the Universe. We experience our oneness with God / All That Is. When your Emerald Child comes to the fore, you reclaim these qualities along with the confidence that comes with knowing you are connected to God / All That Is.

Your fearlessness, flexibility, spontaneity, creativity, curiosity, enthusiasm, and confidence allow you to respond in accordance with the needs of the moment. If the moment calls for fierceness, then fierceness is what rises. If the moment calls for tenderness, then tenderness is what you feel and bring. You may find that one moment requires courage, the next caution, and the next abandon, and you respond in all of these ways. You allow each moment to speak for itself, and you respond spontaneously with clarity, balance, humor, and kindness.

When your Emerald Child becomes available to you as an adult, so does the mind with which you first encountered life, a mind unwounded and unafraid. The mind of the Emerald Child is enchanted by life, and drawn into life by a sense of its endless possibilities. Devoid of judgments, it is spacious, flexible, and expansive. Because it does not judge what you are experiencing, you have no need to withdraw from that experience. You remain totally present and available, observing and learning from everything you see. Your Emerald Child uses words like fantastic, excellent, awesome, amazing, great. He says things like, "Go for it," "No problem," "I can do that," "I want that," "Hallelujah," and "I did it!"

In the mind of your Emerald Child, there is no distinction between what is real and what is imagined. When you see life through the eyes of your Emerald Child, you see the possibility of magic in everything. You see the truth and possibility in everything that is imagined. You see the miraculous in everything and everyone, including yourself. When he is operating in your life, you feel no restraint in reaching for whatever you set your heart on. The world belongs to you. The possibility of failure and the need to follow other people's rules do not deter you from your goal. The path you travel from inspiration to fruition is extremely direct. You see it, you reach for it, and you make it yours. But the means you employ to obtain what you want are always informed by the wisdom and experience of your Nurturing Parents and your Intuitive Self.

When your Emerald Child assumes a larger role in your life, you regain your free-spirited, inquisitive nature. Your behavior changes because you take up his acceptance of himself, his delight in himself, his innate sense of freedom, his love and trust in God/All That Is, his belief that he deserves to be happy. You lose your shyness and your need to put yourself down or diminish your light in any way. His innate trust in the goodness of life becomes part of your wisdom. When he is present in you, you do not withhold yourself out of fear that someone will judge you as imperfect. Your Emerald Child feels perfect just as he is. When he is available to you, you sing even though you may not have the best voice. You dance even though you may not be the best dancer. But above all, you enjoy yourself regardless of what you are doing, and regardless of whether or not you are the best at it. Your capacity to celebrate life knows no bounds.

YOUR PARTNERSHIP WITH THE UNIVERSE

It is through the process of integrating all your aspects of Self that you become an adult—not simply a grown-up person in the physical sense or by virtue of the scope of your responsibilities, but an "adult" in the truest and largest sense of the word. Who is this adult? How does he behave? What motivates his behavior? And what are his goals?

Years ago I met a man who moved through the world as I wanted to move. His name was Franklyn Smith. In terms of the theories we have explored, Franklyn was the quintessential integrating, emerging adult. He was continually exploring and healing the wounds of his past. His Suffering Child and his Critical Detractor Child were no longer a major influence in his life. He rarely reacted to a situation from the perspective of those two aspects. Franklyn's sense of himself, his view of the world, and his actions were primarily derived from the influence of his Nurturing Parents, his Emerald Child, and his Intuitive Self. Through study, meditation, and service, he constantly enhanced his relationship with God/All That Is.

Franklyn was a man who seemed guided at every step by a quiet, gentle, yet powerful voice inside himself, a man who thoroughly delighted in himself and in everyone he met. Though he died some years ago, my friend Franklyn has been sitting on my shoulder throughout the process of writing this book. Indeed, who he was and what I learned from him runs throughout this book. Franklyn inspired me to be bring the same impeccability I brought to my work into every moment of my life. He taught me to look with a curious eye on every situation I found myself in without bringing a personal agenda to cloud what I was experiencing. He encouraged me to be playful and to trust in the Universe. He reminded me that each of us has some extraordinary gift to contribute to the Universe, and he convinced me that I would discover mine.

Perhaps if I tell you more about him, you will be able to see him more clearly. As you read about him, see if you can come in touch with his energy. See if you can visualize how this man walked and talked. Can you awaken within yourself the qualities he expresses?

When I met Franklyn he was in his early thirties. Much of his behavior was prompted by a feeling of unconditional love and respect for everyone he met. In his early teens he began to study the esoteric practices of several religions. Meditation was a daily activity. Through his studies and meditations, Franklyn developed a deep appreciation for the interconnectedness of all things. He truly believed that whatever happened to his brothers and sisters—and to the world—also happened to him. So, he wished everyone and everything well.

Meeting each day with curiosity, he came to every situation with the intention of understanding the deeper meaning of what was going on. Free of agendas and projections, he was able to see the true nature of most interactions. He responded to each moment with appreciation, humor, and a desire to have a positive effect on the circumstances in which he found himself.

When we first met in Washington, D. C., Franklyn was the manager of the Smithsonian Gift Shops in the museum in which I worked as conservator. As the shop grew, his responsibilities became more administrative and highly computerized. He no longer had the time to participate in the comings and goings of the shop itself. Salespeople were hired to take his place behind the counter. He missed the contact he once had with travelers from all over the world who came into the shop. After much soul searching, he decided to quit his job and look for a position that would put him in touch with people again. He became a waiter in a large restaurant in one of the major Washington hotels.

Franklyn had never waited tables before, but he was determined to become the best waiter he could be. During his first few weeks on the job he carefully studied his new work environment. He paid close attention to all the activities in the kitchen and the dining areas. He studied the personalities of the chefs and other waiters, and developed relationships with them. He examined every detail of what makes a good waiter. Franklyn saw himself as a gracious host, not an unwilling servant, and he brought an awareness of detail that all good hosts bring to their guests. Within a very short period of time he was making more money than he had been making at the museum, and by the end of his third month on the job he won the Waiter of the Month Award.

One Thanksgiving Day all of his studying and most especially his way of being in the world helped to turn a difficult situation into a very satisfying one. A couple and their six-year-old daughter had been guests at the hotel for about a week. Every morning they would come into the restaurant for breakfast. The parents were very hard to please, and the child was extremely undisciplined. She was rude to her parents and to the waiters. By the time Thanksgiving Day came, none of the waiters wanted to serve this family. But someone had to serve them. Everyone agreed that Franklyn was the best man for the job.

The family came in and was directed to his station. As he was taking their order, Franklyn noticed that the parents were very absorbed in each other. It seemed to him that they barely realized their daughter was with them. They gave her order without consulting her about what she would like. The young girl repeatedly pulled on the sleeve of her father and then her mother as they were telling Franklyn what to bring for her. He continued to observe these family dynamics, without judgment, while he patiently took their orders. Because he knew that they had been so difficult to please, he was very careful to note all their special requests.

When he finished taking their orders, he turned and headed toward the kitchen. He passed the buffet table where a large, sculpted ice turkey had been placed in celebration of the holiday. Suddenly, from the corner of his eye he saw a fork fly across the aisle, and heard a collective gasp as it hit the ice turkey in the middle of its plump belly. Turning gracefully, he headed back toward the table, bending to pick up the fork as he went. With total composure, he stopped in front of the young girl and looked down at her. She looked back up at him with a belligerent look that said, "I dare you." Ignoring her challenge, he made a slight bow, and in the respectful tone he used to address everyone, he said, "Will you be needing a clean fork, Miss, and is there anything else I can get for you?"

First, a look of confusion spread across her face, then a silent communication passed between them as he continued to look at her without sarcasm or rancor. His look, his tone of voice, and his posture let her know

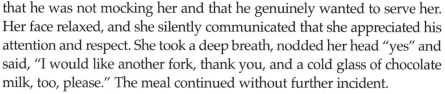

that he was not mocking her and that he genuinely wanted to serve her. Her face relaxed, and she silently communicated that she appreciated his attention and respect. She took a deep breath, nodded her head "yes" and said, "I would like another fork, thank you, and a cold glass of chocolate milk, too, please." The meal continued without further incident.

Throughout this situation Franklyn remained relaxed and centered. The fork throwing incident did not trigger his Suffering Child or his Critical Detractor Child. Instead it elicited his Nurturing Parents, his Intuitive Self, and his Emerald Child. Feeling compassion for the child and her parents, the Parent Who Listens encouraged him to interact with her, to meet her. In doing that he witnessed her Suffering Child. The Parent Who Leads reminded him that by tuning into his Intuitive Self he could discover what action would best resolve the incident. His Intuitive Self guided his response, making it possible for the young girl to join him in the "larger playing field" that he was occupying. His Emerald Child saw the humor in the whole situation, so he did not get hung up on the little girl's bad behavior. He responded in a way that healed both the child and her parents, and restored harmony to the moment. Although I have broken this event down into its separate parts, Franklyn, as an integrating, emerging adult, was able to spontaneously move through this entire sequence of events within seconds.

In the days that followed, there was no more fork flinging or rudeness. Whenever the family entered the restaurant, they asked to be seated at Franklyn's station. He made it his custom to first ask the young girl what she would like to order. Then he took her parents' orders. When they checked out of the hotel, they tipped him handsomely.

Franklyn came to his work and to all of his life with clear motives and intentions. He wanted to be present to each moment, to have meaningful interactions with people, to be an instrument of peace not suffering, to bring gentleness, compassion, and humor to his life and his relationships, and to make a reasonably good living. Money was always his secondary goal. In all areas of his life, he was primarily motivated by a genuine desire to be of service to God/All That Is. He accomplished all of these things and in the process became a teacher to all who were close to him.

Whether he was managing a gift shop or waiting on tables in a restaurant, my friend Franklyn was contributing to his world in a valuable way. His unique contribution was not so much a function of what he did, but how he did it. His deep awareness of himself, his attention to detail, his compassion for everyone he met, his respect for peoples' differences, his desire to transform dissidence into harmony, added to the balance of good in the world.

Franklyn lived according to "the Tao" or "the Way." The Tao is an Eastern philosophy that advocates a life of harmony achieved through silent observation and an intuitive, spontaneous response to whatever is occurring. In a very special little book entitled *The Tao of Pooh*, Benjamin Hoff explains to his readers that "the Tao is simply a way of appreciating, learning from, and working with whatever happens in everyday life. From the Taoist point of view, the natural result of this harmonious way of living is happiness."[9]

In his exchange with the little girl who threw the fork, Franklyn was practicing "the Tao." He appreciated her and elevated the situation in which he and his guests found themselves so that everyone learned something from it. He worked with what he had—his own ability to remain centered, three difficult people whose reputations preceded them, flying silverware, a love for his job, and a sincere desire to be of service—and turned an embarrassing situation into an occasion for a very meaningful exchange.

In shaping the outcome of that situation, Franklyn helped to create a very specific energetic experience for everyone who was directly involved and for those who witnessed the event. He exercised his role as a co-creator of the Universe and chose to respond in a way that promoted harmony and a playful resolution. Every day each one of us is faced with the same opportunity. Each one of us is also a co-creator of the Universe, one half of a very special partnership that exists between us and God / All That Is.

Naturally it is easier to follow the Tao in certain moments than it is in others. If you live simply, in a house in the woods, surrounded by the beauty of nature, with quiet time for contemplation, doing work that you love, and keeping company with kind, intelligent people, then you may find it easier to appreciate and work with whatever presents itself in the course of your everyday life than someone whose life is quite different. The single mother who struggles to make her paycheck meet the needs of her family, the teenager who is in the hospital once again because of complications due to AIDS, the social worker who must find foster homes for children who are being abused by their parents—these people's everyday circumstances make it harder for them to come to each moment embracing the opportunity to appreciate, learn from, and work with whatever life presents. But each of us, regardless of how difficult or easy our lives are, are accountable for what we create in the Universe. By continually becoming aware of ourselves, by nurturing ourselves, by remembering that we are one with God/All That Is, and by forgiving ourselves when we forget to do all of these things, we can become trustworthy co-creators.

Every day, each of you has many opportunities to shape the world in which you live, to make a contribution that will make a difference. As your Nurturing Parents, your Emerald Child, and your Intuitive Self become stronger within you, you recognize those opportunities more readily and you have a greater appreciation for the gifts that you can bring to each moment.

In the Safeway where I shop in Seattle, I witness people making their special contributions every day. The men and women who check out my groceries always have a friendly smile and a kind word. They are patient and helpful. The hundreds of people who interact with these men and women are being served in the largest sense of the word. Everyone they speak with walks away feeling a little better than they did before their encounter.

One day I watched an elderly woman going through her coupons, trying to find the right ones to match her purchases, while the line behind her continued to grow. The man at the checkout counter waited patiently, never once making this woman feel as if she needed to hurry. Instead he called for the manager to open another register so the rest of us would not have to wait. This man was adding critical mass to the good in the world. By taking control of the situation, he avoided creating agitation in the elderly woman by rushing her, or among us by keeping us waiting. Instead he created a sense of calm, and taught us all something about kindness and patience.

At the other end of the spectrum, the heart surgeon who is indifferent to the suffering of his patients, or whose primary interest is in making money to support a certain lifestyle, is not as likely to transform the world for the better as the person who bags our groceries with kindness and a true desire to serve.

We can make important contributions no matter what our work and no matter what our station in life. The men and women who bag our groceries can have as profound an effect on humanity as a great healer or political leader. Hundreds of people pass before them each day. If they perform their jobs filled with resentment or boredom, those energies will be felt by the people they serve, and carried away with them. On the other hand, if they bring to their work a genuine desire to be of service, then each person they come in contact with will be uplifted as a result of interacting with them. The good will that such a person extends can affect many people in the course of but a single day.

For each of us to truly serve one another, we must discover what motivates our behavior, and what our true intentions are. What impact could each of us have on our world if everything we did was motivated by a deep feeling of well-being? What impact would we have if kindness, gentleness, patience, and respect motivated our behavior instead of fear, greed, competition, or indifference? What makes it possible for us to act from a place that is characterized by positive energy? The answer lies in pursuing our own healing process.

When you do the healing work that allows your Nurturing Parents, your Emerald Child, and your Intuitive Self to come to the fore in your life, you are naturally drawn to return to the world the treasures which you have been given. When you do this healing work, you feel so vibrant, so vital, so grateful for being alive that you want very much to contribute something useful to the world in which you live. And when you notice that you are giving something back, no matter what the arena, no matter how seemingly small, you feel a deep sense of satisfaction.

When you pursue this personal healing, you realize that you are responsible for what you create in the world, from moment to moment and over the course of a much longer period of time. You recognize that who you are and what you do has a tremendous impact on your family, the people you work with, your community, your country, and this planet that we call home.

The process of healing personal wounds also reunites you with God/All That Is. You recognize your connection to Spirit and to a higher power, however you define that. This understanding creates a deep sense of security and a desire to act in a way that supports and enhances our world. Your desire to be of service to the world moves you to actively pursue self-knowledge so that you are continually aware and in charge of what you create.

When you move beyond your own personal healing process, you recognize that your greatest contribution is the support you give to others in their efforts to reach their fullest potential. Moving beyond your own personal healing process places you in a position to contribute to the world in a way that enhances its evolution toward Universal Goodwill and Peace.

Now,
Breathe deeply and gently.
Let your body soften.
See yourself within the space that surrounds you.
Feel yourself within the space that surrounds you.
Who is doing the seeing?
Who is doing the feeling?
That person is co-creating our world.

About the Author

Renee Welfeld is a teacher and practitioner of body/mind therapies with more than twenty years of experience. In her private practice, workshops, and classes, she combines her formal training with the lessons of her own life to help people understand the body, mind, and spirit connections in their own lives.

NOTES

EPIGRAPH

From Stanley Keleman, *Somatic Reality* (Berkeley: Center Press, 1979), 118, by permission of the publisher.

1. From Erich Fromm, *The Art of Loving* (New York: Harpercollins Publishers, 1956), 105, by permission of the publisher.

2. Genesis 2:7.

3. From John Kabat-Zinn, M.D., *Full Catastrophe Living — Using the Wisdom of Your Body and Mind to Face Stress, Pain, and Illness* (New York: Bantam, Doubleday, Dell Publishing Group, 1990), 2, by permission of the publisher.

4. From Dianne M. Connelly, *The Law of the Five Elements*, Rev. Ed. (Columbia: Traditional Acupuncture Institute, 1994), 13, by permission of author and the publisher.

5. From Robert Firestone, Ph.D., *The Fantasy Bond—Effects of Psychological Defenses on Interpersonal Relations* (New York: Human Sciences Press, 1985), 111, by permission of author and the publisher.

6. *Ibid.*, 92.

7. From Gay Hendricks, Ph.D., and Kathy Hendricks, Ph.D., *Conscious Loving* (New York: Bantam, Doubleday, Dell Publishing Group, 1990), 125, by permission of the publisher.

8. *Ibid.*, 124-25.

9. From *The Tao of Pooh* by Benjamin Hoff. Copyright (©) 1982 by Benjamin Hoff; text and illus. from *Winnie-The-Pooh* and *The House at Pooh Corner*, CR 1926, 1928 by E.P. Dutton, (©) 1953, 1956 by A. A. Milne. Used by permission of Dutton Signet, a division of Penguin Books USA Inc.